Towards the Planned City

Comparative Studies in
Social and Economic History 3

D1338824

To Moyra, Isabel, and Edgar

Comparative Studies in
Social and Economic History

General editor: *J. R. Kellett*

Towards the Planned City

Germany, Britain, the United States and France 1780-1914

ANTHONY SUTCLIFFE

BASIL BLACKWELL · OXFORD

First published in 1981 by
Basil Blackwell Publisher
108 Cowley Road
Oxford OX4 1JF
England

British Library Cataloguing in Publication Data
Sutcliffe, Anthony
    Towards the planned city. — (Comparative studies
    in social and economic history; no. 3).
    1. Cities and towns — Planning — History
    I. Title   II. Series
    711'.4'09   NA9090

ISBN 0-631-11001-1
ISBN 0-631-12599-X Pbk

Typeset by Janice Buchanan, Gerrards Cross, Bucks
Printed in Great Britain

Contents

General Preface

Comparative Studies in Social and Economic History is a new series committed to the systematic examination of major historical themes in differing settings of time and place. All too frequently there has seemed to be no middle way between the learned monograph dealing with an historical episode in one narrow context and the more ambitious study generalizing at random from a bewilderingly wide-ranging background. Yet certain clear insights can be gained by a more controlled group of parallel and comparative studies. It is possible by means of concise individual *case studies* to underline those elements which are unique and particular to each topic's manifestation in a given time and place.

Each author in the present series will provide a framework for analysing a particular historical episode or problem in changing settings, and will also suggest a personal perspective in the opening and closing chapters.

Other comparative studies in preparation or published consider the experience of industrial disputes in Britain and America, the development of broadly-based municipal authorities in the Victorian city, and economic change in five widely differing peasant societies.

The present inquiry examines the progress of urban planning, both in theory and in practice, in Germany, France, Britain and the United States, and the distinctive contributions made by each country to the ideal of ordered city growth.

J. R. K.

Preface

This book has been written in response to John Kellett's invitation to join his series with a volume of comparative studies on the nineteenth-century urban problem. My first inclination was to examine the ways in which the difficulties generated by rapid urbanization were perceived and then tackled in Britain and two or three other industrializing countries. Such a scheme would almost certainly have cast Britain, the first to enter the industrial urbanization process, in the role of principal innovator, and placed the main emphasis on the field of public health, in which Britain outshone the world from the 1840s until the 1870s and even beyond. Discussions with the editor persuaded me to settle instead for the more precise topic of the rise of modern urban planning, which shifted the emphasis to the more arcane period of the late nineteenth century, demoted Britain from world leadership, and allowed more stimulating international comparisons to be made. In the execution, the book has had to include some general consideration of environmental policies earlier in the nineteenth century, but only in so far as has been required by the historical problem here addressed.

The problem can be simply stated. During the last few years before the First World War, the debates on the urban environment in Britain, Germany, France and the United States, as well as in a number of other industrial countries, generated a new expression. In Britain it was 'town planning' and in the USA, 'city planning'. 'Städteplanung' was the German equivalent, while the French coined a linguistically independent term, 'urbanisme'. The expression was used to describe the deliberate ordering by public authority of the physical arrangements of towns or parts of towns in order to promote their efficient and equitable functioning as economic and social units, and to create an aesthetically pleasing environment. New coinages, of course, sometimes disguise very old ideas, and antecedents of urban planning may be traced back as far as early Antiquity. However, the novelty of the 'town planning' hailed in the early 1900s lay in its relevance to industrial urbanization. There was no precedent for the rapidly expanding towns of the industrial age, nor for the massive shift in the balance between rural and urban populations. It was not merely a question of overall size and rate of growth, important though these were as generators of problems. The towns also had to adapt to rapidly changing technology and social patterns, as a result of which the character and functions of whole districts could change within a few years, placing new demands on the building stock, communications and general services. The accommodation of poorly-paid manual workers, a much larger element in industrial than in pre-industrial towns, was a persistent problem. The idea of controlling certain aspects of this development by public authority was all the more distinct from pre-industrial precedents in that the industrialization process as generated in Britain, and to a large extent too in the forms in which it implanted itself elsewhere, was associated with the wide acceptance of the ideal of free economic competition and private ownership of all the factors of production, including land. The suggestion that public control might be exercised over the use of private land in towns was in this respect potentially a revolutionary one.

The nineteenth century provides many examples of the rapid spread of revolutionary ideas within and between regions, states and continents. Was urban planning such an idea, a revelation convincing enough to command almost simultaneous acceptance in each of the four countries studied here? How far was it, on the other hand, a mosaic of national and even local developments of theory and practice, specific to the immediate problems encountered in each area, and moderated by varying attitudes to the issue of social reform in general? To what extent were its apparently international features the product of common elements in the world urbanization process rather than of the diffusion of ideas? In looking at four countries, and at the distinct manifestations of an international movement of urban planning, the attempt is made here to provide the outline of an answer.

The scope of this inquiry has required me to draw heavily on the work of other historians. Members of the Planning History Group will no doubt recognize those points at which their written or oral contributions to the Group's meetings have added to my understanding, and my main debt of gratitude is to them for the stimulating debate on the growth of modern town planning which they have maintained since we first came together in 1974. My thanks are also due to Nicholas Bullock for bibliographical material and other valuable information drawn from his work on Germany, and to Lutz Niethammer for allowing me to browse in his library of German housing reform texts. A. J. Travis has kept me in touch with his study of Tony Garnier, and Alvin Boyarsky kindly allowed me to read his thesis on Camillo Sitte. Paul Laxton lent me a rare pamphlet on slum clearance in Liverpool. Martin Hawtree kindly allowed me to draw on his thesis on the history of the British town-planning profession, and Michael Day was good enough to permit me a sight of his thesis on Raymond Unwin. Lynn Hibbert enlarged my understanding of Herriot's Lyons. Lately, Andrew Lees has provided me with much useful bibliographical information, and Gerhard Fehl has been a constant help and stimulus. I am grateful to John Kellett for his ready attention and much-abused patience. Christine Marland and Beryl Moore typed the manuscript with good humour and accuracy.

In the selection and preparation of the illustrations I owe a debt to Brigid Grafton-Green, Joe McKenna, Dawn Orr, Sabine Preuss and Fritz Schmoll, who suggested material to me, and to Jim Davies, Chris Holmes and Ron Swift, who photographed some of my choices. Russell Walden is to be thanked for risking his life on the Eiffel Tower to take one of the plates. I am grateful to the following institutions for permission to reproduce material from their collections: Birmingham Reference Library, Hampstead Garden Suburb Archives, and Landesarchiv Berlin. Finally, I am delighted to acknowledge the generous support of the Douglas Knoop Research Fund of the University of Sheffield.

Anthony Sutcliffe
University of Sheffield

One

Introduction
The Context of Urban Planning

This book discusses one aspect of public policy in a century of revolutionary change. Fundamental to that change was the industrialization process, the unprecedented movement of economic and social development which allowed man to multiply the productivity of his labour, thus freeing himself, at least for a time, from humble subservience to the forces of nature. This industrial revolution was accompanied by an urban revolution. Urban settlements, in the sense of nucleated communities depending for their existence principally on activities outside the primary sector, had existed for thousands of years, but their low productivity permitted only a small minority of the total population to live in them. Industrialization promoted a massive increase in this proportion. New techniques multiplied the productivity of human labour in manufacturing, while better local transport permitted its concentration in towns, where considerable economies of organization could be achieved. Associated agricultural improvements generated surpluses of food, raw materials and labour which fuelled the growth of the towns. More efficient long-distance transport reinforced the process, allowing the industrialized regions to dominate an increasingly integrated world economic system. Within those regions the urbanized proportion of the population could consequently rise sharply towards a position of majority and even near totality (see Weber, 1899; Lampard, 1973).

The heartlands of these industrial and urban revolutions lay in Europe and North America. In the former, industrialization spread from its eighteenth-century cradle in Britain to a number of regions on the continent, most of them centred on coalfields or on existing large urban centres. In North America, industrialization began on the eastern seaboard and spread westwards, principally into the great mid-western region around, and to the south of, the Great Lakes. In both continents extensive regions were scarcely affected directly by industrialization, but overall the continents registered marked townward shifts in the distribution of their populations. These shifts were especially pronounced in the four leading industrial countries of Britain, Germany, France and the United States. When the nineteenth century opened, two-thirds of the population of Britain, the most urbanized country of the four, still lived in the countryside. On the eve of the First World War, four-fifths of the population of Britain, and nearly two-thirds of that of Germany, lived in towns. In France and the United States the equivalent proportions were approaching one-half.

Far more, however, was involved in the nineteenth-century urbanization process than a simple transfer of population from the country to the town. Greater productivity permitted a marked increase in the total population of the industrializing areas. The aggregate population of Britain, Germany, France and the United States thus rose from 64 millions in 1800 to 207 millions a century later (Mitchell, 1975, 19—27; McEvedy and Jones, 1978, 287). In consequence the aggregate numbers of towndwellers in the four countries rose in massive proportions. Moreover, the attractions which drew population into the towns tended to increase in strength in proportion to the size of town. This tendency was especially marked after mid-century, when the railways greatly accelerated and cheapened the movement of bulk goods, liberating much manufacturing from the coalfield districts, and tertiary activities began to generate a rapidly growing proportion of total employment. As a result the networks of urban settlements came to be dominated by a growing number of giant cities the populations of which surpassed, in some cases very considerably, those of the largest urban centres of pre-industrial times. In 1800 no city in Europe or North America had exceeded the population of one million which is a conservative estimate for the city of Rome in the early centuries of our era. By 1900 thirteen agglomerations had done so: London, New York, Paris, Berlin, Chicago, Vienna, St Petersburg, Philadelphia, Manchester, Birmingham, Moscow, Boston and Glasgow (Chandler and Fox, 1974, 19, 330).

These great metropoli stood at the head of urban networks in which numerous regional capitals, ports and manufacturing centres far surpassed in population their equivalents in medieval and early modern times, with some of them already pressing towards the million mark. In 1800 there had been twenty-two towns with more than 100,000 inhabitants in Europe, and none in North America. By 1900, excluding the giant cities mentioned above, there were over 150 such urban areas in the two continents, including sixteen of over 500,000 inhabitants (Chandler and Fox, 1974, 19, 36, 300—32). In several cases, including Birmingham—Black Country, Lille—Roubaix—Tourcoing, and the Ruhr, two or more once-distinct towns had merged to form a continuous built-up area. This was the phenomenon to describe which Patrick Geddes, the pioneer urban scientist, coined the term 'conurbation' at the turn of the century.

The bigger the town, the more it tended to diverge in its economic, social and physical structures from the urban centres of pre-industrial Europe. Two related features, above all, marked it out as something new: its centrifugal dynamic of growth, and its division into areas of distinct function. In the pre-industrial town the wealth-generating institutions, among which trade and administration were very prominent, and manufacturing somewhat less so, had tended to concentrate in the centre, in association with the homes of the most prosperous and powerful of the population. The poor tended to live on the outskirts. Such an arrangement, especially when combined with a static population, generated little peripheral expansion, a characteristic which was confirmed by the fortification ring which surrounded most European towns. Areal distinctions within the town, which were in any case not very marked, were usually based on the preference of various trades for particular districts, or on social divisions generated by the rivalry of great families (see Sjoberg, 1960, as qualified by Burke, 1975).

Industrialization transformed this structure by stimulating manufacturing which, at least until the mid-nineteenth century, tended to locate in the central areas of towns. The attendant smoke and noise, and the presence of numerous rough and poor workers, drove out the rich and the middle classes. While the manual workers took up residence in increasing numbers near their central employments, the property-owning, managerial and professional classes came to favour the outskirts. As time passed, changes in the organization of production, improvements in urban transport, and the generation of a suburban environment which offered some of the advantages of the countryside, led a growing proportion of the urban population to participate in this outward movement. An explosion of the town's area resulted as the richest members of the population moved onto cheap land and took pleasure in maximizing the areas which their households enjoyed for their personal use. Meanwhile, the competition between productive functions for central land generated a segregation of uses in the inner districts. This was paralleled, in residential areas, by the segregation of socio-economic groups which resulted from their differing economic capacities to compete for desirable land. Thus under the impact of industrialization the town came to express in spatial form the major components of its economic and social structures, a process which encouraged, and was encouraged by, a much more efficient land market than had existed in the pre-industrial period (Johnson, 1967, 105–62; Pahl, 1970, 36–68).

Admittedly, some features of this model are to be found in certain European towns — particularly the larger ones — before the industrialization period (see Burke, 1975). It must also be said that the model corresponds most closely to the English and North American experience. On the continent of Europe (and also in Scotland) certain divergences can be noted, particularly in respect of the character of urban physical expansion (see Dickinson, 1961). The built-up areas, especially of large towns, tended not to expand as readily there as they did in the Anglo-Saxon countries. Until the middle decades of the nineteenth century the fortifications which continued to ring numerous towns were perhaps the major single restraint on outward growth. In the second half of the century their influence waned as they fell into disuse or were removed, but in many towns a new restriction replaced them. This was the factory belt, product of the rapid implantation of mechanized industry in an era of highly efficient railway communications. In consequence the outer districts of towns did not greatly attract the rich and the more prosperous of the middle classes, who preferred to retain a central residence often combined with a country house some distance away. This left only the lower middle classes and manual workers to sustain the momentum of suburban expansion. The movement was too weak to break down in any great measure the high residential densities which had built up during the first half of the nineteenth century, and in most of the larger towns the majority of residents continued to live in flats or apartments, even in the peripheral districts. This vertical development complicated the emergence of socially-differentiated areas and contributed to patterns of behaviour which differed somewhat from those observable among British and North American towndwellers (see Sutcliffe, 1974b).

This second model of urban development during industrialization corresponds particularly closely to the experience of Germany and France, with the exception of those northern regions of France and north-western regions of Germany which bordered on Belgium and the Netherlands. Here, densities were lower and small houses predominated (Stübben, 1907, 18–19). Elsewhere, at least in the larger towns, the tall apartment block sustained its relentless advance until the end of the century. Only in the early 1900s did a distinct movement of low-density suburbanization begin to take shape. However, this divergence from Anglo-Saxon experience did not make the process of industrial urbanization in France and Germany any the less revolutionary. On the contrary, the rapidity of industrialization in Germany after mid-century generated a faster and in some ways more disruptive urbanization than Britain had known (see Köllmann, 1969). France, her total population nearly stagnant, urbanized more slowly overall, but her industrial districts registered rates of urban growth comparable to those of similar areas in the other industrializing countries (see Carrière and Pinchemel, 1963; Sorlin, 1969).

This urban revolution both stimulated and required important adjustments of public policy in relation to the physical environment of towns. Before industrialization the authorities had generally intervened very little in urban physical development (though certain significant exceptions to this generalization will emerge below, particularly in the chapter on Germany). With industrialization, new problems arose and old ones were intensified. The drainage was swamped, and traditional water supplies were exhausted. Pollution of air and water became very serious. Canals and railways, often pushed into the most central areas, disrupted established patterns of settlement and movement. Thoroughfares became congested, and cheap housing overcrowded. To some extent these were economic problems, in that they restricted a town's capacity to produce wealth. However, most of them also had social implications in that they tended to shorten the lives or increase the discomfort of some or all of the urban residents.

These problems placed the authorities in a dilemma. Wherever it took place, industrialization was generally preceded or accompanied by a reinforcement of individual freedom and private property rights. At the same time, it came to be widely believed that the rational pursuit of self-interest by the individual was the most efficient means of securing the general happiness of society. The individual, it could be argued, was free to protect himself and his dependants from the dangers of the urban environment. Any attempt to protect him in spite of himself was doomed to failure and might even do harm to the general interest. On the other hand, it was usually recognized even by those inclined to take so purist a view that certain aspects of the urban physical environment could not safely be left to the free play of private interests. In four areas in particular, self-interest could not be guaranteed to move the individual to action sufficient to secure the general well-being of the community because the results of his activity or the lack of it frequently affected his neighbours more than himself. These areas were: streets and other public thoroughfares, drainage and sewerage, fire-resistant building, and atmospheric pollution. Furthermore, many urban authorities had been active in these areas before industrialization, so that much of the experience and legal precedent necessary to the continuance of this intervention in more taxing circumstances had been accumulated. Consequently, this rudimentary public intervention in the urban environment generally remained impervious to even the most extreme forms of non-interventionist ideology. It was on this foundation that urban planning developed.

From the earliest stages of industrialization we can detect a clear tendency for public intervention in the urban environment to intensify and to extend itself. It took two main forms. One was the direct provision by the public authority of common facilities such as thoroughfares, drains, sewers, water and, towards the end of the nineteenth century, gas, electricity and public transport. The other was the imposition of obligations on the owners of urban property and, to a lesser extent, on those who used it. The development of this intervention was the product of technical and political processes, principally of the latter. Neither process operated purely at local level. Technical innovations were readily diffused from town to town and from region to region within the industrializing world. Political decisions affecting the urban environment were made partly by the authorities of the individual towns, but partly too by superior authorities responsible for broader areas. In this latter respect the formulation of urban environmental policy diverged increasingly from pre-industrial custom. As the proportion of the total population living in towns increased and urban activities generated a growing proportion of total wealth, and as better communications linked town to town, and town to country, more closely than in the past, the problems of the urban environment came increasingly to concern the whole of society.

When urban problems rose to be considered at a superior political level they encountered deliberative and executive institutions which were much less the product of urban initiative than were the municipalities and other town authorities. Much of the character of these institutions had been formed before industrialization, at a time when towns were of much less importance. Far from transforming or replacing them, the wealth generated by industrialization generally had the effect of sustaining these institutions, sometimes against the immediate interests of the towns themselves.

When industrialization began, Europe was already well on the way to organizing itself into a small number of nation-states in which territorial unity and coherent public policy were sustained by a strong, central government. The example was set by France and Britain, which had been developing on national lines since the Middle Ages. By the eighteenth century these two countries were not only the dominant political and military forces in Europe, but in much of the rest of the world as well. By the early nineteenth century Western Europe and North America had come largely under the sway of ideas generated in Britain and France. Britain's Industrial Revolution and its associated individualist ideology marked out the path of progress in terms of physical techniques and economic organization. The French Revolution and its aftermath projected over much of Europe a political system and ideology which greatly strengthened the appeal of the nation-state while demonstrating, much more clearly than did the British example, how it might most effectively be organized. Indeed, Napoleon Bonaparte contributed directly to the political reshaping of Europe by combining numerous small territories to form a number of new states, with centralized governments on French lines. The process was further promoted after his final defeat in 1815 by the principal victors, Britain and Prussia.

To most contemporary observers these new arrangements looked like progress. The abolition of petty princedoms, both lay and ecclesiastical, was considered a major encouragement to economic and social advance. In most of the West European states which emerged from the Congress of Vienna personal freedom and private property rights were securely established, with the abolition of feudal institutions in the countryside, and of guild organization and other restrictions on enterprise in the towns. Elected assemblies representing the holders of private property were endowed almost everywhere with extensive legislative power. However, even after 1815 Britain and France continued to dominate Europe. The new states were too small to rival them. Even Prussia, whose rise since the seventeenth century had made it France's main rival on the continent of Europe, laboured under major limitations caused by its awkwardly arranged territories and its short and inconvenient coastline.

Consequently, the first half of the nineteenth century saw the development of powerful movements of national unification in Germany and in Italy. These movements were strongly supported by the individuals and corporate interests which favoured economic development on the lines pioneered in Britain. In Germany, a federation of self-governing states had been established by the Congress of Vienna in 1815. Though weak at first, it was reinforced by the German customs union (*Zollverein*) set up in 1834. Increasingly dominated by Prussia, the movement for German national unification reached its culmination in 1871 with the creation of a German Empire of twenty-five federated states with its capital in Berlin. In Italy, national unification was crowned by the movement of the capital to Rome in 1870. Austria, irrevocably defeated by Prussia in 1866, stood apart as the leading territory of the now anachronistic Austro-Hungarian Empire of the Habsburgs. Switzerland and Belgium succeeded in preventing the appropriate ethnic sections of their populations from being incorporated into the big nation-states, and the Netherlands retained their independence. However, the area and population of these three territories were insignificant in comparison with the four great nation-states of Britain, France, Germany and Italy which dominated Europe after 1871.

Thus the stage was set for the growing political, military and economic rivalry between the four increasingly industrialized nation-states which would end in 1914 with the outbreak of an unprecedentedly destructive armed conflict. By annihilating a large part of the labour force and accumulated capital of Europe, the First World War would raise serious doubts about the suitability of the nation-state for economic development and the general promotion of the happiness of humanity. Indeed, some of these misgivings were already being expressed before 1914, particularly by those interested in the well-being of the principal nodes of economic development, the urban areas. However, in the period covered by this study urban government was effected increasingly under the aegis of institutions of national government. What then were the implications of these arrangements for the administration of towns, and particularly for the control of the urban environment?

Two major systems face us, the one of two main tiers and the other of three. In Britain the urban administrations stood for most purposes in a position of direct responsibility to the central government. After 1888 the smaller towns were made responsible in many respects to an intervening tier of county administrations, but the medium-sized and large towns were allowed to retain full local autonomy as county boroughs. In France, after the general reorganization of territorial administration in the 1790s and early 1800s, the position was very similar. Though complicated by the interposition of the *départements*, the system allowed considerable administrative independence to the urban *communes*, and in most matters of town administration the *départements* acted, under their centrally-appointed prefects, as agents of the central government rather than as representatives of regional interests. In Germany, on the other hand, the federal system confirmed in 1871 interposed a tier of largely autonomous regional (state) governments (*Länder*) between the municipalities (*Stadtgemeinden*) and the imperial administration. Each state possessed an elected legislature (*Landtag*), responsible for nearly all domestic matters. In Germany, therefore, these state governments were the direct mentors of the towns. However, the association between domestic policy and national objectives, which grew closer as economic development and international rivalry proceeded, tended to draw the imperial government more directly into urban affairs.

A similar system prevailed in the United States. Evolving in circumstances very different from those of Europe, the former British colonies had settled for a federal structure in the 1770s. Confirmed by the Civil War of 1861—4, the federal system presided over the rapid urbanization which occurred in the United States during the second half of the century. The federal government intervened somewhat less in American urban affairs than did the imperial administration in Germany. Less involved than the European states in military rivalries, never under threat of relative national economic impoverishment, and administering a territory whose people enjoyed the highest living standards in the world, the federal government could largely restrict itself to resolving legal disputes, leaving all other aspects of urban policy to a debate between the various state and city administrations.

The scene is now set for detailed examination of the development of the public control of the urban environment in four of the most important national units in the nineteenth-century industrializing world. It is only right that we should begin with the one which by the early twentieth century was widely recognized as the world leader in urban planning, Germany.

Two

Germany
From Town Extensions to Comprehensive Urban Planning

'Germany...', wrote Patrick Abercrombie in 1913, 'has concretely achieved more modern Town Planning than any other country...' (*TPR*, 1913, 99). Few would have questioned this judgement by the leading British expert on world town planning, except perhaps for some young iconoclasts in Germany itself (see e.g. Hegemann, 1913, 151–61, 272–312, 394). How had Germany achieved this unquestioned position of world leadership in urban planning?

Industrialization and its attendant urbanization can provide only part of the answer. Certainly, German industrialization was in many respects a more rapid and revolutionary process than in Britain, France and even the United States. It generated massive urban growth, particularly in the larger towns. It did not begin, however, until the middle of the nineteenth century and it is unlikely that so advanced a planning would have emerged in the following fifty years had not the urban administrations inherited a pre-industrial framework of intervention which could be elaborated to meet new needs.

The basis of this intervention was the general power to lay out new streets around the existing built-up areas. Applied in a partial and rudimentary manner until the mid-nineteenth century, it began to be developed thereafter into a more ambitious instrument, in step with accelerated urban growth. A number of administrative obstacles remained until the 1870s, when most states began to grant their urban authorities strengthened powers to lay out extensive street networks in developing areas at reduced cost to the public purse. There followed a period of consolidation during which most German towns expanded into thoroughly planned street-systems while their authorities did little to extend their control of the use of private land. From the 1890s, however, a new acceleration of urban growth combined with certain social and political developments threw into relief various tensions in the city-building process. The town authorities responded by adopting a more active role in the shaping of the urban environment as a whole. Developing almost without interruption until 1914, this more ambitious intervention came to be known as 'Städtebau' — the process of controlled town-building, or town planning (see Hartog, 1962; Albers, 1975a).

THE PRE-INDUSTRIAL ORIGINS OF URBAN PLANNING

Paradoxically, the crucial power to plan new streets was a product of the weakness of German towns and their local administrations, not of their strength. The roots of this weakness are to be sought in the later Middle Ages. It had become clear by the end of the fifteenth century that the Holy Roman Emperor, titular sovereign of most of the territory which would form the German Empire in 1871, could no longer hope to unite the territories ruled by his vassals into a single, national state comparable to the kingdoms of England and France. Many of the larger towns had taken advantage of this fragmentation of authority by establishing themselves as virtually independent territories, usually under the emperor's patronage. Most towns, however, were forced by depopulation and economic difficulties in the later Middle Ages to accept progressive incorporation into the territorial states (Barraclough, 1957, 373–81).

The final ruin of the towns was effected by the Thirty Years' War (1618–48), which disrupted trade and industry, undermined what was left of imperial authority, and confirmed the territorial princes (*Fürsten*) as absolute rulers. The free imperial cities, without a local ruler to support them, were exposed to the full blast of the war and most fared badly. Within the princely states some towns escaped serious dislocation and retained a measure of commercial prosperity, but they paid the price of utter subordination to the territorial administrations in all but the pettiest of local matters. Their government generally remained in the hands of magistrates elected by the citizens, but the formal appointment of the magistrates rested with the princely authority. So circumscribed was the initiative of the magistrates that they acted in effect as local agents of the State. This subservience was especially marked in some of the larger territories to emerge from the Thirty Years' War. In Prussia, which ended the war as the dominant power in north Germany, the towns were completely under the thumb of the State (Barraclough, 1957, 376–7, 389).

Many of the larger towns were now extended and rebuilt as princely capitals (*Residenzstädte*) for the more than 200 states which emerged from the war. The palace-town of Versailles, built to the south-west of Paris by Louis XIV from the 1670s, was an influential example. Its broad avenues, emphasizing the dominance of the palace over the town, were echoed in various forms throughout Germany. Although urban populations were generally stagnant in Germany in the seventeenth and eighteenth centuries, the presence of a court required the building of at least one completely new district in most of the *Residenzstädte*. The rulers would normally lay down the street pattern of such districts and sometimes they imposed a standard design on the houses. The result, as at Kassel, Karlsruhe and Mannheim, was often an impressive layout of squares, avenues, parks and vistas in the baroque manner which completely transformed the town (Mellor, 1978, 112). Elsewhere, the medieval cores survived beside extensive new suburbs as at Berlin, where a carefully planned suburb, the Friedriche Vorstadt, was laid out in 1688, and extended in 1721, by the Electors of Brandenburg (Hegemann, 1963, 44–60).

Princely intervention in the shaping of towns was greatly facilitated by the survival of the legal arrangements for the development of urban land which had evolved in the Middle Ages. Under this traditional land law, all the land within a town's direct jurisdiction was owned communally and leased to users. Under absolutist, princely rule, ultimate ownership passed to the State. Occupiers of urban land, whether built or unbuilt, thus became vulnerable to a variety of arbitrary interventions in the free use of their plots. In practice, princely powers were formalized and were rarely enforced in a capricious manner, while established built-up areas were left largely undisturbed. In the new districts, however, the princes had no difficulty in reserving the land necessary for public thoroughfares, other open spaces, and public buildings. This advantage encouraged the princes to plan in a grand and extensive manner, and a high proportion of the new building in German towns in the late seventeenth and the eighteenth centuries consequently occurred in carefully laid-out town extensions.

During the eighteenth century the absolutist power of the princes encountered growing criticism as the thinkers of the German Enlightenment put forward the ideal of a society based on an association of secure, equal and free individuals. The kings of Prussia, who were beginning to benefit from a quickening of the economic pulse within their extensive territories, particularly in the Rhine provinces in the west, were among the first to make concessions to the swelling demand for more secure property rights. After a series of modest reforms the Prussian Crown promulgated its *Allgemeine Landrecht* (general territorial code) in 1794, under the immediate influence of more turbulent developments in France. An attempt to create a single legal and administrative system for the motley territories ruled by Prussia, the *Allgemeine Landrecht* conceded the right of private property in land. However, it reserved the right of the State to acquire, or limit the use of, private land in the common interest. It went on to define, more clearly than in the past, the powers of the local administrative organs of the State (the *Polizei*). Among them it included the power to establish *Fluchtlinien*, the boundaries of areas of land to be reserved for use as new public thoroughfares in and around the towns.

The *Allgemeine Landrecht* thus codified the practice of town-extension planning. In doing so it put a powerful tool of environmental control into the hands of the urban authorities well in advance of the period of sustained urban growth in which it would become especially useful. For the time being, however, the exact nature of urban government remained unclear. In particular, the *Allgemeine Landrecht* failed to clarify the division of authority between the municipal authorities and the local *Polizei*. It took defeat by France in 1806 to prompt a more radical reconstruction of the Prussian State. Many of the reforms enacted thereafter aimed at the regeneration of Prussian society on the basis of greater individual and communal liberty. Typical was the municipal ordinance (*Städteordnung*) of

1808, which created powerful, elected municipalities for all urban communities (text in Engeli and Haus, 1975, 104—34). Though still subject to a degree of State supervision, the towns were now empowered to pursue their own good as they saw fit. In most towns the local *Polizei* was delegated to the municipalities, subject only to certain State checks. Only in Berlin and Potsdam did the police authorities continue to be administered directly by the Prussian government.

It was not, however, the intention of the Prussian government that the useful practice of town-extension planning should now lapse. Not only did the *Polizei*, now under municipal control in most cases, continue to fix the *Fluchtlinien*, but each municipality was required by the *Städteordnung* to set up a building committee (*Baudeputation*) to take care of numerous aspects of the physical form of the town, including street-paving, drainage and the maintenance of public walks. In towns of more than 10,000 inhabitants the municipalities were empowered to appoint a paid *Baurat* (town surveyor) who would sit in the municipal executive (*Magistrat*) and in the building committee. Consequently, most of the elected urban authorities were in a position, after 1808, to pursue the policy of town-extension planning which previously had depended on State initiative.

The other German states made a similar transition from absolutism in the early nineteenth century. The military successes of Napoleon Bonaparte prompted the radical reorganization of a German state system which had proved powerless to resist him. Between 1803 and 1806, the year in which the Holy Roman Empire was formally abolished, the number of German states was reduced from over 230 to around 40. In the west, Bonaparte himself set up Westphalia and a number of other new states with institutions based on those which had emerged in France since 1789. Elsewhere, the incorporation of small territories into larger states, and the general reform of institutions, were undertaken largely under German initiative, but the French example infused most of the new arrangements. Although Bonaparte ensured that none of the new states was large enough to rival France, the abolition of the episcopal territories and nearly all the free imperial cities ensured that Germany was composed of states capable of sustaining political and legal institutions comparable to those of the established European nation-states. Within two decades of the final defeat of Napoleon, urban self-government had emerged virtually everywhere on lines comparable to those established in Prussia (Hofmann, 1974, 32). Thus throughout Germany the powers to plan town extensions, and the rudimentary building regulations which had emerged under absolutist rule, passed into the hands of the municipalities, either outright or in the form of municipal influence over the local *Polizei*.

At first the municipalities made little use of their powers. Most towns grew only slowly until the 1840s and even beyond (Weber, 1899, 80—8). The spread of their built-up areas was hampered in many cases by the reform of rural land-ownership and the rearrangement of plots which followed the initial abolition of serfdom during and immediately after the Napoleonic period. Near many towns, including Berlin, common lands were not fully allocated to private owners until mid-century, and the market for building land in the districts affected was almost completely paralysed until this process was complete (Thienel, 1973, 23–8; Matzerath and Thienel, 1977, 175). In most towns, including some of the very largest, municipal service neither attracted enterprising elected representatives nor stirred the electorate, and the powers of local self-government were taken up lethargically. Urban government did not begin to awake from these slumbers until the 1840s and 1850s, when industrialization began to impinge upon it (Sheehan, 1971, 118–19).

INDUSTRIAL URBANIZATION AND THE APPLICATION OF LOCAL POWERS UP TO 1875

Between the 1830s and the early 1870s Germany passed through the first phase of its industrialization process (Ritter and Kocka, 1974, 12–13). Expanding investment in industry and trade was associated with the growth of economic and political integration among the German states, which culminated in the foundation of the Prussian-dominated German Empire in 1871. A major shift of population towards the towns set in from the 1840s. By 1871 36.1 per cent of an imperial population of just over forty-one millions resided in urban areas (Hohorst *et al.*, 1975, 22, 42–3, 52).

Even in these early stages, the German industrial urbanization process was more rapid than Britain's had been in the later eighteenth century. In Britain many of the most advanced processes had expanded in the countryside where waterpower was cheap and plentiful. In Germany steam power was already cheaply available when industrialization began, and from the 1840s the attraction of urban manufacturing locations was reinforced by the railways. Indeed, these stimuli to the concentration of production very soon produced urban growth rates which showed a propensity to increase in proportion to the size of the town. Consequently, a higher proportion of the total increase in the urban population occurred in large established towns than in the equivalent early phase in Britain (Lee, 1978, 281). Only in the Ruhr, and to a lesser extent in the Saar and Upper Silesia, did the emergence of new urban settlements, necessary for the exploitation of coal or iron ore, play a major part in the urbanization process. Elsewhere, sea- and river-ports predominated among the handful of completely new, founded towns; notably Bremerhaven (1827), Ludwigshafen (1863), and Wilhelmshaven (1869). Consequently, a number of towns soon reached quite an impressive size for a country which until the 1840s had been economically more backward than its western neighbour, France. The largest by far was the Prussian and imperial capital, Berlin, with nearly a million inhabitants in 1875, but Hamburg and Breslau both had over 200,000 residents and Dresden and Munich were approaching that figure (Hohorst *et al.*, 1975, 45). In 1871 4.8 per cent of the population of the German Empire lived in towns of over 100,000 inhabitants, and a further 7.7 per cent in towns of 20,000–100,000 inhabitants (ibid., 42–3, 52).

Industry's preference for larger towns accentuated the demand for manufacturing and residential accommodation in localities where land- and house-rents were already high. There were a number of obstacles to the satisfaction of that demand. During the first half of the century the main problem was the reform of rural landownership which followed on from the abolition of serfdom. The redistribution of common lands took decades to complete, and while it lasted the land market in the vicinity of many towns was seriously disrupted. Moreover, land reform did little to produce parcels which could convert readily into building sites. The authorities took advantage of the distribution of the commons to reconstitute peasant holdings, but much rural land remained divided into tiny plots. In western Germany, in particular, divided inheritance had produced a pattern of strips which often were no more than two or three metres wide. Entirely unsuitable for building, they could, in the hands of tenacious peasant owners, paralyse the outward growth of the towns.

Ring fortifications, consisting of extensive earthworks and a *glacis* (field of fire) on the outside, were another difficulty. Some towns, notably in the west and north-west, and including Düsseldorf, Bremen and Frankfurt, had removed their fortifications in the Napoleonic period (Wurzer, 1974a, 11–12; Kabel, 1949, 44–5). After 1815 the growing integration of the German states had discouraged the upkeep of earthworks around many towns but few had actually been removed. Moreover, the defences of certain strategic towns, particularly in Prussia, were strengthened or extended. At Cologne, for instance, a new line was built in the 1820s, and Königsberg was refortified in the 1840s (*Städtebau*, 1909, 125; Dickinson, 1961, 84). Even in towns which were not seriously defended, the survival of the fortifications, with their infrequent and narrow gates, seriously discouraged the movement of population and employment to the suburbs.

Further problems occurred in the organization of the housing supply. During the early stages of industrialization in Britain the capital market for residential building had been largely independent of that for industrial capital. Many small investors had chosen to put their funds into housing in their own localities for the lack of any attractive and secure alternative. In consequence, plenty of new housing, ramshackle though much of it was, was provided in the growing towns of Britain between the late eighteenth century and the middle of the nineteenth. Local, small-scale investment in housing was the rule in Germany too until the middle of the nineteenth century, but thereafter the sharp upsurge in urban demand coincided with the creation of a largely unified capital market in which housing had to compete directly for funds with commerce and industry. A similar development in Britain was cushioned by the strength of the building societies which had grown up since the later eighteenth century, but in Germany few such intermediate sources of capital existed and a large part of funds for building had to be sought from the banks. Although the actual construction of residential buildings remained organized on a small scale, the development of building land tended to fall into the hands of large, highly-capitalized companies

(*Terraingesellschaften* or *Baugesellschaften*) closely associated with some of the big investment banks. Their services were often very valuable in buying up plots from their peasant owners and rearranging them into parcels suitable for building. However, unless they were subjected to strong municipal control they tended to monopolize the limited supply of building land and push up its price.

The high cost of land and capital for building bore very heavily on individual earnings, which for the lower-middle and working classes were markedly lower than those enjoyed in Britain in the middle decades of the nineteenth century. Most of the growing number of German towndwellers consequently disposed of considerably less floorspace than people of equivalent employments in British towns. Single-room dwellings were the norm in many of the larger towns, and there was much sharing and taking-in of lodgers. In the older districts, many of the more substantial houses of the pre-industrial era were divided into rooms and small apartments. In the newer areas, multi-family buildings were constructed in increasing numbers (see Niethammer, 1976).

Berlin took the lead in this multi-storey housing. The first *Familienhäuser* (blocks of tenements for poor workers) were speculatively built in the outer districts in the 1820s (Thienel, 1973, 149). From the 1840s the building of tall blocks became increasingly common in Berlin as the pressure on land increased. It now became customary to build up the interiors of the sites with tenements arranged around one or more courtyards, and these depressing buildings prompted the coinage of the term *Mietskaserne* — rental barracks. From the 1850s the *Mietskasernen*, which continued to be built mainly in the industrial suburbs, were joined by *Mietshäuser* — more comfortable blocks of apartments for middle-class occupation in the inner districts (ibid., 135). The average number of residents per building plot in Berlin increased markedly; already thirty in 1815, it rose to forty in 1840 and to forty-eight in 1861 (Hartog, 1962, 29).

By the middle of the century blocks of flats were multiplying in other large German towns. They were particularly prominent in the eastern industrial centres, such as Breslau, but they also gained ground in the west. They did not penetrate to the same extent into medium-sized and small towns, and in north-western Germany, particularly in and around Bremen, an established tradition of single-family houses proved very resilient. Even the smaller towns, however, generated numerous two- and three-storey buildings (*Bürgerhäuser*) designed to accommodate four, six or more families in separate apartments (Eberstadt, 1909, 57—8).

Growing residential densities and overcrowding were compounded in many towns by poor sanitation and water supplies, which had received little attention from the effete post-Napoleonic municipalities. Despite a stirring of concern in the 1830s, prompted by the first European cholera epidemic of 1831–2, and again in the later 1840s when a new visitation of cholera coincided with political unrest, urban sanitation was not greatly improved. The main difficulty was the high capital cost of sewerage and water schemes. A waterborne sewerage system was included in the general reconstruction of Hamburg after the disastrous fire of 1842, and Frankfurt and a few other towns began to follow this example in the 1850s and 1860s. Most, however, lagged behind their British equivalents in this respect into the 1870s and even beyond. Instead, they concentrated on ensuring that new districts were built in a healthy manner, by using and developing the existing police powers to plan new thoroughfares and thus to delimit suitable street-blocks. This intervention had the additional advantage of stimulating new building by imposing a degree of order on the fragmented agricultural plots and prompting their rearrangement into convenient building sites.

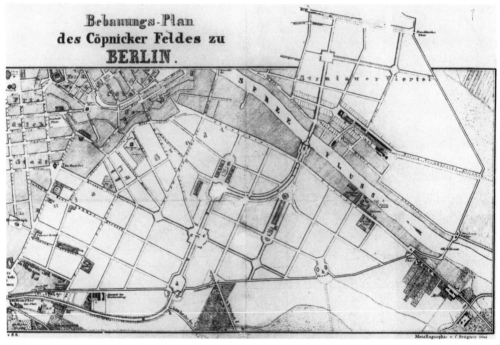

1   *German extension planning in the first half of the nineteenth century: the Köpernicker Feld and the Stralauer Viertel, Berlin, in 1843. This was the largest area available for street planning by the* Polizei *until the completion of rural land reform in 1850. (Landesarchiv Berlin)*

The initial example was provided by Berlin. Already the largest city in Germany in 1815, Berlin grew faster than most in the 1820s and 1830s. The city council, like most others in Germany, was largely indifferent to the problems caused by growth. However, because the Berlin *Polizei* remained under direct State control the Prussian government was able to order it to prepare street plans for a number of new districts in continuation of the tradition established by the kings of Prussia in the seventeenth and eighteenth centuries. Work on these planned extensions began as early as 1825 and the first of the new streets were laid out, in the Friedrich-Wilhelm-Stadt, in around 1830. Further development was restricted by the incomplete state of rural land reform, but the experience confirmed the Prussian government's confidence in this relatively cheap form of environmental control (Hegemann, 1963, 192; Thienel, 1973, 29–30). When environmental problems welled up more generally in the 1840s the government did not hesitate to encourage other towns to plan their own extensions. It also strengthened their powers to do so.

The first major step was a law of 1845 which supplemented the street-planning procedure by empowering the urban *Polizei* to supervise the creation of building sites and to refuse permission for any new building which would constitute a danger for the community or an obstacle to police supervision (Hartog, 1962, 107). In 1850 the Prussian law on police administration confirmed the powers of the *Polizei* to fix the lines of new streets (ibid., 106). By this time, however, the municipalities were beginning to respond to the demands of the industrial era. In the interests of efficient administration, the government decided in 1855 to give them the main initiative in the preparation of extension plans. The *Polizei* still retained certain technical functions and the plans had to be confirmed by the State before compulsory-purchase powers for the thoroughfares could come into force, but after 1855 the last word in any dispute was the elected municipality's, except at Berlin and Potsdam (Kabel, 1949, 55).

This extension of municipal authority was part of a broader effort by the Prussian government, pursued in a series of ordinances between 1831 and 1856, to strengthen urban administration to meet the challenges of population growth and industrialization (see Engeli and Haus, 1975). More active urban government did not however mean more democratic government. On the contrary, the Prussian government acted (apart from a brief period of liberalization after 1848) to ensure that the more powerful municipalities remained docile agents of the State. In addition to new central controls, it enhanced the powers of the municipal executive (*Magistrat*) at the expense of the elected town council (*Stadtverordnetenversammlung*), which was reduced virtually to advisory status. It also remoulded the local franchise (which was already restricted by fiscal and legal qualifications to a minority of the adult male population), in order to ensure beyond all doubt that, however many manual workers flooded into the towns, the councils would continue to be dominated by the rich (Hennock, 1973, 299–300; Engeli and Haus, 1975, esp. 12–16, 180–2, 370–2; see also Hofmann, 1978). This effect was achieved by the three-class electoral system (*Dreiklassenwahlrecht*), which was introduced in the Rhineland in 1845 and in the rest of Prussia in 1850. Municipal taxpayers were ranked according to the size of their fiscal contribution and the resulting list was divided into three groups, each of which contributed one-third of the total tax revenues. Each group was then allowed to elect one-third of the council, subject to the proviso that at least half of those elected should be house-owners (Hofmann, 1964, 76–81; Sheehan, 1971, 120).

Thus strengthened, the Prussian municipalities responded to the unprecedented urban growth of the 1850s and 1860s by launching with some vigour into the planning of town extensions. At Düsseldorf, for instance, a planned extension of

1831, covering ninety-nine hectares, was supplemented in 1854 by one covering 376 hectares (*Städtebau*, 1905, 29). At Bielefeld, a much smaller town, the first extension plan of the century was prepared in 1857 (Hofmann, 1964, 13). In Berlin, the biggest extension plan of all, designed to cater for a century's growth all round the existing city, was drawn up between 1858 and 1862. However, various practical difficulties reared their heads. The arrangements for the compulsory purchase of land to form the new streets were unclear, and often involved the municipalities in compensation which they regarded as unfairly high. In addition, the cost of laying out and surfacing the streets, and of installing the underground services, fell entirely on the municipalities. Meanwhile, the owners of the surrounding land enjoyed a huge unearned betterment value. During the 1860s the heavy cost of town extensions became a constant municipal complaint, and the Prussian government began to consider means of lightening the burden (Hartog, 1962, 107–8). However, opposition from propertied interests in the Prussian parliament (*Landtag*), which since 1849 had also been elected by the three-class system, prevented the enactment of reforms.

Matters came to a head in the early 1870s. Many municipalities had begun to recoup some of their costs by undertaking extensions in association with private development companies (*Baugesellschaften*). From 1870 the successful war with France, the resulting reparations, and the creation of the German Empire stimulated the national investment boom which had begun in the later 1860s. A wave of new extensions were now undertaken. When, in 1873, the over-heated German economy was hit by the world economic crash, most of the *Baugesellschaften* went bankrupt and many municipalities were left seriously overstretched. Their renewed demands for the relief of their financial burdens now fell on more receptive ears in Berlin. The Prussian parliament was in one of its more positive phases, boldly adapting the institutions of the State to further Prussia's leadership of a united Germany. As a result, the government was able to put through two laws, in 1874 and 1875, which set up a framework for town-extension planning which was to endure in Prussia until after the First World War.

The less important of the two was the *Enteignungsgesetz* (expropriation law) of 1874. Although it clarified the compulsory purchase of land and buildings for all projects of public utility, it retained some of the defects of previous practice, which had been based on the Prussian law of 1838 regulating railway enterprises. In Germany, as elsewhere in Europe, the legislators had been at pains to ensure that compulsory-purchase powers granted to private or public railway concerns for the construction of their lines could not be used to acquire further land in the vicinity for resale at an enhanced value once the lines were in operation. When applied to the building of new streets, this principle greatly restricted the municipalities' powers to acquire land beyond what was needed to form the surface of the thoroughfares. Not only did this limit their capacity to shape the built environment, but it prevented them from recouping, by the resale of building sites, acquisition costs which were normally much higher than those incurred by the railway companies. Even in 1874, the Prussian legislators chose to regard the *Enteignungsgesetz* primarily from the point of view of railway-building. Consequently, although the law provided the first firm basis for the acquisition of land for streets in town extensions, it did nothing to stimulate the development of more active and constructive municipal intervention. Indeed, this point was vainly made in the *Landtag* debates by a minority of speakers representing municipal interests and the growing public health reform movement (Berger-Thimme, 1976, 203–6).

These criticisms were partially met by the law relating specifically to town extensions which was passed in 1875. This was the *Fluchtliniengesetz* (law on street lines). Although much of it merely codified or slightly modified existing procedures, it strengthened the powers of the municipalities to draw up extension plans and confirmed that it was their duty to do so. It made automatic the compulsory purchase of land reserved in the plans for new streets, and allowed the cost of building, draining and lighting the new streets to be transferred onto the owners of the frontage sites (text in Stübben, 1907, 617–20; English translation in Aldridge, 1915, 84–7). These reforms greatly reduced the cost to the municipalities of carrying out town extensions. However, the *Fluchtliniengesetz* conceded nothing to demands for powers to acquire compulsorily, in the interests of public health, land lying off the new streets (Berger-Thimme, 1976, 206–12).

THE CONSOLIDATION OF EXTENSION PLANNING, 1875–c.1890

The *Fluchtliniengesetz* confirmed the planning of individual new streets and of town extensions as an everyday municipal activity in Prussia. Other states followed a similar course. Indeed, Baden (1868) and Württemberg (1872) had passed comparable legislation before Prussia. Most of the other states had adopted equivalent enactments by the early 1880s (Berger-Thimme, 1976, 149–50). Many towns took advantage of the power, which was offered to them in Prussia and certain other states, to refuse permission for any new building which was not sited on a municipally planned street deemed ready for development. When suburbs spread outside the municipal boundaries, the neighbouring authorities usually prepared street plans to cater for the influx. Consequently, after the 1870s very little new urban building took place in Germany outside the municipally-planned street networks. For the municipalities, early provision of services saved expense (and higher taxation) later on. For those involved in the building process, street planning was on the whole welcome. As earlier in the century, it helped the developers to form fragmented plots into building sites. In addition, now that piped water, sewerage and gas supplies were coming to be expected by tenants, it helped the builders to know that these services would be available on completion of the houses.

This regularization of extension planning coincided with another important stimulus to the outward growth of German towns. This was the removal of the ring fortifications. Confidence in the efficacy of ring defences began to wane from the 1850s, and after the unification of Germany in 1871 the military authorities were generally willing to agree to the defortification of all but key frontier towns. Numerous ring earthworks were thus removed in the 1870s, often in association with town-extension schemes (Hartog, 1962, 27). In those towns where the army insisted on retaining the fortifications, it was often prepared to build a new line to encompass suburban growth, as at Mainz after 1872, Strasbourg in 1875–9, and at Cologne in the early 1880s and again after 1906 (Dickinson, 1961, 84–5; Hartog, 1962, 65–71). With rural land reform now complete everywhere in Germany, there were from the 1870s no longer any artificial restrictions on the outward spread of most towns.

Despite these encouragements, the practice of extension planning did not greatly advance in the 1870s and 1880s. After the early 1870s German urban expansion slowed in response to the relatively depressed condition of the world economy. Between 1871 and 1890 only about eight and a half million people were added to the urban population of Germany (Hohorst *et al.*, 1975, 22, 42–3, 52). In supervising their accommodation, the municipalities concerned themselves primarily with sanitation. In somewhat belated emulation of British experience and that of Hamburg, Frankfurt and other pioneers in Germany, they began in the 1870s to instal modern water-supply and sewerage systems. Above ground, they concentrated on superficial cleansing and on laying out broad streets which (or so they hoped) would permit the free circulation of air and adequate natural lighting for dwellings. Their extension plans reflected these limited, though important, objectives.

In their detailed planning most towns continued to emulate Berlin. In 1858 the Prussian government had ordered the Berlin police authorities to produce a large-scale extension plan. The work was entrusted to James Hobrecht (1825–1903), a young official in the police building department with a training in architecture and civil engineering. Hobrecht's huge *Bebauungsplan* (physical development plan), published in 1862, was sufficiently far-sighted to remain in force, with only minor revisions, until 1919 (Matzerath and Thienel, 1977, 176; see Heinrich, 1962). The scale of Hobrecht's planning far exceeded anything previously attempted in Berlin. All the streets in the plan were between twenty-five and thirty metres wide and the blocks, in order to reduce street-building costs, were immense. Many of them measured 200 metres by 300 or even 400 metres (Eberstadt, 1909, 58–62). Apart from the streets, the only public spaces were a number of huge squares. It would appear that Hobrecht, and initially the police authorities as well, saw the planned street network as only a skeleton, to which narrower sidestreets and generous planted spaces would be added when building took place (Hegemann, 1913, 153; see Radicke, 1974). In practice, however, such refinements were neglected. The police authorities, which until 1875 remained responsible for building the streets, cut costs to the minimum and the municipality followed their example thereafter. In consequence, the plan greatly aided the spread of the *Mietskasernen*, which could be built on the broad streets up to the maximum height allowed by the building regulations, while spreading deep into the interiors of the blocks via a succession of small courtyards.

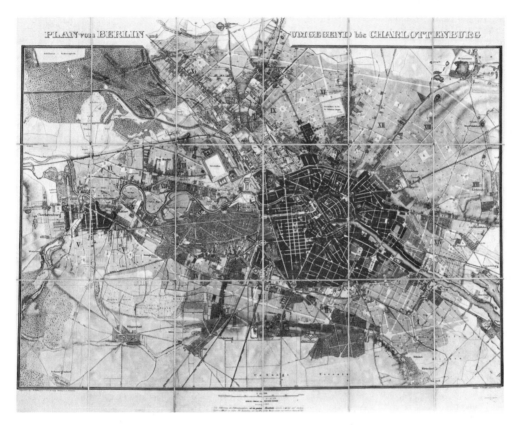

2   *Berlin: the Hobrecht extension plan of 1862. Note the continuity of planning between the Köpernicker Feld, now largely built up, and the suburban ring planned by Hobrecht. Large blocks and wide streets dominate the scheme, and the only open space is the market square provided for each district. Existing royal parks and other public open lands have, however, been incorporated. (Landesarchiv Berlin)*

The Hobrecht plan soon aroused criticism among Berlin housing reformers, notably in an article by Ernst Bruch, a social statistician, published in the *Deutsche Bauzeitung* in 1870 (Albers, 1975a, 15, 38–9, 54, 61, 65). However, its combination of cheapness and efficiency greatly recommended it to other towns. Berlin's example was widely followed in the urban building boom of the late 1860s and early 1870s. When extension planning was firmly established in 1875 it remained the model for many new projects and in some towns it continued to dominate during the 1880s. In Düsseldorf, for instance, a plan for the extension of the whole city was introduced in 1884, supplementing earlier schemes which had dealt with only segments of the periphery. The planned area totalled 2,400 hectares. Assuming an average density of 250 people to the hectare, it provided space for a population of 600,000 people — nearly six times the current population of the town. In its uniformly wide streets and lack of open space it repeated all the defects of the Berlin plan (*Städtebau*, 1905, 29—30).

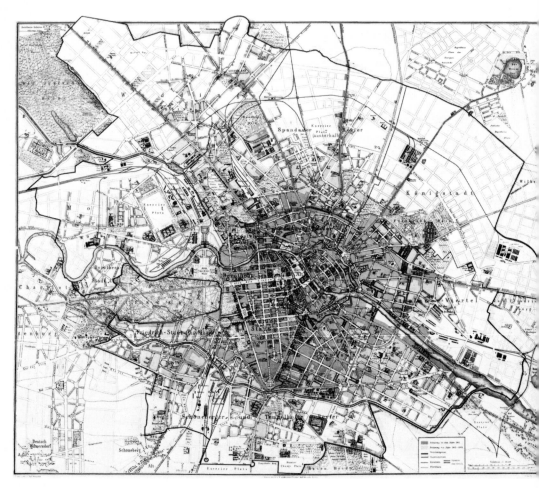

3   *Berlin: the spread of building, 1861—76. The dark-grey areas were built up before 1861, and the light-grey were built between 1861 and 1876, after the introduction of the Hobrecht plan. Note the concentrating effect of the plan, with extensive planned areas, such as Königstadt in the north-east, completely untouched by the builders. (Landesarchiv Berlin)*

The weaknesses of this crude form of extension planning began to stimulate debate in specialist circles in the early 1870s. One of the effects of national unification was to prompt the foundation of a number of professional and social-reform associations to coordinate or supersede bodies which had previously operated within the individual states. Particularly interested in the urban environment were the *Verband deutscher Architekten- und Ingenieurvereine* (Confederation of German Associations of Architects and Engineers), which was founded in 1871, and the *Deutsche Verein für öffentliche Gesundheitspflege* (German Association for the Promotion of Public Health), set up in 1873. Less directly involved was the *Verein für Sozialpolitik* (Association for Social Policy), founded in 1872. These three bodies generated distinctive but overlapping approaches to the urban question.

4   *Berlin* Mietskasernen *of the later nineteenth century. This dense, multi-storey building pattern was greatly encouraged by the crude application of the Hobrecht extension plan and its associated building regulations. (Photograph by courtesy of Franziska Bollerey and Kristiana Hartmann)*

The *Verband deutscher Architekten- und Ingenieurvereine* was a professional organization which grouped the various local and regional associations of architects and engineers which had grown up in Germany since the foundation of the Berlin association in 1824 (*Centralblatt*, 1889, 335–7). Separate organizations existed, both locally and nationally, for architects on the one hand and engineers on the other, but the *Verband* and its constituent associations reflected a willingness among German architects, unparalleled among their British and French equivalents, to combine with engineers to discuss matters of mutual interest. These covered a wide range, including industrial design and transport, but the shaping of towns figured prominently in their proceedings, and local branches of the *Verband* were particularly strong and active in the large cities.

The *Verein für öffentliche Gesundheitspflege* reflected the growing concern for environmental hygiene which had greatly advanced in the 1860s and early 1870s. More overtly a reforming body than the *Verband*, it counted among its adherents members of a variety of professions, municipal officials, politicians and social reformers (Hartog, 1962, 24).

The *Verein für Sozialpolitik*, finally, was the creation of a group of educated reformers drawn from the upper and middle classes. They were commonly known as *Kathedersozialisten* ('chair socialists') as so many of them were university professors. The *Verein* advocated the resolution of the social problems associated with industrialization by an extension of public intervention in the workings of society and the economy. From its origins it showed a lively interest in the improvement of the urban environment. Although anti-socialist and even conservative in its political tendency, it looked favourably on the growth of municipal activity and on land reform (Hartog, 1962, 63; Marschalk, 1978, 63; Berger-Thimme, 1976, 122–3).

While comparable organizations existed in other countries, those of Germany were unique in the direct influence which they exercised on the formulation of urban policy. This influence was a product of the distinctive nature of German urban government, and the marked professionalization of public life. When rapid urban growth began to place greater burdens on the municipalities in mid-century, the larger towns were forced to appoint more salaried officials to replace the leisured citizens who had previously filled all but the most onerous executive positions on the *Magistrat*. This process was connected with the extension of the executive's control over policy-making, and by the 1870s the senior salaried officials were beginning to find themselves in a position of some power. Although their numbers did not normally outweigh those of the unpaid members of the *Magistrat*, they generally served there longer (in Prussia they were appointed for twelve years, compared to six for the unpaid members).

Most powerful of all the salaried men was the *Bürgermeister* (in the larger towns, *Oberbürgermeister*). In Prussia and most other states the *Bürgermeister* was appointed by the government from a shortlist drawn up by the town council. He was normally expected, by both government and council, to have administrative experience and appropriate professional qualifications, usually in jurisprudence. In the Prussian province of the Rhineland, and in some other parts of Germany, the *Bürgermeister* had enjoyed strong executive powers since the early nineteenth century, in emulation of the French institution of the *mairie*. Elsewhere, his official status was merely that of chairman of the *Magistrat*. As the century wore on, however, the influence of Rhenish practice, and the growing scale of municipal responsibilities, tended to strengthen the power of the *Bürgermeister* throughout Germany. His long term of office helped him to build up close control over his municipality's policies, either directly or through the growing corps of officials which he supervised. The big-city *Oberbürgermeister*, in particular, were men of some standing in national as well as local affairs. In Prussia, many of them represented their towns in the upper house of parliament (*Herrenhaus*) after 1848. Birth, education, military record and personal contacts made most of them worthy members of the upper-middle class. Security of tenure allowed most of them to steer clear of party politics in their towns, and some maintained a non-political stance at national level. Nearly all, however, were through personal inclination or self-interest strong supporters of the Crown's policies, and many were openly of National Liberal tendency. These virtues made them highly effective promoters of their towns' interests, and as such they enjoyed great respect both in their councils and among the citizenry in general (Hofmann, 1974, 26–56; Hennock, 1973, 299–300).

The development of environmental policies was thus determined to a large extent by the salaried officials. Certainly, they could not ignore the powerful economic interests represented in the town council and among the unpaid members of the *Magistrat*, but they held an initiative which their counterparts in England, the 'servants' of sometimes narrow-minded and ignorant councils, were denied (see Hennock, 1973). In using that initiative, they were very open to influence from the professional and reform associations, in which they were allowed to participate fully. Even some of the *Oberbürgermeister*, most notably Franz Adickes (1846–1915), *Oberbürgermeister* of Frankfurt between 1891 and 1911, played an active part in their debates. Far more numerous, however, were officials directly concerned with the environment. The associations kept them in touch with developments in other towns and states, and helped them to see their own activities in the context of social policy as a whole. They could use the associations to drum up support for extensions of powers or other reforms which they needed in their towns. Activity in the associations could allow the abler official to build up a national reputation and so move easily to a better post in a larger town, or even into state or imperial politics and administration. For the less gifted man, the associations offered the chance to maintain his awareness of professional opportunities elsewhere in Germany, and to build up a vicarious experience of administrative procedures which varied greatly from state to state (and, within Prussia, from province to province).

Also attracted were the numerous independent professionals who were involved with urban administration as consultants, competition entrants or representatives of private interests. The rapidly growing towns made heavy calls on such people, who were spawned by Germany's highly-organized system of technical education. They were joined in the associations by many of their educators — professors in technical subjects in the expanding high schools and universities. Particularly prominent in the later nineteenth century was Reinhard Baumeister (1833–1917), professor in the school of engineering at Karlsruhe Polytechnic. Many of these professors themselves engaged directly in urban affairs as elected representatives or consultants. Such was the level of expertise in the associations that the state and imperial legislators among their members often invited them to take part in drawing up bills and regulations.

The associations first began to make their influence felt during the Prussian debates on urban powers in 1874 and 1875. At this early stage, however, they did not seek a major modification of the Hobrechtian model of town-extension planning. The *Verein für Sozialpolitik* was as yet scarcely aware of the possibility of creating an educative or integrative urban environment. The *Verein für öffentliche Gesundheitspflege*, for its part, was concentrating on persuading the municipalities to provide good sewers and water supplies, and wide streets, so it regarded the *Fluchtliniengesetz* as a step forward. Only the *Verband deutscher Architekten- und Ingenieurvereine* struck a contentious note, in a resolution which it passed in 1874. Entitled 'Fundamentals for town extensions in their technical, economic and police aspects', it reflected a general fear among the members of the *Verband* that any encouragement of extension planning would lead to the drawing up of a rash of ill-considered schemes by inexperienced personnel. At worst, the plans might discourage building and put architects out of work; and there was a distinct danger that excessive rigidity on Hobrechtian lines might limit the freedom of designers working for private clients (text in Stübben, 1907, 643—4). Consequently, the resolution urged that municipalities should restrict themselves to planning the main lines of communication and establishing basic health standards for new building, leaving market forces to shape everything else. Local and sidestreets should be planned only when building was about to take place, or left entirely to the discretion of the developers. If the plan sought to allot a special character or function to any district, it should do so in accordance with existing circumstances in the area, and compulsory direction of its development should be limited to the exclusion or regulation of industry under general public health powers.

These recommendations were largely reflected in the technical advice on the implementation of the *Fluchtliniengesetz* which was issued to Prussian municipalities by the Minister of Commerce in 1876 (text in Stübben, 1907, 620—3). They were also incorporated into Germany's first extension-planning manual, Reinhard Baumeister's *Stadterweiterungen in technischer, baupolizeilicher und wirthschaftlicher Beziehung* (Town extensions: their links with technical and economic concerns, and with building regulations), which also appeared in 1876. Baumeister had presented the report on which the *Verband*'s 1874 resolution had been based and, with James Hobrecht now heavily involved in creating a modern sewerage system for Berlin, Baumeister emerged as the leading expert on extension planning in Germany. However, Baumeister's main experience up to this point had been in railway-building and his book was more notable for its caution than its precision.

This subdued note was generally maintained in the municipal practice of extension planning in the 1870s and 1880s. Thanks to growing experience and the advice of the associations, the worst of Hobrecht's errors were avoided in a growing number of towns (Baumeister, 1876, v). A greater variety of street-widths was used and very large blocks were avoided (see Baumeister, 1887, 4—5). However, the authorities hesitated to extend their control over private land. Some of the larger towns, encouraged by the *Verein für öffentliche Gesundheitspflege*, tightened up their building regulations to counter some of the worst abuses of the proliferating *Mietskasernen*, but little was done to encourage the building of smaller houses and the provision of more open space, private or public. Indeed, some of the people who lived through these years later looked back on them as something of an interlude. For instance, in 1904 two Hanover officials, trying to excuse the defects of a district of their city which had been planned as late as 1888—9, wrote:

> At that time Paris, Brussels, etc., with their disregard for the shape of the street-blocks, their traffic arteries running straight across the city from one side to another, and their inevitable star-junctions, passed as good examples. Sitte's book, Stübben's text, and Henrici's fine plans had not yet appeared. The scanty literature of town planning (*Städtebau*), with the sole exception of Baumeister's manual, was scattered in a number of different journals, and active professionals in responsible positions felt that they had little more to draw on in their planning work than their own experience and the prevailing attitudes of the time. (*Städtebau*, 1904, 37—8)

THE EMERGENCE OF COMPREHENSIVE URBAN PLANNING TECHNIQUE, c. 1890—1914

This relatively placid phase began to come to an end around 1890. Underlying the change was the resumption of rapid economic growth which began to make itself felt from the later 1880s. Germany now emerged as Britain's major industrial and military rival in Europe. Urban growth accelerated in consequence; between 1890 and 1910 over fifteen and a half million people were added to the urban population of Germany, nearly twice the increase registered in the previous two decades. In 1910 60 per cent of the population of the German Empire resided in towns. Most of the growth continued to occur in the larger centres. Towns of between 20,000 and 100,000 inhabitants had accommodated 7.7 per cent of Germany's population in 1871; in 1910, 13.4 per cent lived in them. In towns of more than 100,000 people, development had been even more spectacular. By 1910, 21.3 per cent of the population of Germany lived in such towns, compared to only 4.1 per cent in 1871 (Hohorst *et al.*, 1975, 22, 42—3, 52).

This growth prompted a considerable expansion of the built-up areas, particularly in the larger towns. Its impact was amplified by two other factors which, though not entirely novel, exercised a markedly enhanced effect after about

1890. These were public transport and the growth of the middle class. The introduction of the electric tramcar from the early 1890s occurred more rapidly and more generally in Germany than in any other European country (see McKay, 1976). Meanwhile, the middle class of non-manual workers was greatly expanded by an influx of white-collar employees generated by Germany's rapid economic development (Crossick, 1977, 20–1). With cheap and rapid transport increasingly available, this middle class came for the first time to play a major, distinct part in the total demand for urban space (Born, 1976, 27). Able to command more residential space than manual workers, and increasingly willing to live in peripheral areas, the middle class helped to promote an expansion of the German town after 1890 which contrasted with the slower, denser outward growth of the 1870s and 1880s (see Baumeister, 1887, 4).

These changes in the spatial implications of urban development were accompanied by a transformation of the social context within which environmental policy evolved. Social tensions, which had been kept under control in the 1880s by Bismarck's ban on the socialist parties, anti-trade union legislation, and welfare measures, welled up again after 1890. With Bismarck dismissed and the Social Democratic Party once more allowed to operate openly, industrial conflicts multiplied and socialist representatives were returned in growing numbers to the *Reichstag*. Among the upper and middle class apprehension mounted of the shifting, pullulating worker masses in the cities. Even if they did not pose a direct threat to the State through revolutionary action, they appeared capable of dragging down the whole of society by their defective morals, slovenly behaviour, and poor physical and mental condition (Hartmann, 1977, 18–19; see also Krabbe, 1974; Vondung, 1976).

The housing question now emerged as an important (though by no means the only) focus of these concerns. Up to the 1880s it had been regarded largely as a matter of sanitation and public health; in the 1890s the new spurt of urban population brought problems of supply, rents and quality of accommodation more strongly to the fore (see e.g. Eberstadt, 1893, 5–23). Housing also came to be seen as more than just a physical matter. It was increasingly incorporated into the general debate on the social question, in which considerations of family life, property ownership and community spirit generated growing attention. As time passed, this new, broader definition of the housing question itself tended to merge into a developing awareness of the total environment as an influence on people's attitudes and behaviour as well as on their physical condition.

The municipalities, encouraged by the state and imperial governments, responded energetically to these new circumstances. As their suburbs spread, they obtained boundary extensions; of the total area annexed by German towns between 1850 and 1918, nine-tenths was taken in after 1885 (Matzerath, 1978, 79; see Rebentisch, 1978). They redoubled their efforts to ensure that adequate public transport was provided (see e.g. Bangert, 1936, 70–1). Most of them refrained from the direct provision of housing, but they were increasingly persuaded that they could stimulate the building of cheap, healthy and socially educative housing by refining and extending their policies of environmental control. This growth of activity, combined with changes in the internal structure of the towns themselves as they divided more clearly into areas of distinct function, gradually generated an awareness of the need for more ambitious municipal strategies of urban development.

A major role in the creation of the necessary expertise was played by the distinctively German institution of the public competition. It was common practice in nineteenth-century Germany (as it still is) to select the designs of important public buildings by open competitions, judged by panels of independent experts. The first important extension of this method to urban planning in German-speaking Europe had been the competition held at Vienna in 1857 for the development of the fortification zone around the old city (Wurzer, 1974a, 14—15). Although most towns in the future German Empire were happy at first to entrust their extensions to their own officials or commissioned consultants, their growing recognition of the complicated issues involved therein inclined some of them to draw more widely on the expertise generated within the professional and reform associations, and in the universities and high schools. The first major city in Germany to organize an extension competition was Cologne. Severely constricted by the Prussian army's fortification line, Cologne had been unable to join in the wave of extension planning in the 1860s and early 1870s. When, in 1880, the army at last agreed to build a new line some 600 metres further out, the municipality found itself short of experience. It therefore decided to hold a competition for an extension plan to cover the whole of the area between the old and new fortifications.

The competition was a great success, with twenty-seven entries. First prize went to a scheme submitted jointly by Joseph Stübben (1845—1936), director of works at Aachen, and Karl Henrici, an architect in the same town. The basis of the plan was a ring street (*Ringstrasse*) six kilometres in length running through the newly-acquired zone, with an associated system of sidestreets and open spaces. Of course, such ring streets had already become the standard replacement for fortifications in Germany and they figured in most of the other entries. Where Stübben and Henrici stood out was in their appreciation that the new zone of building would alter the structure of the whole city. They clearly distinguished a business area in the south and a villa district in the north. They also proposed a rationalization of the railway system and changes in the building regulations (Wurzer, 1974a, 26).

So novel was Stübben's approach that he was invited to Cologne to direct the implementation of his plan. He took up this offer in 1881 and within a few years his work at Cologne had established him as Germany's leading planner. He also began to play an active part in the associations, where he urged that effective planning of the outer areas of a town could be carried out only in the context of a development strategy for the whole. This view was encapsulated in a set of 'Guiding principles of town extension with particular respect for hygiene' which he put through the *Verein für öffentliche Gesundheitspflege* in 1885 (text in Stübben, 1907, 644—5):

> Every developing town requires for its outward extension and the improvement of its inner areas a unified, comprehensive physical development plan (*Stadtbauplan*). Attention should be given in the plan to suitable street widths, the appropriate routing of the streets, open spaces, means of transport, planting (rows of trees, front gardens, and planted squares) and public gardens, a drainable and flood-free situation (or one protected against flood), water-supply and drainage systems, the purity of natural watercourses, the suitable size of building sites, and sites for public buildings and other municipal establishments.

Stübben went on to develop this principle in a massive textbook, *Der Städtebau*, which appeared in 1890, completely supplanting Baumeister's extension-planning manual of 1876.

The movement towards the planning of entire towns was thus firmly established in advanced circles before the great spurt in urban growth in the 1890s. It was then further reinforced by two influential competitions, at Vienna and Munich, both held in 1893. At Vienna a big boundary extension in 1890 had incorporated some established suburbs and competition entrants were asked to produce, not an extension plan, but a general regulating plan (*General-Regulirungs-plan*) for the whole city. The Munich brief required a *Generalbebauungsplan* (general development plan), with no limit of area. The results were a triumph for Stübben and his approach. At Vienna his entry shared first prize with that of Otto Wagner, the leading Viennese architect. Of the four equal first prizes awarded at Munich, one went to Stübben's former associate, Henrici, whose entry was singled out by the jury as the most aesthetically satisfactory (Wurzer, 1974a, 26—8).

Although the winning entries at these competitions confirmed beyond all doubt that an entire city could be developed in accordance with a single scheme, they stopped some way short of comprehensive urban planning. As the work of pure architects, or of architects with supplementary training or experience in urban engineering, they concentrated on communications and public space, rather than on the use of private land. Proper consideration of the latter awaited developments in a separate field of environmental control, that of building regulations.

Despite the general transfer of town extension powers to the municipalities, building controls had, in most of Germany, remained the province of the *Polizei*. Even though, in practice, the police authorities were subservient to the municipalities in most towns, this division of powers had delayed the evolution of a fully integrated environmental policy for both public and private land. By the 1880s most of the larger towns had responded to the growing public health movement by enacting building codes the main purpose of which was to control the worst excesses of large tenement blocks. However, while banning the extreme horrors of the *Mietskasernen*, these regulations added needlessly to the construction costs of smaller buildings and contributed to the proliferation of the tenement block, which reached its climax in the later 1880s (see Baumeister, 1887, 18).

This development horrified the German housing reformers. Ever since their emergence as a distinct group in the 1840s, under the leadership of Victor Aimé Huber (see Rauchbach, 1969), they had advocated the single-family house as the ideal residence for the German worker (see e.g. Sax, 1869). Yet by the late

5   *Houses in the best-known of the Berlin* Villenkolonien, *Grunewald. Though welcomed by housing reformers as a means of breaking down the Berlin high-density building pattern, the villa colonies were never more than retreats for the rich. Low-density suburbanization was to remain a minority movement until the turn of the century. (Landesarchiv Berlin)*

1880s the flat had become the normal dwelling even of the middle classes in the larger towns. Only the very rich could afford to live in the 'villa-colonies' which had sprung up round Berlin and other large cities since the 1860s. The further the small house was removed from the reach of the working man, the more virtue the housing reformers (nearly all of whom belonged to the upper and middle classes) saw in it. In the 1880s and even more in the 1890s it came increasingly to be seen not merely as a healthy home conducive to a happy family life, but as an encouragement to thrift, residential stability, self-improvement, and acceptance of the existing social order. In a Germany increasingly dominated by finance capital, more and more non-socialist reformers were prepared to single out urban land and building speculators and their supporters, the big investment banks and selfish property interests in the municipal councils, as the main opponents of harmonious social progress.

Responding to this shift of opinion, the reform associations began to advocate what came to be known as *abgestufte Bauordnungen* or *Staffelbauordnungen* (stepped, or differential, building regulations). The idea was that full heights and an intensive use of sites should be allowed in the central districts where land values were high; in the outer areas, however, lower buildings, covering smaller proportions of the sites, should be required. The first resolutions to this effect were passed by the *Verein für öffentliche Gesundheitspflege* and the *Verband deutscher Architekten- und Ingenieurvereine* in the later 1880s, under the principal influence of Baumeister, Stübben and Franz Adickes, at that time *Oberbürgermeister* of Altona (Hartog, 1962, 111). Though a lawyer by training, Adickes had built up considerable experience of urban planning through his involvement in the harbour extension at Altona in the 1880s. He had also become a firm opponent of land speculation. In 1891 he took up the post of *Oberbürgermeister* of Frankfurt, a city of low-density traditions where the spread of the tenement block was causing grave misgivings (Bangert, 1936, 25–7). Taking full advantage of the executive powers vested in him by the Rhineland municipal constitution, he pushed through, before the end of the year, Germany's first comprehensive set of differential building regulations. Frankfurt was divided into an inner and an outer building zone. In the former, the maximum height was fixed at four storeys. In the outer zone the regulations were designed to produce much lower and less densely constructed buildings. However, it was clearly recognized that regulations designed to produce low-density residential building might hinder the creation of premises for non-residential uses which, quite properly, might wish to locate in the outer areas. Consequently, both zones were divided into residential, mixed and industrial districts (Hartog, 1962, 112; Bangert, 1936, 49–51).

The new Frankfurt regulations had revolutionary implications for the development of German urban planning. Before 1891 the courts had normally been prepared to rule that a landowner's right to use his property as he wished, which was enshrined in the *Allgemeine Landrecht* in Prussia and in similar codes in the other states, could be limited by general building regulations designed to protect the public interest. It had, however, been assumed that the public interest was the same throughout the whole of the area governed by the regulations. That some landowners should be more restricted than others merely as a result of the location of their property within the town was a different matter altogether. The only precedent was provided by the powers, which local authorities in most German states had enjoyed since the 1860s, to prevent the establishment of noxious industries in certain areas. The courts, however, chose to draw on this precedent in ruling in favour of Frankfurt and other pioneering towns which were taken to law in the early 1890s (Hartog, 1962, 112). Consequently, differential building regulations were allowed to spread without hindrance throughout Germany and by the early 1900s most of the larger towns had adopted them (see Logan, 1976, 380–1).

The towns soon found, however, that the differential regulations required them to adopt a much more sensitive and scientific approach to urban development than had previously been their wont. The designation of a particular use for any district had implications for the size of the blocks and the width and arrangement of the streets. Industrial areas, for instance, required wide streets and large blocks; in residential districts the opposite was generally the case but the layout of land for shops and other services often raised problems. If too much or too little land was designated for a given use the whole of the land market could be distorted and all building held back. The separation of residence and employment required consideration of public transport, working hours and incomes. Initially, many towns found these problems beyond them and made huge mistakes, or took refuge in strategies so vague and flexible as to be almost worthless (Stübben, 1920, 114). However, the associations rose to the challenge by providing a forum of informed discussion. A series of resolutions were passed in the 1890s, notably by the *Verein für öffentliche Gesundheitspflege*, urging the urban authorities to grasp the nettle and advocating various extensions of public powers, most notably in the compulsory purchase of land for open space, slum clearance and the rearrangement of building sites (*Umlegung*) (see texts in Stübben, 1907, 647–51).

In 1900 powers and procedures very similar to those advocated by the *Verein* were incorporated for the first time in a general enactment of a German state. This was the general urban development law (*allgemeine Baugesetz*) passed by the Saxon parliament (Albers, 1975b, 63). It conferred general planning powers on urban authorities for both new and established districts. Not only were the authorities empowered to lay out streets and provide drainage and other underground services, but they could also set aside land for open spaces, playgrounds and other communal uses including churches and schools. The law also codified and supplemented the existing powers of compulsory purchase so that they could be used, subject to certain checks, to acquire land needed for any public purpose. Authorities were empowered to fix maximum heights and control the arrangement of buildings erected on private sites, forbidding industrial and commercial premises where they considered these inappropriate (text in Stübben, 1907, 626–30). During the next few years most of the other states followed the Saxon example and enacted general planning laws (Berger-Thimme, 1976, 150). The main exception was Prussia, where conservative interests in the *Landtag* had become a major obstacle to all social reforms. However, the Prussian government partly compensated for this deficiency by the ministerial circular of 20 December 1906 and other orders encouraging the urban authorities to adopt more ambitious and sensitive policies of environmental control (*Städtebau*, 1909, 79; Heiligenthal, 1929, 27–8).

It was thus in the early 1900s that urban planning came to be fully recognized in Germany as both a useful and a practicable municipal activity. The term 'Städtebau', first popularized by Stübben and Sitte around 1890, by now had general currency. In many of the larger towns the *Baurat* had been joined, or replaced, by a *Stadtbaurat*. Town planners (*Städtebauer*) now began to regard themselves as a distinct profession; special training courses sprang up, competitions multiplied, and technical literature proliferated (Albers, 1975a, 89–90). A major milestone was the launching, in 1904, of *Der Städtebau*, the first journal in the world to be devoted exclusively to town planning. Its founders, Camillo Sitte and Theodor Goecke, were partly motivated by the hope that *Der Städtebau* would ensure the victory of the 'artistic' tendency in planning, which Sitte in particular represented (see Collins, 1965), over the more bureaucratic, materialistic and philistine elements. However, they were sufficiently aware of the social, economic and technical aspects of planning to aspire to serve the whole field. In their first editorial they described *Städtebau* as 'a...great field of technical, artistic and economic (*volkswirtschaftlich*) activity, ...only recently recognized and promoted as a single, complete entity' (*Städtebau*, 1904, 1). It was, they continued, both a science and an art, drawing contributions from a multitude of cooperating specialists, including engineers, economists, artists, doctors, sociologists, historians, archaeologists and administrators.

Among the growing number of books which reflected this comprehensive approach were Ludwig Hercher's *Grossstadterweiterungen* (The Planned Extension of Cities) (1904), and Eugen Fassbender's *Grundzüge der modernen Stadtbaukunde* (Foundations of the Modern Science of Urban Planning) (1912). Meanwhile, Stübben published the second edition of his *Der Städtebau* in 1907, incorporating recent work by other authors. Hercher provided the first comprehensive formulation of the functions of the *Städtebauer*, and went on to advocate a strategy of development based on encouraging commercial functions in the centre and residence in the outer areas, the two being linked by fast traffic routes which would also attract commercial activities (Albers, 1975a, 26; Stübben, 1907, 316–18). Fassbender put forward a similar view of the town but developed a more scientific approach than either Stübben or Hercher to the preparation of the plans (see Wurzer, 1974b).

The impact of this expanding literature was reinforced by an innovation, the town-planning exhibition. The practice of organizing exhibits relating to environmental matters had grown up during the nineteenth century with the international exhibitions (see below, p. 165). Within Germany it first became common in the early 1900s in connection with the national housing reform congresses, but the first big extension of the idea to town planning as a whole came in 1910. In that year a large town-planning exhibition was put on in Berlin as part of a campaign to promote the regional planning of the Berlin area (see below, p. 45). Later in the year the exhibition moved to Düsseldorf at the invitation of the municipality. It was such a success there that in 1912 Düsseldorf held another exhibition as part of an international congress on urban policy (*Städtebau*, 1913, 14). Theodor Goecke hailed this exhibition and congress as a sign that *Städtebau*, which had been 'still in children's shoes' a decade previously, had now come of age in Germany (*Städtebau*, 1913, 20).

PLANNING AND THE GERMAN CITY IN THE LAST YEARS BEFORE THE WAR

In an institutional sense, German town planning had indeed come of age by 1914. In terms of physical achievement, however, its results were still only partial. To some extent, planning practice remained constricted by lack of knowledge; there were signs of the growth of a distinct urban science from the 1890s, particularly in the work of Theodor Goecke, Rudolf Eberstadt, Paul Voigt, and other economists, but most planning decisions continued to be based on experience derived from practice (Hegemann, 1913, 151–2). Much more restricting however were the limitations which remained on the powers and the freedom of action of the planners.

The great development of public control of the urban environment since the 1870s had occurred in a political atmosphere that was generally favourable to the free enjoyment of private property and to rapid economic growth directed mainly by private interests. These interests — capital, land and the better-paid professions — dominated the representative institutions of Germany throughout the period. In the *Reichstag*, which was elected by full manhood suffrage, they faced a growing challenge from the main working-class party, the Social Democrats, from the early 1890s. They nevertheless retained control there, with support from the growing lower-middle class, until the war. In any case, the *Reichstag* was only a partial arbiter of social policy, much of which remained in the hands of the *Land* governments and the municipalities. In most of these, more demanding electoral qualifications allowed wealth to remain in easy control. Its position was particularly strong in Prussia thanks to the three-class electoral system.

To some extent, it must be said, the power of wealth was moderated by the central and local institutions of the State. Although principles of *laisser-faire* economics, drawn largely from the orthodoxy generated in Britain since the later eighteenth century, had been of great influence in Germany, especially in the early industrialization period, they had never reduced the State's domestic field of action to the rudimentary level achieved in Britain. The states of nineteenth-century Germany, and especially the dominant Prussia, inherited traditions of practice from the absolutist period which proved very durable. Before unification, Prussia and some of the other states actively promoted economic development to sustain their political and military ambitions. Some participated directly in the industrialization process, notably by building and operating railways and water-ways. After 1871 the imperial and state governments, eager to protect their institutions from being undermined by the social tensions generated by industria-lization, showed a willingness to rein in the increasingly powerful capital and land interests. In the interests of economic development as a whole, which had to fuel the Empire's increasingly voracious political ambitions, they also acted to reduce friction between competing private interests (see Medalen, 1978, 93—4). In these respects the late nineteenth-century German State was prepared to engage in economic and social planning to an extent unparalleled in Britain. In doing so, moreover, it enjoyed the general support of private owners of land and capital who, thanks to the social stability and efficient productive environment which the State could normally guarantee, were assured of the secure and profitable enjoyment of their investments together with the extra degree of social status which their alliance with an unusually pompous State could confer upon them.

Most of the development of urban planning in Germany before 1914 occurred within the area of public activity defined by this consensus. It was on the whole not the product of pressure by the consumers of the urban environment, the vast majority of whom were manual workers or low-paid, propertyless white-collar employees. Admittedly, the emergence of growing Social Democratic minorities in the municipal councils after 1891 coincided with a general extension of municipal activity, even to the point where the expression 'municipal socialism', imported from Britain, began to be used in all seriousness in the early 1900s. Their presence, however, did little more than generate a more acute awareness of social tensions among the wealthy interests which dominated the councils, and the in-creasingly State-influenced bureaucrats who were so influential in the *Magistrat*. They thus merely accentuated a process of reform which had been under way since the 1870s. Most of the growth of urban environmental control was therefore the product of an incremental process of technological and administrative evolution rather than of political conflict. It was not surprising that paid officials and asso-ciations of professionals and social reformers could take the lead in this process. However, when environmental control reached the limits of the area of compe-tence freely accepted by the State and the wealthy private interests, it encountered almost insurmountable political obstacles. These obstacles were particularly in evidence during the years of acute social tensions and mounting international insecurity from the early 1900s, and in some respects the evolution of urban environmental control failed to maintain its momentum in the new century.

Typical of the opposition which reforms disruptive of private interests could encounter was that generated in Prussia by *Umlegung* — the compulsory re-arrangement of private plots to produce sites capable of bearing healthily-designed buildings. A precedent for this activity existed in the rural land reforms of the first half of the century, and after being suggested in rather general terms by Baumeister in his manual of 1876, it began to figure in the proposals of the associations in the 1880s and 1890s. Although its advocates often presented it as a merely technical instrument which would improve the efficiency of the urban development process to the advantage of all participants, the landowners viewed it with suspicion. Under existing arrangements many owners made huge profits by charging inflated prices for parcels without which neighbouring owners could not form sites suitable for building. Not only were they loth to lose this opportunity, but they also feared that municipal intervention would undermine the whole of the speculative land market. As urban land values mounted, to levels far in excess of those common in England, the reformers for their part increasingly presented *Umlegung* as one element in a general programme of land reform designed to reduce the cost of housing land by breaking the grip of interests now identified as 'speculators'. The boom of the 1890s brought matters to a head and the landowners, who generally had benefited from, and had supported, a town-extension planning which enhanced the value of their sites, now hardened in their opposition to all land reforms, including the relatively innocuous *Umlegung.*

The leading figure in what soon became the *cause célèbre* of pre-war urban policy was Franz Adickes, the reforming *Oberbürgermeister* of Frankfurt. Building in Frankfurt was particularly afflicted by the ridiculous dimensions of many of the peasant strips. Supported by a council which, like many in Germany, still retained a strong tradition of benevolent liberalism (see Sheehan, 1971, 120), Adickes was encouraged to seek *Umlegung* powers from the Prussian parliament. As he himself sat in the upper house as the representative of Frankfurt, he intro-duced there in 1893 a bill designed to confer the necessary powers on all local authorities in Prussia. He was supported by many of the other big-city *Ober-bürgermeister* who sat in the *Herrenhaus*, and after amendment the bill was passed. It then sank without trace in committee proceedings in the lower house, where urban property interests were more strongly represented.

In 1901 Adickes tried again. By this time, three state parliaments had enacted general *Umlegung* powers — Hamburg (1892), Baden (1896), and Saxony (1900). Moreover, Adickes now had government support. Nevertheless, prudence dictated that his new bill should be limited to the city of Frankfurt alone, and should omit the powers of zonal compulsory purchase which had been a bone of contention in 1893. Thus emasculated, the bill had an easier passage, becoming law in 1902, but the lower house inserted a number of amendments which greatly restricted the use of *Umlegung* in Frankfurt before the war. Meanwhile, growing demands for the general introduction of *Umlegung* failed to produce any response from the Prussian parliament after 1902 (Berger-Thimme, 1976, 213—20; *Städtebau*, 1905, 41).

Prussia also failed to develop compulsory-purchase powers suitable for comprehensive urban planning. Landowners tolerated the compulsory purchase of land for streets, which enhanced the value of their sites. They could not, however, be persuaded that the compulsory purchase of land for open space and slum clearance, increasingly advocated by reformers from the 1890s, was in their interests. The Prussian *Landtag* therefore resolutely ignored growing demands from the reformers for a new compulsory purchase law to replace the *Enteignungsgesetz* of 1874. Defenders of the *status quo* maintained that towns could always seek special powers for specific clearance schemes, and suburban parks and public gardens could often be provided out of the municipalities' own estates. However, the paucity of slum clearance in Prussia before 1914 can almost certainly be attributed in part to the lack of general powers for the acquisition of whole areas. Even street improvements remained few and far between, owing largely to the high acquisition costs imposed by the 1874 legislation (Gurlitt, 1904, 24). Some of the other state parliaments, less dominated by urban property interests, made certain concessions to the reformers' demands, but these were insufficient to encourage their towns greatly to diverge from Prussian practice (*Städtebau*, 1905, 38–9; Stübben, 1907, 362–73; Wurzer, 1974a, 22).

The early 1900s also saw a strong reaction by builders and landowners against the use of differential building regulations to reduce densities. In many cases the land uses and building types prescribed by the regulations corresponded to the landowners' intentions, and as such they were tolerated or even welcomed as a creator of order in the development process (see Mancuso, 1977). However, those municipalities which responded to the housing reformers by trying to crack down hard on the *Mietskasernen* often found that they had a fight on their hands. Mannheim, for instance, introduced in 1901 new regulations which were generally considered to place greater restrictions on the free development of private sites than those of any other town in Germany. Huge areas were reserved for houses with gardens, and unusual efforts were made to reduce densities in the central areas when rebuilding occurred there. The regulations immediately provoked a violent agitation by local property-owners and businessmen, orchestrated by the local Chamber of Commerce and Association of Manufacturers. Legal proceedings dragged on for a few years and eventually resulted in a toning down of the regulations (*Städtebau*, 1904, 46–7). At Chemnitz an attempt by the authorities in 1905 to ban the construction of *Mietskasernen* was foiled by the local Builders' Association, which appealed successfully to the Saxon government (*Städtebau*, 1905, 41–2). In many other towns meanwhile, and particularly in those of Prussia, comparable proposals were torpedoed by property interests within the municipal councils.

These continuing defects of German urban policy were reflected in the efforts of the environmental reformers, which continued to gather momentum after the turn of the century. The 'housing question' (*Wohnungsfrage*) maintained its development as the main focus of concern. In 1898 a number of strands in the housing, public health and land reform movements coalesced in the foundation of the *Verein Reichswohnungsgesetz* (Association for an imperial housing law). This new body, the creation of a small group of prosperous Frankfurt social reformers, was a direct descendant of the *Verein für Sozialpolitik*. Its prime mover, Karl von Mangoldt, was at the time secretary of the *Institut für Gemeinwohl* (Institute for the Common Wealth), a disseminator of information on the social question set up by the wealthy Frankfurt merchant, Wilhelm Merton.

The initial aim of the *Verein* was to persuade the *Reichstag* to add a national housing policy to the established national social-welfare insurance scheme. Standardized building regulations, stronger slum clearance powers, and more generous financial help for the public utility housing companies, formed the core of this policy. The *Verein* hoped that by appealing to the more democratically elected *Reichstag* they could bypass the vested interests in the state parliaments. Unfortunately, the *Reichstag* had entered a more conservative phase since the mid-1890s and it could not be persuaded to intervene. Consequently, in 1904 the *Verein* decided to broaden its scope under the new title of *Deutsche Verein für Wohnungsreform* (German Association for Housing Reform). As part of its new effort to influence local authorities and the *Länder*, it convened the first housing congress ever held in Germany, at Frankfurt in 1904. Over 800 people attended, and the *Verein*, going from strength to strength, organized several more such meetings, some of them associated with exhibitions, before the war. It even gained a degree of support from members of the reforming wing of the Social Democratic Party (Berger-Thimme, 1976, 39–54).

One of the biggest problems faced by the *Verein* was the continuing high cost of building land in German towns. Indeed, the German land reform movement, once interested mainly in the plight of the peasant, was now shifting its emphasis to urban land. This evolution was reflected in, and greatly encouraged by, the foundation of the *Bund deutscher Bodenreformer* (Union of German Land Reformers) by Adolf Damaschke in 1898. A former schoolteacher who had become a land reform enthusiast in the 1890s, Damaschke sought support from much the same social groups as the *Verein für Wohnungsreform*. Eager to co-operate with other reform associations, Damaschke claimed a membership for the land reform movement, including affiliated bodies, of over 210,000 in 1905 and 800,000 in 1911 (Berger-Thimme, 1976, 71–119). The growing strength of Damaschke's movement encouraged the *Verein für Wohnungsreform* to highlight the land question, and Von Mangoldt himself published an influential study of the urban aspect of the problem, *Die städtische Bodenfrage*, in 1908.

The polemical writings of Damaschke, Von Mangoldt and other agitators were supported by more scientific studies. Outstanding was the work of Rudolf Eberstadt, the Berlin University economist and *Kathedersozialist*, who had published widely on land and housing reform since the early 1890s. In 1907 he followed up his much-respected *Städtische Bodenfragen* (Urban Land Issues) of 1894 with *Die Spekulation im neuzeitlichen Städtebau* (Speculation in Modern

Town Planning). Then, in 1909, he published a work of synthesis, *Handbuch des Wohnungswesens und der Wohnungsfrage* (A Handbook on Housing and the Housing Question). Far from admiring the sophistication of German *Städtebau*, Eberstadt argued that in all but the most enlightened towns it tolerated or even promoted the inflation of land values which lay at the root of the housing problem. No mincer of words, Eberstadt was inclined to overstate his case, and by the end of the first decade of the twentieth century he was in the thick of a lively controversy with academics and publicists more favourable to the land and building interests. However, their refutations failed to deflect the housing and land reformers. For one thing, Eberstadt was basically right; for another, land reform was an ideal issue around which to rally a broad front of support. Liberal manufacturers, the lower-middle classes, and non-Marxist elements in the working classes could readily be persuaded to unite against the non-productive landowner and the financier who abetted him in his speculative activities. This alliance of labour and capital over an issue of social reform corresponded precisely to the approach to social progress and harmony long adopted by the *Verein für Sozial-politik* and other reformers from the middle and upper classes. Damaschke's motto, 'Neither Mammonism nor Communism', summed up its appeal. Indeed, this anti-socialist undercurrent reinforced the doctrinaire Marxist wing of the Social Democratic Party in its distrust of the land and housing reform movements.

This indifference of part of the Social Democrats, combined with a rallying of conservative interests, helped to prevent the enactment of major land reforms by the *Reichstag* and the state parliaments between the turn of the century and the war. In consequence, what increasingly became known as the *Spekulationsring* remained largely intact in many towns. The *Spekulationsring* was the belt of unbuilt land round the larger towns within which land values were dominated by the huge estates built up by the development companies with support from some of the big investment banks. In these gloomy circumstances, many of the housing reformers were persuaded that the only solution was to jump over the speculation ring and build cheap housing outside. If their basic theories were correct, the competition of this cheaper housing would undermine house and land rents in the cities, and rout the speculators (see e.g. Baumeister, 1876, 25).

The economic attractions of this strategy were reinforced by an increasingly persuasive vision of a semi-rural housing environment. Already in the 1890s the proliferating advocates of urban parks had begun to ally with those who were beginning to call for public conservation of areas of natural beauty. After the turn of the century their agitation was reinforced by a largely new demand, for children's playgrounds and sports fields (Hennebo, 1974, 77). Even the growing interest in the preservation of historic monuments played its part, for it contributed to the perfection by German architects of a vernacular style, of asymmetrical buildings with steeply pitched roofs, which was ideal for low-density housing schemes. At a deeper level, the whole movement of urban decentraliza-tion was linked to the progress of national sentiment and a growing distrust of the big city as a social milieu (see Lees, 1979). Consciously or unconsciously, many reformers were strengthened after 1900 in their conviction that rural Germany and its traditions held the key to individual responsibility, social harmony and national might. By the end of our period the views of Otto March, the leading campaigner for Berlin regional planning, had become typical:

> For a man to live under his own roof in close contact with nature strengthens his love of home life and of his country as well. On the other hand, to house an intransigent proletariat in the back courts of city tenements is to create a serious danger for the State. Constantly moving house as they do, the denizens of the cities lose that feeling of domestic roots which, in time of peril, makes it the most natural thing in the world for a man to defend house and home with his own life. (*Städtebau*, 1913, 31)

The purest expression of the semi-rural ideal was the *Deutsche Gartenstadtgesellschaft* (German Garden City Society). It was founded in 1902 by a group of well-off Berlin intellectuals of socialist inclination who belonged to the *Neue Gemeinschaft* (New Community) movement, a literary circle centred on the brothers Heinrich and Julius Hart. In the 1890s *Neue Gemeinschaft* had founded a small rural retreat at Friedrichshagen, near Berlin, as part of its general advocacy of a return to nature, cooperation and traditional craft and community values. The creation of the *Deutsche Gartenstadtgesellschaft* was prompted by the success of Ebenezer Howard's Garden City Association in Britain since 1899 (see below, pp. 64–8), and reflected a general admiration in Germany for English suburban housing and the artistic and intellectual products of the Arts and Crafts Movement. Much like its English counterpart, the *Deutsche Gartenstadtgesellschaft* soon chose to water down its original ideals in order to play a more influential role in the housing reform movement. In 1904 it appeared at the Frankfurt housing congress and won strong support for its ten basic principles of urban reform, the first of which was: 'A far-reaching solution of the housing question is possible only in association with a methodical strategy of urban decentralization and planned settlement' (*Städtebau*, 1905, 24–5). It never seriously advocated garden cities of the size and economic independence favoured by Howard, and the handful of settlements promoted by the society before 1914 were all satellites of large cities. Only one, Hellerau, built near Dresden from 1908, approached economic self-containment. Most, far from attempting to set up cooperative production of craft products on the lines of Hellerau, were merely communities of high-standard housing created by public utility building societies or enlightened employers (see Hartmann, 1977).

Whatever it lost of its original radical social reform ideals, the *Deutsche Gartenstadtgesellschaft* certainly confirmed the existing decentralizing inclinations of the German housing reform movement. After 1904 the *Deutsche Verein für Wohnungsreform* put much of its effort into campaigning for planned decentralization, and proposed strategies for achieving this end multiplied. Decentralization appealed especially to the *Baugenossenschaften* — the societies building cheap housing for mainly working-class tenants. Their activities had begun to expand in the later 1890s after the imperial government had allowed the state social-insurance funds to advance loans to them, and had granted them limited liability status under the cooperative societies law of 1889 (Thienel, 1973, 166—74; Berger-Thimme, 1976, 55—7). However, in the larger towns expensive land continued to thwart them in their ambition of building cottages with gardens. In the absence of imperial and state action, the *Baugenossenschaften* began to seek municipal aid in the form of cheap land and/or cheap transport.

Some of the more enlightened municipalities were prepared to meet these demands, at least partially. Since the early nineteenth century they had been allowed to purchase land and to hold it without any specific purpose in view. By the early 1900s most had accumulated extensive estates; at Munich, for instance, 23.7 per cent of the land within the city boundary, and an even larger area outside, belonged to the municipality (*Proceedings of the Third National Conference*, 1911, 19). Parts of these lands were used for public purposes as the towns expanded, and the remainder was normally sold off to the highest bidder. From the 1890s, however, Frankfurt and certain other towns began to use their reserves of land to keep down suburban land prices by making some of it available at low cost to the *Baugenossenschaften* and others building for working- or lower-middle-class occupants (Rebentisch, 1978, 109; Bangert, 1936, 51—3). Ulm set a particularly bright example by extending its land-purchase programme into a general strategy of urban development using the leasehold system (*Erbbaurecht*). By 1914 Ulm had even begun to provide municipal housing on municipal land, and so had Freiburg, Frankfurt, Düsseldorf, and a few more (*Städtebau*, 1913, 31: Berger-Thimme, 1976, 141; Stübben, 1907, 31). Most municipalities remained more cautious, and as the *Baugenossenschaften* built no more than a few dozen houses a year in most towns, general levels of suburban land values were scarcely affected by the release of land to them. However, municipal attitudes towards the private land market definitely hardened in the early 1900s. Frankfurt led the way with its *Umsatzsteuer* (property transfer tax), set up in 1904. The rate varied from between 2 and 25 per cent of the increased value of a property between sales, the lower rate applying if the increase was between 15 and 25 per cent, and the higher rate if the increase was more than 55 per cent (Bangert, 1936, 59—60; *Proceedings of the Third National Conference*, 1911, 24). By 1910 the *Umsatzsteuer* had been adopted by over 600 local authorities in Germany (Berger-Thimme, 1976, 101—2).

If most towns had reservations about municipal housing, very few were averse to municipal transport. Fortified by Germany's long tradition of state railway enterprise, they did not hesitate to municipalize their private electric tram networks after the turn of the century if these failed to meet the needs of the outer districts. Whether the trams were municipal or private, the municipalities redoubled their efforts in the early 1900s to extend cheap and frequent services to the suburbs. Indeed, with trams increasingly routed on separate reservations along the wide radial streets of the planned suburbs, and the other forms of traffic appropriately organized to use the rest of the thoroughfare efficiently, German towns found themselves leading the world in traffic engineering. Here again, however, municipal transport efforts provided only a partial solution to the land problem as few tram routes extended any great distance outside the built-up areas.

Overall, the action of the municipalities, technical improvements in transport, and the growth of middle-class demand for low-density housing combined to produce a tendency towards somewhat lower densities in the development of most towns in the last years before the war. In the newer extension plans it became general practice to distinguish between main traffic arteries and residential streets, and a combination of *Staffelbauordnungen* and market forces encouraged commercial uses to gravitate towards the former. Narrower streets and smaller blocks suitable for small houses could then be planned on the cheaper land between the radiating arteries. The lower densities and smaller traffic flows in the residential areas allowed winding streets and asymmetrical junctions to be included on the lines proposed since the early 1890s by the followers of Camillo Sitte. In theory, the use of the increasingly popular vernacular style of residential architecture could allow these districts, even in large cities, to recreate the intimacy and modest scale of the traditional German small town. This effect, strongly encouraged by *Der Städtebau* and many of the big authorities on town planning, was increasingly sought in the years after 1900. Some towns even went as far as to modify their existing extension plans and building regulations to make such pleasant neighbourhoods possible; Düsseldorf did so in about 1905, and Munich in 1908 (*Städtebau*, 1905, 29–31; Egli, 1967, 324). However, these developments and changes favoured mainly the middle classes. Up to 1914 most new working-class housing, especially in the larger cities, continued to be provided in large flatted blocks.

Furthermore, by 1914 a great gulf had opened up between the more enlightened towns and those which remained largely in the grip of property-owning interests. The chief standard-bearer was Frankfurt, pioneer of almost every major environmental control innovation after 1890 thanks to the leadership of *Oberbürgermeister* Adickes and the compliance of a liberal-reformist council. Trailing at the rear of the column was Berlin, with four million people in city and suburbs the largest city in Europe, after London, in 1914. In Berlin the Hobrecht plan of 1862 was still in force. Differential building regulations had been introduced in only a handful of districts within the city. If they had been applied in a rudimentary form to the suburban municipalities in 1892, it was only as a hurried attempt by the State *Polizei* to correct the harmful effects of their Berlin area building regulations of 1887, which had encouraged the construction of *Mietskasernen* in districts previously occupied by villas. In fact, the *Mietskasernen* remained the predominant form of construction even in the suburbs, and the Berlin area remained more securely in the grip of the land speculators than any

other city in Germany. No extension of the city boundaries had taken place since 1861, initially because of municipal opposition to the incorporation of the poorer industrial suburbs, and since the 1890s owing mainly to State reluctance to strengthen a potentially socialist municipality (Herzfeld, 1962, 295–6).

From the early 1900s a campaign built up among housing and planning re-formers in the Berlin area to secure the comprehensive planning of the whole conurbation. A single development strategy, combined with an integrated trans-port system, could, it was thought, break down inflated land values in both the city and the suburbs. The publication of a tract, *Gross-Berlin*, by the two Berlin architects' associations in 1906 led to the establishment of a special body, the *Ansiedlungsverein Gross-Berlin* (Association for the Development of Greater Berlin). In 1909 the *Ansiedlungsverein* issued a policy statement calling for a regional plan to coordinate planned decentralization to a ring of new settlements, to be built on publicly acquired land by large *Baugenossenschaften* and served by a new, State-built transport system (*Städtebau*, 1909, 24–5, 127). In the following year the two architects' associations, with some municipal support, promoted a Greater Berlin planning competition (see Hegemann, 1911). The competition produced the most impressive entries ever seen in Germany, some of them the work of multi-disciplinary teams including economists and transport experts (Hegemann, 1913, 155–7). Yet the competition, and the big exhibition which followed it, produced no more than a sop from the Prussian government in the form of the *Zweckverband Gross-Berlins*, an *ad hoc* union of local authorities with virtually no initiating power. The creation of a single Greater Berlin autho-rity was not to come about until 1920, in very different political circumstances (Herzfeld, 1962, 297; Engeli and Haus, 1975, 21; Werner, 1978, 10–20). Indeed, in the last years before the war German reformers were preparing themselves for a long struggle over Berlin, which they rightly saw as an important influence on the development of town planning in the rest of Germany and even abroad. As Werner Hegemann, organiser of the Berlin planning exhibition, put it in 1911:

> Berlin is now becoming an international battleground in the struggle for the beneficial arrangement of this completely new world in which we have been living since modern techniques in industry and transport first came into effect. (Hegemann, 1911, 7)

In Germany, then, some important planning battles still remained to be won on the eve of the First World War, and German towns still had a long way to go

6 *Part of the extension plan for Chemnitz (now Karl-Marx-Stadt), Saxony, c. 1910. This plan was exhibited by Stübben at the RIBA town planning conference as an example of the most enlightened and technically competent big-city planning of the period. Detailed building plans for suburban districts such as this were normally drawn up shortly before development, within the guidelines laid down by the extension plan. Note the distinction between traffic and residential streets, the generous planting and open space, and the insertion of sites for public buildings. Complemented by the* Staffelbauordnung, *this plan would secure comprehensively planned development. (RIBA, 1911, 796)*

before they conformed to the artistically and scientifically shaped entities glimpsed in the writings of the leading planning experts. In Werner Hegemann, moreover, Germany had produced an expert who professed to believe that in many aspects of urban environmental policy German practice and achievement lagged behind those of other industrialized states. What then *had* been happening elsewhere? Let us look first of all at a country much admired by Hegemann, and until recent years the source of so many of those 'modern techniques in industry and transport' — Great Britain.

Three

Britain
Public Health, Suburbanization
and the Example of Germany

However much we individually may like or dislike the particular style
and the detail treatment adopted by the Germans, we cannot but feel
the highest admiration for the skill and the thoroughness displayed in
their town planning work;...and, while there is much in their work that
one would not wish to see copied in English towns, there can be no
question as to the immense benefit to be derived from a careful study
of that which has been accomplished in a field where they have been
working earnestly for many years and where we are in comparison mere
beginners.

Raymond Unwin, *Town Planning in Practice* (2nd ed., 1911), p. 112

Town planning has been studied in German towns for so many years
that it is somewhat remarkable that German methods have not attracted before now the attention of English visitors.

City of Birmingham, *Report to the General Purposes Committee of the
Deputation Visiting Germany and Austria, May 25th–June 5th, 1910,
for the Purpose of Studying Town Development* (1911), p. 5

Municipal extension planning, that foundation of German *Städtebau*, was almost
entirely unpractised in Britain until shortly before the First World War. The first
general powers permitting it were contained in the Housing, Town Planning, Etc.
Act of 1909. This statute was the main legislative product of a campaign, which
had begun at the turn of the century, for more constructive public intervention
in the shaping of British towns. During the campaign 'the example of Germany'
was much cited, and in essence the 1909 Act confirmed the adoption of a foreign
innovation on which, in Britain too, the subsequent development of comprehensive urban planning has been based.

Much of the interest of the British experience lies, however, not in the events
surrounding the belated adoption of a rudimentary planning tool, but in the previous blissful ignorance of it. In most respects the environment of the 'unplanned'

British town in the later nineteenth century was not palpably inferior to its German equivalent. On the contrary, many German reformers regarded British urban conditions as distinctly superior to those of their own country (see Sutcliffe, 1980). Britain's advantage, in their view, lay in its prolific town-building process, which had secured the single-family house as the norm not only for the middle class but also for the majority of workers. Supplemented by slowly expanding public provision of services, and moderated by rudimentary regulation of the use of private land, this process produced an environment which in the later decades of the nineteenth century was not fundamentally questioned in Britain. Only from the turn of the century did it come to be regarded as incapable of meeting the full needs of British towndwellers. This new attitude was partly the product of rising expectations but partly too of growing defects in the town-building process itself.

BRITISH URBAN GROWTH AND THE DEVELOPMENT OF PUBLIC INTERVENTION UNTIL THE END OF THE NINETEENTH CENTURY

From the middle decades of the eighteenth century industrialization began to generate rapid urban growth in Britain. In England and Wales, the richest and most populous components of the United Kingdom, the urbanized proportion of the population rose from between 20 and 25 per cent in the early eighteenth century (Holderness, 1976, 15; Chalklin, 1974, 3—4) to about 33 per cent at the time of the first national census in 1801. By 1851 it had risen to 54 per cent (Law, 1967, 131). At the same time, the total population of the country increased very quickly; in England and Wales it passed from nearly nine millions in 1801 to roughly double that figure in 1851. So during the first half of the nineteenth century some six and a half millions were added to the urban population of England and Wales. Scotland, meanwhile, followed a comparable evolution, with just over half its population living in towns by 1851 (Weber, 1899, 59).

   Throughout this first century of industrial urbanization, public authority did little to control the evolution of the urban environment. Many of the new centres of advanced industry, such as Manchester and Birmingham, rose so rapidly from the status of village or small market town that they possessed no municipal organization at all. To provide a modicum of government, they had to develop their existing parish or even manorial institutions. Moreover, the possession of borough status was not in itself a guarantee of effective administration. In some important industrial centres and sea ports, of which Liverpool is the most striking example, the corporation acted energetically to promote economic growth and protect the environment (see White, 1951). In many others, however, such as Leicester, unrepresentative and corrupt municipalities failed to respond to economic and social change (see Simmons, 1974, I).

It was to counter the defects of existing urban administration that groups of townsmen began, from the mid-eighteenth century, to petition Parliament to set up new local institutions capable of adapting the physical environment to the needs of the industrial era. A precedent already existed in the turnpike trusts which were authorized to charge tolls on public roads in return for modernization work, and Parliament responded readily to this new request. Between the mid-eighteenth and mid-nineteenth centuries it set up several hundred local boards of improvement commissioners with powers to perform defined tasks such as paving, lighting and drainage (Webb, 1922, 235–349). Such boards were set up even in incorporated boroughs and until the middle of the nineteenth century they did more to control and improve the urban environment than any other public institution.

In 1832 the system of election to the House of Commons was reformed to give fuller representation to the economic and professional elites of the new centres of industry and communications. This change led directly to the Municipal Corporations Act of 1835, which reformed 178 of the existing corporations and allowed unincorporated towns to obtain borough status. Over the following forty years, sixty-two new boroughs were incorporated in this way (Smellie, 1957, 30–3). Thus, by the middle of the nineteenth century most of the larger English towns possessed their own magistrates, elected council and mayor. At first, however, most of the improvement commissions remained in being alongside the reformed corporations. The concentration of environmental powers in municipal hands did not begin until the Public Health Act of 1848, which proposed to grant extensive sanitary powers to new local authorities known as Local Boards of Health. It was open to the boroughs to apply for recognition as Local Boards of Health and most did so, either to take advantage of the proffered powers or to prevent the establishment of a rival authority. Most of the surviving improvement commissions now began to disband, handing over their powers and functions to the strengthened municipalities. Thus from mid-century, in most of the larger towns, control of the environment at last came to be vested in a single elected authority (see Fraser, 1979, 163–7).

This concentration of authority did not, however, immediately promote more active public intervention in the environment. In many towns death rates had risen to a peak by mid-century, but in the absence of a full understanding of the causes of disease, and in the face of the increased expenditure which the new responsibilities brought with them, municipalities generally left as much as possible to private enterprise. It was universally accepted that the municipality had to provide a drainage system, but water could be provided profitably by private initiative and in most towns the supply was not municipalized until well into the second half of the century. In London, private control of water survived until 1904 (Robson, 1948, 116). Most councils acknowledged the duty of keeping existing thoroughfares clear and adequately surfaced, but they normally left the creation of new streets to the landowners. Moreover, they scarcely interfered at all in the use of private land and buildings.

These arrangements may appear derisory in comparison with the town-extension schemes already being pursued by numerous German municipalities in the 1850s. They were, however, partly a reflection of the generally high quality of British urban development. Real earnings were much higher than on the Continent, while rural land passed much more freely into the hands of the builders thanks to the dismantling of the remaining feudal institutions and the economic rationalization of agriculture which had preceded and accompanied industrialization. The leasehold system, which had come into use in many towns since the early stages of industrialization (see Aspinall, 1978), probably helped to discourage speculation and high land costs. Most towns had no fortifications to restrict their outward growth. Capital and enterprise flowed freely into residential building (see Chalklin, 1974; Chapman, 1971). The result was a standard of housing which, for all social classes, greatly excelled that enjoyed by their equivalents in German and French towns. Residential densities, in particular, were much lower, except in Scotland (see Best, 1973, 402–5). The single-family house was the norm, arranged contiguously in terraces and courts for working people, and increasingly in detached or semi-detached villas for the middle and upper classes (see Lloyd and Simpson, 1977). Outside London few houses exceeded three storeys in height, and by mid-century two storeys were becoming the norm in the new districts of most towns.

Even the street system evolved adequately in most towns. The basic network of radiating roads, the product of the Middle Ages, was conserved and enhanced from the sixteenth century by parish highway surveyors. From the early eighteenth century their efforts were increasingly supplemented by the turnpike trusts, which continued to look after many roads in urban areas until the municipalities took over from them in the middle of the nineteenth century (Webb, 1913, esp. 210–13; Webb, 1922, 274). Thanks to concentrated landownership, developers in most towns were usually able to provide adequate sidestreets to serve new building. Indeed, some of the districts developed in London and the provinces for middle- and upper-class residence were designed to a standard which has not since been surpassed (see e.g. Olsen, 1964). In these circumstances, public intervention in the town-building process was much less urgently required than in Germany.

For all this, a definite tendency towards more ambitious public intervention emerged during the last three decades of the nineteenth century. The main stimulus, apart from mere administrative accretion, was continuing concern about public health (see Ferguson, 1963–4), supplemented by an enhanced perception of the deficiencies of much working-class housing. From around 1870, stimulated or directed by national legislation, most municipalities sought to improve their sewerage systems and water supplies. They also began seriously to restrict the free use of private land, principally by drawing up codes of building regulations which were embodied in local by-laws. In England the main precedent was provided by the regulations applied to new building in London after the fire of 1666 (Simon, 1890, 102). In the bigger Scottish towns, such regulations had an even longer pedigree (see Rodger, 1979). The first half of the nineteenth century had already seen some extension of the building regulations in London and the bigger provincial cities, but it took the Towns Improvement Clauses Act of 1847 and the Public Health Acts of 1848 and 1875 to promote their widespread adoption and to extend their concerns from fire safety to public health. After the 1875 Act the Local Government Board published a model set of building by-laws which was adopted in its entirety in many of the towns which previously had enforced no regulations, and which influenced the evolution of existing building codes. So from the later 1870s most urban building in England and Wales was governed by regulations which in their essentials did not vary greatly from town to town. In Scotland, too, more restrictive and standardized regulations emerged.

As the building regulations grew in ambition, they sought increasingly to regulate the arrangement of houses and the spaces around them. The main objective at first was to ensure thorough ventilation. During the early decades of public health concern, between the 1840s and the 1870s, most medical authorities held to the anti-contagionist, or miasmatic, theory of disease transmission, according to which most diseases were transmitted by the vapours emitted by putrefying matter. To counter these dangers in an urban environment, it was considered crucial to establish a free movement of air within and around the home. This end could best be achieved, it was thought, by ensuring that each house faced a broad street and had an open space behind it, so that draughts could blow right through the house. Consequently, we find the Towns Improvement Clauses Act suggesting a width of thirty feet for all streets used by wheeled traffic, and twenty feet for non-traffic streets. By the later nineteenth century, most towns imposed a width of thirty-six or even forty-two feet on new residential streets, which was normally far more than vehicular usage required.

The imposition of open areas behind each house was more strongly resisted, for by the 1840s the 'back-to-back' arrangement, by which two rows of houses shared the same rear wall, had become the normal type of workers' housing in most of the larger industrial towns and ports. After a vain effort by housing reformers to secure a national ban on the building of back-to-back houses in the early 1840s, little progress was made until the 1860s, when a number of influential towns took this step in their own by-laws. Further encouragement was provided by the model by-laws issued by the Local Government Board, and by the 1880s most towns had banned the building of back-to-backs. The normal requirement was that an open space of a given area be provided behind each house, which had the effect of ensuring that half or more of each site remained unbuilt.

As the nineteenth century wore on, the interaction between increasingly stringent regulations and the efforts of developers and builders to make the most of their land tended to produce a standard layout not only for workers' housing but even for much middle-class housing. Residential streets were arranged in parallel lines with the minimum of cross-streets, producing building blocks in the form of elongated rectangles. The streets were lined by unbroken rows of two-storey houses standing on or slightly behind the street-line. The interior of each block was occupied by the back yards or gardens, divided by low walls. Access to these back yards was provided either by a narrow alley running the whole length of the block parallel to the streets, or by a series of narrow passages or tunnels through the rows of houses from the street. In Scotland, the entrenchment of tenement living produced a very different housing environment, but there too the by-laws had produced a standard, rectilinear street of four-storey tenement blocks by the later part of the century.

Whatever criticisms may be levelled at the residential layout produced by the by-laws, it was certainly not chaotic. In this respect, the Prussian *Fluchtliniengesetz* of 1875, and similar German legislation, offered no advantage over British arrangements. Where the British approach fell short of the German was in the creation of anything more ambitious than the purely residential street. Because public health, and the surroundings of the house, were the primary considerations of the building by-laws, they did not normally allow certain streets to be designated as major arteries and allotted more than the standard minimum width. Even in those towns where the by-laws allowed a variety of widths to be imposed, the greatest width — usually fifty feet — was not much more than the normal minimum width for purely residential streets (Aldridge, 1915, 210; Unwin, 1911, 244). Anything more would have angered the land-owners who, in contrast to common German practice, normally were required to cede their completed streets to the local authority without compensation. A few towns obtained special powers to establish main traffic streets; Barrow-in-Furness, a new industrial town which was planned almost from scratch by its promoters, obtained powers to require widths of up to eighty feet in 1875. Liverpool, perhaps England's most consistently enterprising authority, obtained powers in 1908 to require streets of any width, subject to the payment of compensation to the landowners in extreme cases (Aldridge, 1915, 666). In most towns, however, neither the developers nor the municipalities were in a position to establish major new traffic routes, and the developing networks of residential streets came to depend almost entirely on the existing radial roads for all but purely local movement.

At the turn of the century the rising volume of traffic, complicated by the electric tram and the motor vehicle, would begin to reveal this defect. Until that time, however, traffic congestion continued to occur principally at bottle-necks in the central areas of towns. Although these were very expensive to remove, adequate powers were available. Under the Lands Clauses Consolidation Act of 1845, municipalities could acquire land and buildings compulsorily for street widening, new streets, and other schemes of public interest. The Towns

Improvement Clauses Act of 1847 further allowed them to impose widening lines on existing streets, to be enforced as and when buildings were demolished. These powers, which were consolidated in the Public Health Act of 1875, allowed gradual progress between the 1840s and the end of the century towards the creation of an efficient street network in the central areas of the larger towns. London was particularly prominent thanks to the efforts of the Metropolitan Board of Works between 1855 and 1889, and communications between the City and the West End were greatly improved (see Gibbon and Bell, 1939, 27–61). Admittedly, much more was achieved in Paris and some of the leading French provincial cities during a much shorter campaign of central improvements in the 1850s and 1860s. However, British towns carried out the minimum of work required to keep traffic moving, and generally undertook more central improvements than did their German equivalents, which were handicapped by inadequate powers.

In one respect, finally, Britain outshone both the Germans and the French. This was in the clearance and redevelopment of areas of slum housing. The general compulsory purchase powers, like those available on the Continent, were tailored to the building and widening of thoroughfares, and did not readily allow the acquisition of land lying off the street. However, in the 1860s and early 1870s a number of towns obtained their own legislation to permit the compulsory acquisition, clearance and redevelopment of whole districts of defective housing. The big Scottish cities took the lead with the Glasgow Improvement Act of 1866 (see Allan, 1965) and similar Acts promoted by Edinburgh in 1867 (see Smith, 1980) and Dundee in 1871 (Ashworth, 1954, 94). Meanwhile, however, Liverpool had obtained comparable powers with its Sanitary Act of 1867. The strength of these Acts lay in the powers extended to the local authorities, or to improvement trusts set up by them, to acquire areas of generally poor housing without having to establish the insanitary state of each and every building. So successfully were they applied, particularly in Glasgow, that Parliament extended them to all English municipalities under the Artizans' and Labourers' Dwellings Improvement Act of 1875. The exact nature of the redevelopment, as for instance in Birmingham's Corporation Street scheme, was in practice a matter for negotiation with the Local Government Board (Briggs, 1952, 77–85). Solutions varied from reconstruction with municipal dwellings to the building of new streets with the remaining land leased for commercial use. Moreover, the powers were very costly to apply. However, they allowed the more enterprising British municipalities to undertake comprehensive schemes of urban reconstruction without, as was usual on the Continent, being forced to resort to a street scheme in order to clear slums. Indeed, they excited much envy abroad, as did the reconstructed areas, especially in London and Liverpool among the English cities, which resulted from their application between the 1870s and the early 1900s.

THE PRE-CONDITIONS OF THE TOWN-PLANNING IDEA

British urban authorities, then, were doing much to shape the urban environment by the later nineteenth century. Meanwhile, urbanization proceeded, with the urban proportion of the population of England and Wales rising to nearly 80 per cent in 1901 (Law, 1967, 131). However, an awareness that the various modes of public intervention could be combined in a single strategy of urban development emerged only slowly and uncertainly.

During the first big public health agitation in the 1830s and 1840s a number of proposals had been aired for the comprehensive designing of towns on sanitary lines. Even in Britain this was by no means an outlandish idea. Most of the necessary architectural and engineering skills had been perfected since the seventeenth century in the development of suburban residential areas on the great landed estates of London and other fashionable towns (see Summerson, 1945; Olsen, 1964), and in the building of big military installations. Indeed, a number of *municipal* planning schemes had been undertaken; at Edinburgh the municipality provided access to, and developed, a completely new district of impressive streets and squares, the New Town, from the 1760s (see Youngson, 1966). More modestly, the Corporation of Liverpool directed the development of a large municipal estate to the south-east of the old town in the eighteenth and nineteenth centuries. One of the most ambitious extension schemes of all was the Crown's Regent's Park and Regent's Street development in London, completed in the 1820s. Here, a former royal hunting-ground was converted to an urban park and residential area, and linked to the town by an impressive thoroughfare, the whole conforming to the designs of one man, the architect John Nash (see Saunders, 1969; Hobhouse, 1975, 26–69). Admittedly, most of these new districts were intended for well-to-do people, but experience of designing residential areas for the poor began to accumulate from the later eighteenth century as a result of the proliferation of factory villages (Creese, 1966, 13–60; Bell, 1969, 163–213). However, the most significant experience of all was gained in the colonies by the military engineers who on occasion laid out complete towns, such as Adelaide, from scratch (Williams, 1974, 389–404).

This accumulated wisdom helped to secure a respectful hearing for the advocates of planned towns when they sought to influence the great sanitary inquiries of the early 1840s. Men like Captain James Vetch of the Royal Engineers, Butler Williams, professor of geodesy at the College of Civil Engineers, and T. J. Maslen, author of *Suggestions for the Improvement of Our Towns and Houses* (1843) and a long-established advocate of the careful planning of new towns in Australia, were mainly interested in planning efficient drainage networks. However, they were also aware of the sanitary and circulatory advantages that an efficient street system could offer, and they drew much inspiration from Wren's plan for post-Fire London and the French *alignement* procedures (see e.g. Williams's evidence to the Commissioners for Inquiring into the State of Large Towns and Populous

Districts, *BPP*, XVII(1844)3, 385—92). In Liverpool, which since the late 1830s had been eager to extend its municipal powers by special legislation (Fraser, 1979, 26—36), it looked for a time as though general extension planning would become normal practice. In 1848 the Borough Engineer, echoing earlier recommendations by the Liverpool branch of the Health of Towns Association, told the Corporation's Health Committee that all extensions to the town should be made in accordance with a fixed plan. In 1850 the Corporation's Improvement Committee invited proposals for an improvement scheme and selected one which included both road and park systems. However, little came of the idea even at Liverpool and in the 1850s the idea of overall planning sank into obscurity as a new wave of complacency swept over British urban authorities (Ashworth, 1954, 25, 63). Although the idea of the completely planned town re-emerged from time to time in the discussions and literature of the urban reform movement, it was usually presented as a paradigm rather than as a serious proposal for action; such, for instance, was Benjamin Ward Richardson's 'Hygeia' proposal of 1876. Indeed, far from bringing comprehensive planning closer to reality, the passage of time in some respects pushed it further away as the building by-laws became more effective and municipal authorities perfected a variety of *ad hoc* arrangements to ensure the coordination of their efforts in various areas of environmental improvement.

The persistence of this unwillingness to view the town and its problems as a whole emerges strongly from the great housing and environmental debate of the early 1880s. After more than a decade of renewed progress in national and local sanitary reform, the highlight of which had been the great Public Health Act of 1875, Britain had entered a serious depression which coincided with a slump in the building industry. Accompanying social tensions raised doubts in many minds about the whole future of British society (see e.g. Jones, 1971, 281—90). Very quickly, the widespread optimism which had marked the 1870s crumbled to reveal underlying doubts about the quality of the built environment and its effects on the physical and moral state of the urban populations. However, the debate never extended beyond the problems of high rents, overcrowding and insanitary housing in the central districts of large towns, and principally of London. A number of partial solutions were canvassed without the emergence of an overall strategy of reform. The main legislative product of nearly a decade of concern was the Housing Act of 1890, which did little more than codify existing powers under which urban authorities could clear slums and build houses for rent. Only in the idea of a deliberate decentralization of population, more seriously discussed in the 1880s than at any time since its first adumbration in the 1840s, was a new element injected (Dyos, 1968, 22). However, the question of cheap transport, on which some progress was made, remained separate from the development of suburban housing. Then, in the 1890s, building and employment revived, the incidence of overcrowding fell, social tensions eased, and housing and the urban environment were less urgently discussed.

At the very close of the 1890s a new urban scare hit Britain. It had much in common with the 1880s episode, with the housing of the poor as the main cause of concern. This time, however, the debate generated the widespread demand for an ambitious, new approach to urban improvement which came to be known as 'town planning'. What, then, had changed since the early 1880s?

Fundamental to the new debate was an intellectual development, the growing belief that man's well-being was largely determined by his environment. This idea had been emerging since Charles Darwin's theories of evolution first became influential in the 1860s. It generated numerous variations and even contradictions, but it retained a common core of thinking in which the physical, economic and social surroundings of man came to be regarded as aspects of a single, all-embracing environment, to which he responded on a psychological as well as a physiological plane. In this new intellectual atmosphere less confidence was placed, from the early 1880s, in the power of the individual to rise above his environment by holding firmly to moral principles (Collini, 1976, 93). To most observers, the biggest threat to the physical and moral health of the individual seemed to lie in the towns, and by the 1890s many were even prepared to believe that environmental factors could override genetic ones to produce a declining quality of human stock from generation to generation. Admittedly, few people had the ability to explain precisely how the environment exercised its influence. Also unclear was how far, if at all, education entered into the equation. However, much of the strength of the environmentalist idea lay in its imprecision. It allowed the house, the yard, the street, the park, the church, the school and the public house to merge into an often hazy image of an urban totality in which the individual was sometimes an observer, and sometimes a participant. It no longer seemed enough to reform the house and its sanitary equipment; the town as a whole had to be transformed.

The victory of this new orthodoxy coincided with a marked change in the evolution of the structure of towns towards a much greater decentralization of population. Certainly, the movement of better-off residents towards the periphery had been a feature of the larger British towns since the early nineteenth century, if not earlier (Dyos, 1961, 34–9). However, suburbanization did not become a mass movement until the end of the century. It was clearly moving in that direction in the 1870s and 1880s, but the crucial acceleration of the outward movement occurred in the 1890s when the last big building boom of the century coincided with the widespread electrification of the tramways and the multiplication of workers' concessionary fares on both the trams and the railways (Dyos and Aldcroft, 1969, 218–22). For the first time, working men joined in large numbers with the growing middle classes in travelling to work by public transport. The idea of solving the housing problem by encouraging the poor to move out of the city centres, which had been intermittently canvassed since the 1840s, at last began to appear realistic in the 1890s. Thereafter, scepticism gave way to enthusiasm as the idea of a spreading city, solving its own problems in an organic, evolutionary process, caught the imagination of many. By the turn of the century, a shift of attention was occurring in reforming circles from the destruction and replacement of central slums to the creation of attractive and freely expanding suburbs.

Decentralization was made all the more plausible and attractive by the perfection in the 1890s of a cheap, low-density mode of design for residential neighbourhoods. This new mode was based on a fusion of the middle-class suburban villa estate, which had been emerging since the early nineteenth century, and the rural cottage and garden. The combination of cheap, lightly-constructed housing with an open layout seemed to offer a healthy and uplifting environment even to working men. The new method was principally tested at two factory villages built by employers eager to encourage the self-improvement of their workers by providing a stimulating environment, backed by educative social institutions. At Port Sunlight, near Birkenhead, the Congregationalist soap manufacturer, William Hesketh Lever, began in 1888 to build a community close to his new factory (see Reynolds, 1948). George Cadbury, the Birmingham Quaker chocolate manufacturer, followed this example when, from 1894, he built the model village of Bournville next to his suburban factory (see Bournville Village Trust, 1955). From there, the style spread to a number of other settlements built by enlightened employers in the later 1890s. Meanwhile, those reformers who placed emphasis on environmental influences were increasingly convinced that the resulting environment of small houses, gardens or allotments, public open space, and social and cultural facilities, combined with proximity of employment, beauty and the presence of a range of social classes, was the one most likely to generate the harmonious, contented society of which they dreamed.

The example of Port Sunlight and Bournville particularly appealed to the growing number of municipal councils which were being attracted during the 1890s into the direct provision of housing for working people. Although general powers to build houses for workers had been available to English municipalities since 1851, most of the small number of municipal dwellings built until the 1890s were intended to replace slums demolished in clearance schemes. Councils built reluctantly, and usually only after private builders had declined to provide the replacement dwellings normally required by the clearance legislation. Despite the growing cost of using these central sites for housing, councils were loth to compete with private enterprise by building on peripheral land. This reluctance even survived the passing of Part III of the 1890 Housing Act which, as a product of interest in decentralization in the 1880s, consolidated earlier legislation under which urban authorities could build houses for working people in peripheral districts. However, during the 1890s, some of the larger municipalities began to consider such suburban housing more seriously. Rising land and property values during the housing boom increased the cost of central redevelopment. Meanwhile, working-class representatives, thanks to changes in electoral law and political consciousness among the workers, were becoming more numerous and more

7   *Aerial view of the mature Bournville (1956). The large gardens and generous public open space of turn-of-the-century Bournville (in the middle ground) contrast with the speculatively-built by-law terraces of suburban Birmingham which were built in the same period (top and top right). The houses in the foreground were added by the Bournville Village Trust after the Second World War. (Aerofilms Ltd)*

8   *(Opposite) Linden Road, Bournville, in 1902 (above) and 1952 (below). Such scenes, appealing to the heart as well as the mind, strongly supported the case for town planning in the early 1900s. (Bournville Collection, Birmingham Reference Library)*

vociferous in the councils. In the big cities, they began to give voice to a growing demand for municipalities to build in the suburbs to counteract the growing unwillingness of private enterprise to build houses for workers, and the resulting rise in house rents. Most councils were reluctant to recognize this case, but the general extension of municipal enterprise in the 1890s gradually made the climate more favourable to public housing.

Especially influential was the municipal takeover of tramways which occurred in many towns in the 1890s. This development was partly fortuitous, in that

under the cautious terms of the Tramways Act of 1870, most tramway companies had been granted short leases of the permanent way (which, as part of the thoroughfare, belonged to the municipality). From the early 1890s, many of these leases began to fall in. It would have been easy to renew them, but in many towns the companies had hesitated to undertake new investment towards the end of their leases and there had been a relative decline in the quality of street transport in the later 1880s and early 1890s. The companies were particularly hesitant to introduce electric traction, which their American equivalents, fortified by long franchises, had widely adopted in the 1880s. It was felt that a renewal of the leases would perpetuate this retardation, and in most towns the great weight of public opinion favoured municipalization. Thus transport was added to water, gas and electricity, which in most of the larger towns had also been brought under direct municipal control by the later 1890s (see Kellett, 1978). It thus became much easier for the municipalities to plan transport services which would encourage workers to live in the suburbs, and the building of municipal housing on the periphery began to be considered more seriously.

The first local authority to inaugurate a suburban housing strategy (though, paradoxically, in the absence of direct control over transport) was the London County Council, in 1898 (Wohl, 1977, 253–5). In the early 1900s, its example was followed by Sheffield, Manchester, and a number of smaller towns. All adopted, in cheapened form, the Port Sunlight/Bournville mode of design, which by now had been further refined by the influential housing architect, Raymond Unwin. Admittedly, not very much housing was provided in this way – fewer than 20,000 dwellings between 1890 and 1909 – but the new departure required much broader vision from municipalities which were now involved directly in purchasing and developing suburban land and in providing access to employment and other facilities (Gaskell, 1976, 187).

Meanwhile, many of those active in housing reform circles remained unconvinced of the necessity of municipal housing. As yet, hardly anyone was prepared to suggest the public subsidization of rents, which seemed likely to lead merely to lower wages. However, the survival of this self-help attitude sustained rather than retarded the general progress towards urban planning. Bournville, in particular, fortified the critics of municipal housing by holding out the hope that a high standard of workers' housing could be provided without subsidy. Certainly, even skilled workers did not find it easy to scrape together the rent for the cheapest Bournville houses, but a virtue could be made of this limitation. To strive after such a house, it was suggested, would improve the character of the working man, and life in the model village would be an educative experience. Bournville thus helped revive the century-old, but recently flagging, cooperative housing movement.

The first step in this renaissance of self-help housing had in fact been taken in 1888, when Benjamin Jones, manager of the London branch of the Cooperative Wholesale Society, had set up Tenant Cooperators Ltd (Ashworth, 1954, 158). The new company was intended to promote cooperative housing schemes cheaply enough to attract lower-middle-class and working-class members, but very little was built until the turn of the century. Then, in 1902, the Ealing Tenants Society was founded to build houses on an estate in West London. The prime movers were Henry Vivian, the future Liberal MP, and a group of middle-class sympathizers (Aldridge, 1915, 417). At first, the Ealing Society intended to build conventional, terraced houses in by-law streets, but it very quickly extended its objectives to the creation of an entire community, with social facilities, open space and a varied layout (*TPR*, 1910, 119). In the early 1900s, similar societies were founded elsewhere in London and in other parts of England. Henry Vivian took over national leadership of the movement, which became known as Tenant Co-Partnership. A new company, Co-Partnership Tenants Ltd, coordinated the various building ventures, while a Co-Partnership Tenants Housing Council decided general policy (*TPR*, 1910, 25–6, 119–24).

This quickening of enterprise by local authorities and cooperative bodies not only in the building of suburban housing but in the design and creation of communities was reflected in a body which linked both interests, the National Housing Reform Council. Founded in 1900, the Council sprang from the efforts of a number of housing reformers, notably Henry Aldridge and Alderman William Thompson of Richmond, to organize and build on a growing interest in housing among the trade unions. At first working-class representatives dominated its committee, though as its influence grew it became more and more of a middle-class organization. The most important milestone in its early development was a meeting which it held with interested MPs in 1903. The meeting led to the creation of a permanent committee composed of MPs and members of the Council, to discuss desirable legislation (*Garden City*, 1(1), 1904, 11). Very soon, the National Housing Reform Council became the acknowledged link between Parliament and the whole of the housing reform movement, and by 1907 a parliamentary lobby of 130 had been built up (Hawtree, 1974, 38–9). Valuing this respect, the Council maintained a catholic interest in a variety of approaches to housing reform in the hope that a common front would more quickly prod the legislature into some kind of action. It was this eagerness to establish common ground which particularly inclined it to the idea of town planning when it was injected into the environmental debate in the early 1900s.

Although the increasing recognition of the possibility of a suburban solution to the housing problem was certainly the main development of the 1890s, the outward spread of towns also had implications for the policies applied to their existing built-up areas. In particular, the traffic load on central streets began to cause serious congestion in London and some of the big provincial towns. Owing to the rise in property values in the central areas, the traditional policy of piecemeal street improvements began to appear expensive and inefficient (see Land Enquiry Committee, 1914, II, 242–84), and municipal engineers began to give more serious consideration to the problem. Liverpool led the way, expanding its central street improvement programme from the later 1890s, and beginning to consider the possibility of building wide roads in advance of demand in the newer areas. By the turn of the century, traffic engineering had become a prime concern of the London County Council and a number of provincial cities.

It is clear that by about 1900 some of the pre-conditions of urban planning had been established in Britain. Municipal enterprise was at a new peak of vigour and respectability. The structural problems of large cities were recognized, if only dimly. British techniques for the layout of residential estates were already winning acclaim abroad, and not least in Germany. Yet an overall strategy of urban development and improvement, comparable to German *Städtebau*, was still lacking. It is quite possible that incremental processes would have generated this comprehensive view of the city within a few years. Incremental processes, however, were by no means the only factors at work. On the contrary, at the turn of the century Britain was more susceptible than ever before to the idea of revolutionary change in social policy, in the form of the wholesale importation of foreign practice.

Beginning in the 1880s, British confidence in the quality of national society, and in British ability to generate solutions to social problems, had begun to wane. This growing uncertainty was partly a function of the rise of economic rivals, notably the United States and Germany. In social policy the United States clearly had little to offer Britain, but Germany's industrial expansion appeared to be proceeding hand in hand with extensive State intervention in economy and society. As Britain was itself moving in this direction, German practices began to command growing attention. In the 1880s it was Bismarck's social insurance policies which particularly caught the eye, but the quality of German education, and especially technical education, had been a source of envy since the 1870s. Of course, the impact of the German example was distorted by growing British fears, dating back to as early as the 1870s, of German military strength and political ambitions (Mander, 1974, 196–204). However, the undoubted growth of anti-German feeling was countered by even more determined efforts by those who maintained that Germany had much to teach Britain to foster contacts between the two countries (Kennedy, 1975, 145). Furthermore, many of those who detested or feared Germany had a sneaking respect for German institutions. Thus by 1900 Britain was very open to German example, and not least in the field of urban policy, where *Städtebau* was now so far in advance of British practice.

THE ENVIRONMENTAL DEBATE AND THE PRESENTATION OF TWO RIVAL SOLUTIONS, 1899–1906

In October 1899 war broke out in Southern Africa between the British Empire and the Boers. The domestic economy was in depression and many of those who flocked to join the colours were unemployed, unskilled young men from the large cities. A high proportion were rejected on physical grounds. The war went badly and the army recruiting drive continued into 1900 and 1901, so that poor news from the front was echoed by reports on the rejection of volunteers at home. The result was a sharp wave of unease in which the whole condition of British society was called into question. Signs of decline and disintegration could be detected everywhere — labour unrest, the running sore of Ireland, rising industrial competition from Germany and the United States, the desertion of the countryside. This new social crisis, though partially obscured by the imperialist context in which it was set, had much in common with its 1880s predecessor. Once again, concern centred on the teeming cities (see e.g. Masterman, 1901, v–x).

It was widely recognized that poverty underlay the poor condition of the recruits, for thanks to the work of Charles Booth and other social researchers poverty was now much better understood than in the 1880s. However, the eradication of poverty on the scale revealed by Booth and confirmed by Rowntree was a daunting task which seemed to require a major reconstruction of society. To improve the environment, on the other hand, appeared to need only minor adjustments to accelerate changes which were already occurring. Moreover, the educative potential of the environment, as understood at that time, held out the prospect of a progressive resolution of social problems by a refined process of self-help. Certainly, environmental reform was only one of many measures canvassed in the social debate of the early 1900s, and only a minority of those concerned with the social question devoted themselves exclusively or predominantly to it. Nevertheless, it enjoyed great prominence, partly because it emerged as a focal point at which a number of reform proposals converged.

Although the idea of urban planning did not emerge immediately, it was clearly foreshadowed by the discussion of several aspects of the environment in the early stages of the debate (see e.g. Haw, 1900). The main environmental problems discussed were: (i) the persistence of overcrowded, unhealthy and relatively expensive housing conditions among the very poor in the town centres; (ii) the shortfall in the provision of new housing for the working classes in general, combined with rising rents; (iii) air pollution; (iv) the lack of parks and play spaces in working-class areas; (v) the visual boredom and ugliness of the working-class and lower-middle-class by-law suburbs; and (vi) the absence of uplifting cultural institutions in working-class areas. To these problems, which were almost universally acknowledged, might be added a seventh, which worried only a minority of observers — the increasing residential segregation of the social classes (see e.g. Masterman, 1901, vi). None of these problems was being recognized for the first time, but several of them now aroused much more concern than in the 1880s. By rising in the general awareness to stand alongside the perennial problem of the slum they helped to extend concern to the town *as a whole* (see e.g. *Improved Means of Locomotion*, 1901, 3). Consequently, social reformers could now be persuaded to consider the possibility that a single strategy of reform might deal with all these problems on a city-wide scale.

Two such strategies were presented, and seriously discussed, during the debate. The first, in chronological terms, was the 'garden city' proposal launched by Ebenezer Howard. The other was the idea of town-extension planning which, in its most persuasive form, was imported from Germany, principally by the efforts of Thomas Coglan Horsfall.

The garden city idea

In 1898 a small book, *Tomorrow: A Peaceful Path to Real Reform*, was published in London. The author, Ebenezer Howard (1850–1928), was a parliamentary stenographer and amateur inventor with long-established interests in Christian Socialism, cooperation, education of the working classes, and land reform (Howard, 1965, 9–20; Fishman, 1977, 31–6). The book put forward the most radical solution to the urban problem to be proposed seriously anywhere in the urbanized world before 1914.

Howard wanted to eradicate the whole of the existing urban network, which he recognized as generating the disproportionate growth of very large cities. It would be replaced by a series of clusters of physically distinct, but economically and socially interdependent, new towns. These new towns would be designed as socially balanced communities incorporating large areas of open space, and would stand on communally owned land — 'clusters of beautiful home-towns, each zoned by gardens' (Howard, 1965, 128). Most of these new garden cities, which would be ringed by an agricultural belt, would not be allowed to exceed the population of around 30,000 for which they were to be carefully planned. However, Howard foresaw an ultimate population of a quarter of a million people for each cluster. As the garden cities grew, attracting population and industry by their pleasant environment, low house rents, and low production costs, the existing towns would wither away until they either disappeared or could be replanned as individual garden cities or clusters.

Howard's model combined two reform ideas which had already generated much interest earlier in the century. These were new communities and decentralization. The idea of setting up new communities as prototypes of an alternative social and economic system had attracted some support from the working and middle classes between the 1820s and the 1840s, when Robert Owen and others founded a number of new communities. None, however, had been a success and from the 1850s the continued growth of towns, the increasing capitalization of production, and the workers' general acceptance of the existing organization of society made this approach appear unrealistic. Marx and Engels denigrated it as 'utopian socialism' and the leaders of the working classes, whether or not influenced by Marxism, concentrated on trade union activity and political reform.

The idea of the alternative community nevertheless survived as a topic of discussion among reformers. It was given minor boosts by the small communities of craftsmen and intellectuals generated by the Arts and Crafts Movement and other middle-class reforming tendencies in the 1870s and 1880s, and by Anarchist advocacy of tiny, self-supporting communities in the 1880s and 1890s (see Armytage, 1961; Hardy, 1979; Darley, 1976). A literary stimulus came from the publication, in 1888, of Edward Bellamy's *Looking Backward*, a vision of a future Boston (Mass.). Ebenezer Howard, as a lower-middle-class intellectual who moved widely in London reform circles from the later 1870s, after his return from an unsuccessful spell as a homesteader in the United States, had bathed fully in these currents. While he was discreet enough not to lay undue emphasis on the cooperative production which he clearly envisaged for his garden cities, he made a point of emphasizing the communal landownership which had been a feature of many earlier proposals for alternative communities.

Land reform, another objective dismissed by the Marxists, had been much canvassed in British reforming circles during the nineteenth century. As in Germany, its urban aspects became increasingly prominent as the population shifted into the towns and the prospect of scratching a living from a smallholding lost its appeal. The agricultural depression brought on from the early 1870s by cheap American grain imports forced the great landowners to look increasingly to their urban estates for financial salvation (see Cannadine, 1977). Meanwhile, it became increasingly fashionable, even in moderate reform circles, to pick out landowners as an exploiting class distinct from other capitalists, a status which rising urban land rents and simple economic theory combined to make appear quite plausible (see Singer, 1941; Douglas, 1976, 15—20). Lecture tours by the American land-tax enthusiast, Henry George, strengthened interest in land reform. By the end of the century the public standing of private landownership had reached its nadir (see e.g. Money, 1905, 75—8), and Howard's proposals for communal ownership were favourably received. They were, nevertheless, the creation of a man who had much of the utopian socialist about him and the garden city idea as a whole touched idealistic chords in many of its supporters — which helps to account for the enthusiastic and even irrational support that it received from some quarters.

The second of the long-established reform approaches incorporated by Howard was a more prosaic one. The idea of moving the poor from crowded town centres to dormitory settlements or self-contained industrial communities in the nearby countryside dated from the 1840s, when the spread of the railway had suggested how it might be achieved (Ashworth, 1954, 123). Indeed, it was put into effect on an impressive scale and with great success as early as the 1850s, when a Bradford textile manufacturer, Sir Titus Salt, built a giant mill and a settlement for 4,000 people in open country several miles outside the town (see Dewhirst, 1960—1). However, few employers were tempted to emulate Saltaire at a time when steam power and the railways were encouraging industry to concentrate in towns rather than forsake them. The idea did not revive until the housing scare of the 1880s when Alfred Marshall, the economist, provided theoretical support for decentralization. In 1883 the Society for the Promotion of Industrial Villages was set up specifically to promote the idea, and although it achieved little, the initiatives of Lever and Cadbury at Port Sunlight and Bournville gave encouragement in the 1890s. Howard's proposals thus appeared more realistic at the turn of the century than they would have done twenty or even ten years earlier. Indeed, Howard had formed the essentials of his garden city theory by 1892, under the immediate impact of Bellamy's thinking, but had been unable to publish it in book form or to win interest for it outside a narrow circle of land reformers (Fishman, 1977, 32–6, 52–4). Moreover, even on its publication in 1898 his book aroused little interest, and it was not until the urban debate burst out in the following year that his ideas, disseminated by the Garden City Association which he and a few supporters founded in June 1899, achieved a wide currency.

However, once the garden city idea had secured a degree of discussion, it proved extraordinarily potent. It impressed, at one extreme, in its comprehensiveness, and at another, in the charm of the local environment which it implied. It was more, even, than a programme of urban reform. The clusters of garden cities with their parks and agricultural belts were presented by Howard as a composite 'town-country' which would solve the problem of rural depopulation which, exacerbated by the agricultural depression, had been causing concern since the 1870s (see Saville, 1957). Indeed, Howard's sweeping vision at first caused him to neglect the internal arrangement of the garden city. However, he and his supporters soon made it clear that they envisaged a housing environment comparable to that achieved at Port Sunlight and Bournville. In espousing this attractive mode of design they greatly extended their sphere of influence, and from 1899 support for the garden city began to extend far beyond the socialistic and somewhat cranky reform milieu which Howard had previously frequented.

This broadening of the garden city's appeal was hurried along, at the expense of a weakening of its more socialistic features, by Ralph Neville, a London lawyer of some influence in the Liberal Party. Neville lent his support to Howard in 1901 and became chairman of the Garden City Association. He was originally attracted to the garden city as an extension of his own interest in industrial co-partnership, a form of profit-sharing in which a firm's employees were granted part of its equity. This arrangement, which was designed to secure the worker's loyalty to his employer, differed radically from cooperation in that direction of the enterprise remained vested in the non-employee shareholders. As such, it had attracted some support on the reforming wing of the Liberal Party, and Neville secured much support for the garden city in that quarter. Neville also introduced Howard to George Cadbury and W. H. Lever, whose social reform activities had now made them national figures. Persuaded by Thomas Adams (1871–1940), the full-time secretary of the Garden City Association who, like Neville, was eager to broaden its support, Cadbury and Lever agreed to sponsor a national conference on the garden city. Held at Bournville in September 1901, it attracted over 1,500 participants and put Howard's ideas firmly in the public eye. It was this success which led to the republication of his book in 1902, under the more specific title of *Garden Cities of Tomorrow* (Fishman, 1977, 54–60).

The Bournville conference, which attracted the full range of housing reformers, foreshadowed the eventual degradation of the pure garden city idea into the more easily realizable concept of the garden suburb. For the time being, however, momentum was maintained on Howard's original track by surprisingly rapid progress towards the creation of a pilot garden city. Sufficient capital was raised by private subscription, mainly among the rich supporters brought in by Neville, to launch First Garden City Ltd in 1903. Almost immediately, a large area of land was purchased on a railway line some thirty miles north of London, and by 1904 development of Letchworth garden city was well under way. A restricted competition in 1904 produced a master plan by the partnership of Raymond Unwin and Barry Parker, two architects who combined experience in the social-istic reform movements of the later nineteenth century with acknowledged success in designing model workers' settlements (see Day and Garstang, 1975).

The plan was a fully-fledged example of comprehensive urban planning. It contained distinct industrial and commercial areas, a rational network of com-munications, a civic centre, a park system, a green belt, housing areas in which densities and layouts were clearly fixed, and an appropriate code of building regulations. It outshone even the best German practice, of which Unwin was only just becoming aware (Day, 1973, 104–5). Of course, we have to remember that all this was possible only because all the land was owned by First Garden City Ltd, and because no existing building by-laws applied to this rural district. However, Letchworth clearly demonstrated for the first time in Britain that a large town, accommodating a variety of firms and with a combination of private and co-partnership housing, could be planned from scratch to secure both amenity and efficiency. Letchworth thus made a point that no model factory village, however well planned, could have done.

The year 1904, however, marked the apogee of the garden city movement in its pure form. It proved easier to found Letchworth than to secure a rapid rate of growth for the town. The Garden City Association did not dare to attempt a second garden city while lessons were still being learned from the first. Howard's supporters had failed in their efforts to persuade the Cooperative Movement to promote a garden city, and no serious effort was made to obtain State support from the Conservative government, even though Howard foresaw that one day the State might take over the garden city programme. Meanwhile, the Garden City Association was increasingly tempted to interest itself in smaller-scale enterprises, including even housing estates built by enlightened employers, co-partnership housing companies, and private landowners, in or near existing towns. Although such suburban accretions were, strictly speaking, the antithesis of the garden city ideal, it was argued by Thomas Adams and many others that they could be welcomed as efforts to improve the environment 'on garden-city lines'. This debate had not been fully resolved within the Association when, in 1904, town-extension planning burst upon the scene.

Town-extension planning

One of the features which distinguished the environmental debate of the early 1900s from that of the 1880s was its gloomy view of the working-class suburb. During the 1890s, particularly in West Ham and other districts of eastern London, the building of miles of peripheral streets for almost exclusively working-class occupancy had done much to dash the dream of a redemption of the poor through decentralization. Their minimum by-law standards and monotonous appearance were widely regarded as reproducing many of the defects of the central slums. This reverse did not discourage the advocates of decentralization from reinforcing their proposals, with Charles Booth's scheme for a city-wide transport strategy foreshadowing full urban transport planning (see *Improved Means of Locomotion*, 1901). However, it could no longer be assumed that cheap and rapid transport would solve the whole urban problem, and it was suggested that some superior kind of design should be imposed on the new suburbs.

During the 1890s news had begun to filter in from Germany about the planning of town extensions. A full description of German practices appeared in Albert Shaw's *Municipal Government in Continental Europe* which, though aimed primarily at an American readership, was separately published in London in 1895. The idea was also discussed by those branches of the land reform movement which favoured large-scale municipal land purchase or land nationalization. However, as Howard had discovered, ideas associated with land reformers scarcely qualified for general attention in the 1890s and when the Boer War debate broke out the concept of suburban planning was still in no more than embryonic form.

One of the clearer formulations of the idea was included by Frederick Lawrence, the young Liberal reformer, in his contribution to C. F. G. Masterman's influential exposé of urban conditions, *The Heart of the Empire*, in 1901. He called for 'certain general schemes setting out the main outlines of any general plan of growth' to be formulated for peripheral districts. Such schemes should include wide streets and avenues and the reservation of large areas for open space (Masterman, 1901, 83). To sustain these districts, Lawrence wanted to see a comprehensive transport scheme on the lines proposed by Booth, and he went on to discuss various means of recouping betterment values. However, Lawrence failed to combine his proposals in the concept of a single urban strategy or plan. He was vague about the content of his 'general schemes' and he ignored most of the practical difficulties which they raised, particularly in respect of relations between the public authority and the landowners. Apparently, he drew most of his inspiration for suburban planning from a hazy understanding of post-1811 street planning in New York (see below, p. 92). Though only a few steps away from the idea of urban planning, Lawrence's proposals lacked both precision and persuasive power.

The resolution of these difficulties, and the development of an effective advocacy of suburban planning, were, like the garden city idea, very largely the work of one man. Thomas Coglan Horsfall (1841–1932), the son of a Manchester industrialist and a staunch Anglican, had early in life fallen under the influence of the Christian Socialists and William Ruskin. Confident that an appreciation of beauty could allow the poor to rise above their squalid surroundings, he became involved in a scheme to set up an art gallery and cultural institute in a Manchester park, which culminated in the foundation of the Manchester Art Museum in 1877 (Creese, 1966, 273). His campaign for funds generated widespread interest in this Ruskinian enterprise, and he went on to read papers on the value of art at the annual congresses of the National Association for the Promotion of Social Science in 1881 and 1882. It was at around this time that he came into close contact with William Morris, and with Samuel and Henrietta Barnett, the leaders of the Settlement Movement, a civilizing mission to the urban poor based on small communities of Christian social workers, which had begun in the 1870s. In 1886 Horsfall inherited the family firm and so arranged its affairs that he could devote most of his time to his reform activities.

It was by now apparent that the Manchester Art Museum, of which Horsfall was treasurer, was failing to make any impact on the great mass of the working class. Like the People's Palace in East London, it became the haunt of the ambitious clerk who appreciated the company of upper-class reformers and do-gooders. Disappointed, Horsfall broadened his interests. While he retained his belief in the value of beauty, the 1890s saw him increasingly interested in education, welfare, housing and the general improvement of the environment. These concerns led him to look abroad, and particularly to Germany. The more he read about Germany and corresponded with officials there, the more interested he became in a *Städtebau* which, as we have already seen, was in one of the most vital phases of its development (see Reynolds, 1952–3; Hawtree, 1974, 224).

During the early months of the Boer War a very high proportion of Manchester volunteers were rejected and the resulting controversy reached the dimensions of a public scandal in the city. Horsfall joined the debate, arguing that more than just poverty, immorality and poor housing were to blame. The following passage epitomizes much of what he said and wrote at this time:

> The causes of the degeneration which goes on in our large towns, and of the high death-rate of many of those towns, are very obvious. The main cause is not the overcrowding of dwellings, though that is a very marked and serious evil, nor excessive drinking, nor licentiousness, nor betting and other forms of gambling, nor the cutting off of light by smoke, nor the horrible filthiness of the air, nor the lack of physical exercise, nor any other of the evils which exist in our towns, though each of those which I have mentioned would by itself almost suffice to cause the ruin of the race.

The chief cause is that, while all these evils exist, there is nothing to counteract the effect of them, that none of the conditions exist for the majority of the inhabitants of the towns which give strong motives to human beings to resist the temptations found everywhere to drink, to gamble, to be licentious, to give up exercise, to exclude fresh air from one's house and so on. The chief cause of evil is that the towns lack the pleasantness, which is the most important condition of cheerfulness, hopefulness, physical and mental health and strength for all classes, for the poorest as well as for the richest. (Horsfall, 1904, 21)

Although Horsfall's emphasis on the need to transcend squalid surroundings recalled his Ruskinian arguments of the early 1880s, he no longer believed that one art gallery could create the required 'pleasantness'. Instead, the whole city had to be transformed. And how? By town-extension planning, which would supersede the British tradition of piecemeal intervention:

What is needed by the authorities is not the power to buy up large tracts of land or the power to build workmen's dwellings, it is the power, and the intelligence needed for the right use of the power, to make and to enforce the strict observance of plans for large areas round every town which is growing... (Horsfall, 1900, 5)

Horsfall had in fact first seriously advocated this solution in a paper to the Manchester Statistical Society in 1895 (see Horsfall, 1895). Like Howard, however, he had found that in the absence of a social crisis such outlandish ideas could not take root. In 1900 all was different; Horsfall was inundated with questions about German practice and was encouraged to find out more about it. Indeed, he knew as yet very little about German planning, despite a study-visit there in 1897, and he redoubled his efforts to master its intricacies.

Meanwhile, Horsfall had helped to found, and had become president of, a pressure group known as the Manchester and Salford Citizens' Association for the Improvement of the Unwholesome Dwellings and Surroundings of the People. The Association gave its support to an inquiry into housing conditions in Manchester conducted by T. R. Marr, a local reformer, and Horsfall decided to prepare a monograph on German planning for publication as a supplement to Marr's work.

It was not until 1904 that *The Improvement of the Dwellings and Surroundings of the People: The Example of Germany*, was ready for publication. Much of it consisted of translations from published German reports and studies. Horsfall seemed eager to convey an impression of varied planning policies in Germany, but the main innovation which he urged as suitable for adoption in England was the extension plan. It should be supported, he argued, by three other reforms drawn from German practice: cheap loans to organizations and individuals building workers' housing; large-scale municipal land purchase; and cheap transport to the outer districts. Throughout the book he flaunted his admiration of German institutions, and advocated many other German reforms which had nothing to do with the environment. Overall, he wanted to see a general reconstruction of

British town government on German lines (including direction by paid officials), to fit it for the great tasks which it would now take up.

Intellectually, Horsfall's work was much less impressive than Howard's and his tedious and repetitive citing of foreign example would have been counter-productive in any decade other than the unusually insecure 1900s. However, the book crystallized in a single strategy nearly all the environmental reform proposals which had been under discussion since 1899. Its applicability to existing towns seemed to offer the prospect of more rapid improvements than Howard's programme, and it quickly came to dominate the whole urban debate.

The first expression of national political support for the idea was obtained at the Leeds Trades Union Congress of 1904 when, at a joint meeting of the National Housing Reform Council and the Workmen's National Housing Council (a purely working-class body), Horsfall moved a proposal calling for the creation of powers to allow municipalities to plan town extensions. It was carried unanimously (Cherry, 1974, 42). In the same year the Inter-Departmental Committee on Physical Deterioration, set up by the government after the Boer War to investigate the suspicion that urban life was leading to the physical degeneration of the populace, published its report. Although it did not support the fears of a general deterioration, it recommended *inter alia* that steps should be taken to prevent the re-creation of poor conditions in the new suburbs (Ashworth, 1954, 168). Also in 1904, the president of the RIBA, John Belcher, introduced town-extension planning into his annual address.

The discussions generated by Horsfall's book were followed with particular interest by John Sutton Nettlefold (1866–1914), a Birmingham industrialist and Unionist councillor. After his election to the City Council in 1898 Nettlefold had made a name for himself by his trenchant criticisms of the Council's muddled housing policy. In 1901 Nettlefold had found himself chairman of the newly-created Housing Committee which, the Council hoped, would either establish a coherent strategy or silence Nettlefold (Sutcliffe, 1974a, 188). Experience in the post not only confirmed Nettlefold's aversion to municipal housing but turned him against slum clearance; instead, he favoured co-partnership building in the suburbs and rehabilitation in the inner districts. He persuaded the Council to abandon its plans for a suburban housing estate on the lines pioneered by the LCC, and he gradually wound down the demolition programme. He held out the prospect of a progressive resolution of the central slum problem by a voluntary movement to the suburbs, encouraged by cheap transport (ibid., 188–9).

It was not, however, until Nettlefold read Horsfall's book that he fully realized that it might be possible to incorporate cheap transport, cheap land and a pleasant environment within a single planning strategy for the suburbs. The idea was a revelation. In 1905 he began to advocate it himself, and he persuaded the Council to send him, with a deputation from the Housing Committee, to visit Germany in the summer of that year. The deputation submitted two reports to the Council, in 1905 and 1906. With a few reservations, they expressed strong admiration of the German urban environment and called for a general plan for all undeveloped land within the city boundaries, extensive municipal ownership of land, and changes in the building by-laws to allow narrower, and therefore cheaper, residential streets. The Council soon discovered that general powers would not permit planning on this scale, and in July 1906 it passed a motion from Nettlefold's Housing Committee calling for national legislation.

Birmingham's conversion to extension planning completed the domesticization of the idea and greatly enhanced its respectability. With other big municipalities, led by Liverpool and Manchester, also interested, extension planning began to be incorporated into local government orthodoxy at the precise time when municipal independence and enterprise were reaching their peak in Britain. Nettlefold, moreover, was a better advocate than Horsfall, as he proved in numerous speeches and in his persuasive book, *Practical Housing* (1908). While acknowledging Germany's example sufficiently to arouse a spirit of emulation in his readers, he eschewed the long quotations and tedious recitations of German achievements in which Horsfall still wallowed. Instead, he demonstrated in simple language how a large British city would benefit from extension planning. He even anglicized the term, coining the expression 'town planning' which by late 1906 was on the lips of most urban reformers (see Cherry, 1975). It was from 1906, therefore, that extension planning began clearly to outshine the garden city as a beneficial and practical step towards the general reform of the urban environment.

PROGRESS TOWARDS LEGISLATION, 1906–9

In December 1905 the Conservative government fell and was replaced by a Liberal administration under Sir Henry Campbell-Bannerman. In January 1906 the new government fought and won a general election on an ambitious social reform platform which included the resolution of the housing question. The new President of the Local Government Board, John Burns, let it be known that he was eager to bring forward an important housing measure within the first couple of years of the new Parliament. Immediately, therefore, the various tendencies within the environmental reform movement began to concentrate their efforts on influencing the new legislation.

The first climax of these endeavours came in November 1906, when Campbell-Bannerman and Burns received a large delegation from the National Housing Reform Council. Valuing its position as the acknowledged mouthpiece of the reformers, the Council put forward a large number of proposals, acknowledging that not all of them had its unanimous support. Most were piecemeal reforms to stimulate the building of workers' housing, and some were of purely rural relevance. Only a small minority of the suggestions related to urban planning as distinct from housing. Alderman William Thompson from Richmond, leader of the delegation and an experienced housing reformer, even made a virtue of

the fact that nearly all the proposals were venerable ones, based on the recommendations of the Royal Commission on the Housing of the Working Classes
in 1885 (Aldridge, 1915, 167).

The planning proposals were partly the product of T. C. Horsfall's activities
as a member of the committee of the National Housing Reform Council, to which
he had been elected early in its existence as the representative of the Manchester
and Salford Citizens' Association (Hawtree, 1974, 39). Horsfall had attended the
Council's meeting with interested MPs in 1903 and thereafter he had sat on its
parliamentary committee (*Garden City*, 1(1), 1904, 11). The main planning
suggestion was that local authorities, either singly or in groups, should be empowered to make plans for town extensions to meet future needs. Such plans
should pay particular attention to main roads, open spaces and sites for public
buildings and workers' dwellings. Supporting it was a proposal that the building
by-laws should be revised to secure more open spaces and larger gardens, to fix
maxima of houses or rooms per acre in various districts, to allow narrower roadways in residential areas, and to avoid unnecessary expense in residential building.
A third proposal called for local authorities to be allowed to purchase large areas
of peripheral land in order to promote its development on the lines adopted at
Bournville. Finally, the delegation suggested that a central commission, or special
department of the Local Government Board, should be set up to study urban
growth over the whole country in relation to existing local authority boundaries,
with powers to set up joint committees for 'Scientific Areas' in order to guide
their development (Aldridge, 1915, 164–6).

The Prime Minister responded encouragingly, but John Burns's grudging reply
foreshadowed the difficulties to come, difficulties which would allow only a
partial triumph for town planning in pre-war Britain. He began by claiming that
most of the reforms sought by the delegation already lay within existing local
powers, or were currently under consideration in Parliament. He dismissed municipal landownership on the ground that the government was already considering
a general land reform measure – an oblique reference, this, to Liberal plans for
land taxation (Douglas, 1976, 139–45). Turning to extension planning, Burns
went out of his way to deride the German example. Once leave the main streets
of a Continental city, he averred, and you encounter squalid alleys. In fact, all
that the delegation secured from Burns was an ungracious undertaking to give
broad attention to the delegation's demands in 1907, when pressure on parliamentary time would be less severe (Aldridge, 1915, 176–80).

Although the leaders of the delegation thanked the two ministers effusively,
Burns's speech had been distinctly discouraging. Admittedly, it might merely have
reflected Burns's glum resentment of the criticism which he was inclined to detect
in the most benign of remarks. However, Burns's general performance as an
administrator and legislator was already disappointing both his ministerial colleagues and his friends in the labour movement. Much had been expected of the
former firebrand trade union leader turned Liberal politician, the first working

man to sit in the Cabinet. However, whether through inexperience or premature decline in his personal capacities, Burns seemed unable to master his senior officials at the Local Government Board. Notoriously conservative and legalistic, they held up progress in all the areas in which Burns had been expected to press forward with major reforms (see Brown, 1977). In the following year Burns was to claim that immediately after meeting the NHRC delegation he had set his officials to work on two bills, one on housing and the other on town planning, with a view to putting both through Parliament in 1907 (*Times*, 8 August 1907). Unfortunately, the destruction of the relevant Local Government Board files during the Second World War makes it impossible to establish the truth of the matter, but nothing in the surviving evidence suggests that town planning had become a priority for Burns in the autumn of 1906. On the contrary, he appears to have seen it, at best, as just one of a number of housing reforms which might be embodied in legislation if his officials could complete the necessary studies and parliamentary time could be spared (Brown, 1977, 127). What seems to have tipped the balance was mounting pressure for extension-planning powers over the following months from the big urban authorities.

At the October meeting of the Association of Municipal Corporations in 1906, the Lord Mayor of Manchester had carried a motion which referred to the need to consider what new powers for the planning of suburbs ought to be given to local authorities (Ashworth, 1954, 180–1; *Garden City*, 1906, 236). This resolution led to the establishment by the Association of a Town Planning Committee under the chairmanship of Nettlefold. The committee drew up a draft town planning bill and in August 1907 Nettlefold led an AMC deputation to see Campbell-Bannerman and Burns about 'the planning of suburbs' (*Times*, 8 August 1907).

By this time Burns was under heavy pressure. In January Campbell-Bannerman had made a widely-reported speech at Glasgow in which he lamented the evils of the concentration of population and stressed the need to set up 'counter-attractive agencies' (*Garden City*, 1907, 293). In April he had made a similar speech in London. Then, in May, the growing planning lobby in the House of Commons had obtained a debate on 'town development'. It ended with the passing of a resolution stating the need for legislation to grant local authorities 'the power of laying out suburbs for building upon a rational plan, which shall include adequate air-space, convenient grounds for recreation, and facilities for locomotion, so preventing the grave evils which result from overcrowding in and around great cities' (*Hansard*, 4th ser., 173, 978–90). Burns had replied, with his usual bluster, that his officials had already drafted two alternative bills capable of providing the powers desired by the House (though he added, gratuitously, that in his opinion the powers already available left very little to be desired). However, the fact of the matter was that no housing or planning measure was anywhere near ready. Indeed, the Cabinet, which had assumed that Burns would be bringing one or more bills forward in 1907, decided in the early summer to postpone the whole matter until the 1908 session, when time would be made available for Burns to present a major measure (Brown, 1977, 127). In this atmosphere, the AMC deputation may well have acted as the final influence concentrating Burns's mind on town planning. Whereas it had appeared in the NHRC submission of the previous year as one group of reforms among many, it was now presented as the key priority of the big urban authorities and one which, thanks to assiduous lobbying, had a good chance of getting through both Houses. It also had the strong support of the Prime Minister, whose reply to the deputation implied that only internal difficulties in the Local Government Board were holding it up (*Times*, 8 August 1907).

Whatever the exact nature of Burns's thinking, he had said enough by mid-summer 1907 to suggest that a measure granting powers to local authorities to plan their suburban areas was imminent. In doing so he indirectly limited his own options. The more the government appeared to favour town-extension planning, the more the housing and environmental reformers concentrated their attention on it, and neglected the more direct stimuli to house-building proposed by the NHRC delegation in 1906. Local authority advocacy now began to be supplemented by professional support. Noting that new work might soon become available in the preparation of extension plans, the three interested professions of architects, civil engineers and surveyors began to dispute the right to direct it. In doing so, they gave the impression to laymen that extension planning was the only reform worth considering.

Of the three professions, the architects did most to catch the public eye. Since the turn of the century they had been increasingly impressed by, and envious of, the monumental products of the American City Beautiful movement (see below, p. 103). The wide adoption of the classical style for public buildings had suddenly civilized American design in the eyes of British architects, who could now begin to admire the massive scale of much transatlantic building. Many of the leading British architects of the day entertained fond hopes that town planning would stimulate a revival of the monumental tradition in Britain. Their visionary schemes for civic centres, boulevards and parks, which multiplied from about 1905, and were widely publicised, added a new dimension to the increasingly numerous plans for residential districts generated by the growth of the co-partnership movement and the housing efforts of enlightened employers. Many of these schemes were both opportunistic and unrealistic, but in the work of Raymond Unwin, in particular, the monumental and cottage modes were convincingly combined to produce a total planned townscape of great persuasive force.

While the prospect of town planning became more attractive visually, so were its virtues as a social panacea more widely canvassed and acknowledged. The idea that the physical proximity of the upper and lower classes would generate a caring, organic community was never much more than a pious hope, but it strongly appealed to the more socially concerned elements among the middle classes during the heightened labour unrest which marked the first decade of the twentieth century. Its most influential prophet was Dame Henrietta Barnett. Discouraged by the constant setbacks endured by the Settlement Movement in its efforts to civilize the poor of East London, she and her husband had begun around the turn of the century to think about reversing the process by bringing the poor to live with their social superiors. Involved in a campaign to protect the leafy heights of Hampstead, North London, where the Barnetts had a weekend house, from impending development with run-of-the-mill suburban terraces, Henrietta hit on the idea of promoting a planned suburb. To this end she set up a Garden Suburb Committee in 1904. Wealthy and titled support was quickly forthcoming, and by the end of 1906 a large area of land had been purchased, Raymond Unwin had produced a master plan, and a private Act had been put through Parliament by Henry Vivian to secure the necessary modifications in the local building regulations (Barnett, 1909, 332–47; Cherry, 1974, 49). Meanwhile, Henrietta Barnett's prolific pen wove the spell of the happy suburb:

> Is this state of things a necessity of our civilisation? As our towns yearly grow in population and show a continuous tendency to spread out, can we hope for nothing more than a repetition of those dreary roads full of trivial villas, those ranks of closely-built gardenless boxes? Must we be content, now that education is bringing all sorts of people nearer together in sympathy, to have classes topographically divided by an arbitrary division depending upon their rent-paying powers? Is it a natural sequence that hundreds of people with multi-form possibilities and varied tastes should be obliged to live in houses exactly alike, so close that there is not room to develop their tastes, or opportunity of turning buried potentialities into facts? (Barnett, 1909, 333)

The brilliant, early success of Hampstead Garden Suburb soon outshone Letchworth. Its planning had most of the virtues of the garden city without its isolation. It struck a further blow against municipal housing, to which Henrietta Barnett was resolutely opposed; at Hampstead, workers' housing was to be provided by co-partnership companies on the cheaper land on the estate. Its location, and Henrietta Barnett's social connections, ensured the support of the cream of London society, some of whom actually opted to live there. As in earlier model villages and suburbs, the technical qualities of the planning rested on unified landownership, but the private Act of 1906 was a real step forward. It confirmed Parliament's support for low-density planning and held out the hope that a general measure, capable of imposing such a mode of development on all landowners, would be favourably received. Above all, Hampstead Garden Suburb suggested that the gradual improvement of existing cities through planned extensions, but without massive construction of public housing, was a policy well worth pursuing.

Even the Garden City Association jumped on the bandwagon. In February 1907 a conference of the Association passed a resolution, proposed by Nettlefold, calling for 'town planning powers' to be granted to local authorities (*Garden City*, 1907, 298–300). Then, in October of the same year, it organized a big conference on town planning at the Guildhall, in London. Among the large attendance were representatives of over one hundred local authorities and all the major professional institutions and reform bodies. Also represented was the Sociological Society which, since its foundation in 1904, had developed a strong interest in the urban environment under the leadership of the Edinburgh biologist and sociologist, Patrick Geddes. The Guildhall conference was the most varied and distinguished town-planning assembly yet held in Britain, but the consensus which the organizers openly sought was achieved only by the virtual jettisoning of Ebenezer Howard's original ideals.

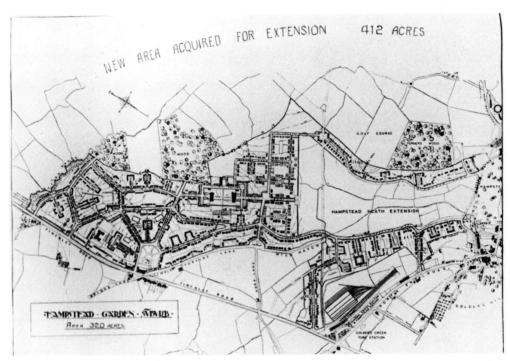

9 *Hampstead Garden Suburb: development plan by Raymond Unwin and Barry Parker, incorporating detailed architectural schemes by Edwin Lutyens. Though a much smaller project than Letchworth, Hampstead gave Unwin and Parker scope to demonstrate their skills in residential site layout. Their pioneering use of cul-de-sacs (closes), footpaths and three-sided courts of terraced dwellings, and their novel methods of integrating houses with open space, reinforced a reputation which, from 1905, rapidly became an international one. (Aldridge, 1915, 407)*

As a basis for discussion the Garden City Association presented a memorandum which, while maintaining that the independent garden city would in the long term provide the best solution to the urban problem, acknowledged the German lead in town planning and called for the expected legislation to permit 'General Development Schemes', municipal land purchase, and cheap loans to approved organizations

10   *Hampstead Way, Hampstead Garden Suburb, in the early 1930s. The houses, which face the Heath Extension, were built before the First World War. As at Port Sunlight and Bournville, the growing maturity of the planting reinforced the attractiveness of the low-density layout. In an early attempt to redistribute betterment value, part of the high ground rent generated by these prime sites was used to subsidize the allocation of land elsewhere on the estate to low-rent, co-partnership housing. (Hampstead Garden Suburb Archives)*

building workers' housing (*Town Planning in Theory and Practice*, 1908, 68–72). This important concession to the main current of opinion was acknowledged with a kindly word by Nettlefold, who moved the conference resolution (which was later carried unanimously) welcoming Burns's promise of legislation:

> Town-planning may be shortly described as the application of the Garden City idea to existing cities and their suburbs — the application of business principles to the solution of the Housing problem. (*Town Planning in Theory and Practice*, 1908, 15)

However, the second part of this sentence was a travesty of Howard's ideas, and the other speakers, none of whom was primarily a supporter of the garden city movement, concentrated exclusively on suburban planning. After the conference

12   (Opposite) *Woodlands, a mining village near Doncaster, built from 1907 to designs by Percy B. Houfton. As an advanced piece of residential planning designed purely for manual workers, it aroused great interest. (RIBA, 1911, 774)*

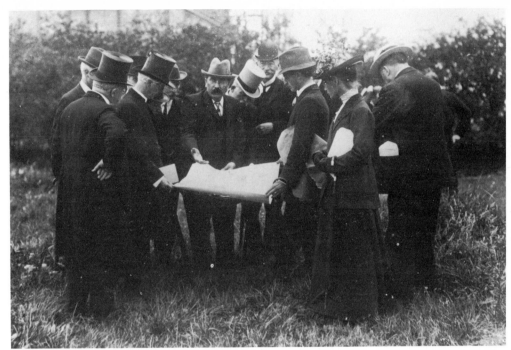

11 *Henry Vivian shows plans of Hampstead Garden Suburb to visiting members of both Houses of Parliament on Central Square, 23 July 1912. The creation of one of the most advanced of the planned suburbs in an increasingly fashionable district of suburban London was of inestimable value to a town-planning movement which relied heavily on parliamentary support. (Hampstead Garden Suburb Archives)*

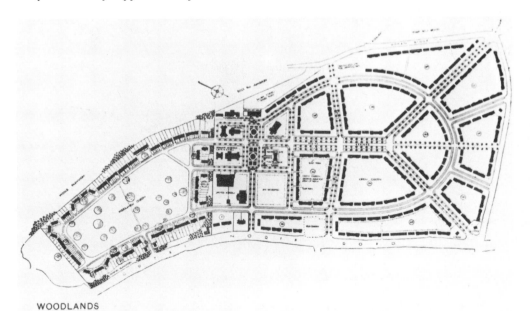

WOODLANDS

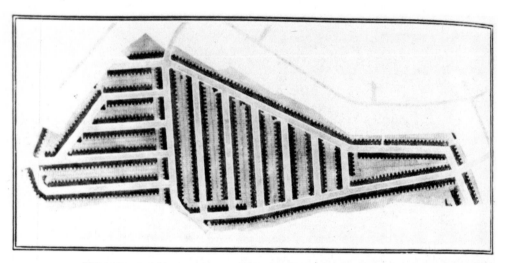

ORDINARY TYPE OF SITE PLAN. SHOWING 40 HOUSES PER ACRE

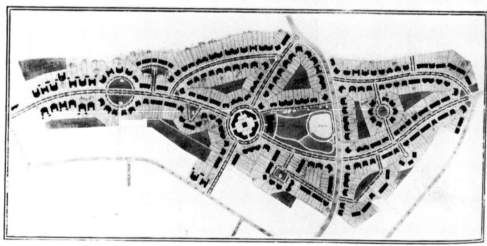

SITE PLAN OF HARBORNE TENANTS. SHOWING 10 HOUSES PER ACRE

HARBORNE TENANTS

13   *The plan of Harborne Tenants, a co-partnership estate built in Birmingham from 1907, compared with a hypothetical by-law layout for the same site. Such comparisons were the stuff of the British town-planning debate, with Unwin leading the argument that lower densities made economic, as well as social and aesthetic sense, owing mainly to savings in road costs. (TPR, 1910, plate 42)*

14 *Houses under construction at Harborne Tenants, c. 1907. Though the layout diverged from the standard by-law grid, paved streets of full width were required by the local authority. (Birmingham Reference Library)*

the Association changed its name to Garden Cities and Town Planning Association, and in 1908 the title of its journal, *The Garden City*, was changed to *Garden Cities and Town Planning*.

It was not only, however, the garden city movement which felt the need to throw in its lot with extension planning. The main mouthpiece of housing reform, the National Housing Reform Council, changed its name in 1909 to National Housing and Town Planning Council. Significantly, the Workmen's National Housing Council, the purely working-class body which worked closely with the NHRC in the early 1900s, had by now parted company with it. Alienated by the Liberal Party's housing policies in both opposition and government, it allied itself from 1907 with the newly-created Labour Party, which was prepared to press for direct State subsidies for housing. Later it would denounce the 1909 Town Planning Act as a mere publicity stunt and a distraction from the realities of the housing problem (Wohl, 1977, 328–9).

THE TOWN PLANNING ACT AND ITS AFTERMATH, 1909–14

The general closing of ranks behind town-extension planning greatly eased the government's task in pushing legislation through Parliament. The Housing, Town Planning, Etc. Bill was introduced for the first time in 1908. As Burns's public attitude had foreshadowed, it was a very mild measure. The housing section lumped together a number of minor changes designed to secure the building of more workers' houses, mainly by voluntary bodies. The town-planning part was more coherent but it did no more than make powers available to urban authorities to prepare planning schemes for peripheral districts in the process of being, or about to be, developed. Existing built-up areas were completely unaffected, municipal land purchase was virtually ignored, and the powers granted were purely facultative, not mandatory. Even this cautious measure met difficulties in committee, and it was eventually withdrawn. Reintroduced in 1909 in an even weaker form, it was further amended in committee and in the House of Lords. However, thanks to the general support of both the Liberal and Conservative parties in the Commons, it became law at the end of the year. Basically, the Act allowed urban authorities to lay down the pattern of main streets, to designate industrial and residential areas, to set aside land for open space and public buildings, and to fix densities and house types in the residential districts. In principle, these powers could allow British urban authorities to emulate the best of German planning practice in their new districts. City-wide planning on German lines remained, however, completely out of the question.

To many reformers the Act was a terrible disappointment. George Cadbury, now a committed advocate of extension planning and a man who thought he had Burns's ear, wrote him a bitter letter lamenting the failure to require *all* towns of more than 50,000 people to draw up plans for the *whole* of their peripheral areas (Cherry, 1974, 64). The neglect of municipal land purchase caused some annoyance which was not allayed by the general land taxes introduced by the Chancellor of the Exchequer, Lloyd-George, in 1909 (Douglas, 1976, 143–4). Burns and other supporters of the Act riposted that too few competent planners were available to sustain a universal planning effort, and that time had to be devoted to preliminary survey work (*TPR*, 1914, 9–10, 57). There was some sense in this view, with which Patrick Geddes, for one, strongly concurred. Nevertheless, as time passed, most observers came to agree that the intricacies of the Act, which were designed mainly to protect private property, were a serious obstacle.

Even the most ambitious of authorities fought shy of preparing a planning scheme for the whole of their peripheral area, and most of those which adopted the Act contented themselves with a small, experimental project. By the end of

15 (Opposite) *The Ruislip town planning scheme was completed in 1913 and approved by the Local Government Board in the following year. The shading on the inset map indicates the maximum permissible number of houses per acre, which varies between four and twelve. A small industrial zone was planned near Northolt Junction Station, in the south of the planned area.* (TPR, *1913, 40*)

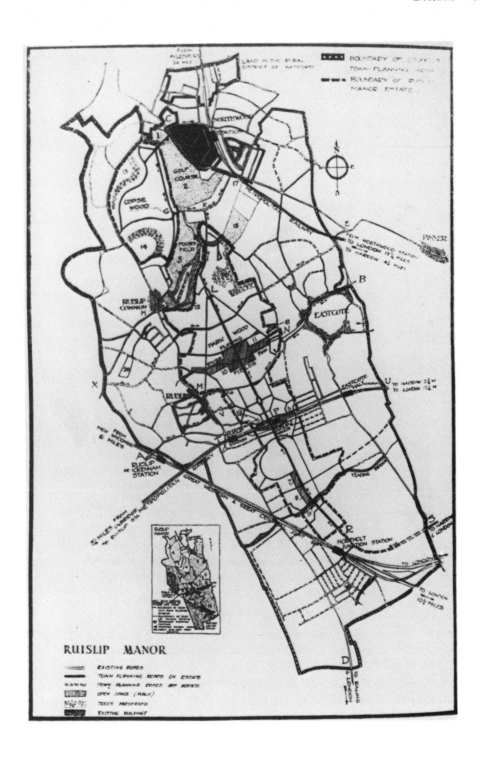

RUISLIP MANOR

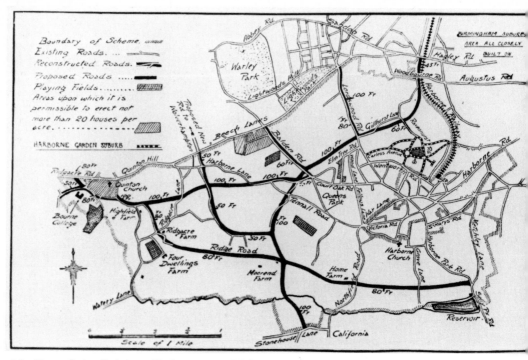

16   *Map of the Quinton, Harborne and Edgbaston town planning scheme, Birmingham. This was the first scheme in Britain to secure the approval of the Local Government Board, in 1913. The plan does not indicate fully the maximum densities proposed for the residential areas, but in other respects its sketchy character fairly reflects the rudimentary nature of the planning carried out in this early scheme. Note the inclusion of the existing Harborne Tenants estate, near the terminus of the railway line. (Aldridge, 1915, 307)*

1913 fifty urban authorities were at various stages of involvement in the preparation of sixty-six town-planning schemes, but only two had been approved by the Local Government Board. Moreover, the areas affected by the sixty-six schemes amounted to less than one-fifth of the total area administered by the fifty authorities (Land Enquiry Committee, 1914, II, 149). Burns himself had stated that the Act was not intended as a means of coercing private interests in the free development of their property, and nearly all the schemes affected areas in which the landowners were perfectly willing to cooperate with the local authority. This meant that most of the districts chosen would in any case have been laid out for low-density housing. Of course, Burns had been saying all along that adequate scope already existed for authorities to reach agreements with the landowners on the planning of suburban districts. Given his attitude, the limited scope of the Act is no surprise. However, even Burns came to agree that the Act's time-consuming procedures and niggling regulations, which were the work of his officials at the Local Government Board and of landowning interests in Parliament, could usefully be simplified.

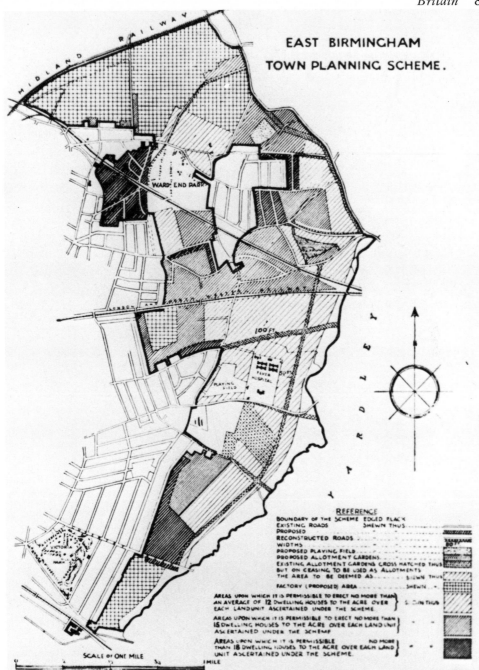

17   *The East Birmingham town planning scheme, approved in 1913. This was the first planning scheme in Britain for a district with an important industrial element. The industrial zones are in the extreme north and south, near the railway lines. The other hatching indicates maximum numbers of houses per acre, and open space. The highest residential densities (up to 18 houses per acre) adjoin the industrial zones. (Aldridge, 1915, 309)*

Slow though progress was towards the formal implementation of extension planning, the years 1909—14 saw a number of important steps in the professional organization of town planning, and in the development of planning theory. The growing dispute between the interested professions was amicably, though only partially, resolved by the foundation in 1913 of an inter-disciplinary Town Planning Institute to supervise the training and examination of town planners (Cherry, 1974, 57—8). In the meantime, however, it had stimulated a number of conferences and meetings at which the rival professions stated their claims, and which had engendered much useful debate. Outstanding was the International Town Planning Conference, claimed to be the first ever held, which the Royal Institute of British Architects put on in London in 1910. Architects were also behind the *Town Planning Review*, the first British journal to be devoted exclusively to town planning. It was published from 1911 by the Department of Civic Design at Liverpool University, which had been set up in 1909 as an offshoot of the School of Architecture there, with funds provided by W. H. Lever. A number of monographs also appeared in response to the unspoken demand from local authorities for advice on how to use the new powers; the most widely read was Raymond Unwin's general discussion, *Town Planning in Practice*, first published in 1909, but others dealt with more detailed aspects of planning.

For all this, the practice of town planning was still at a very rudimentary stage in Britain when war broke out. The absence of powers to draw up development plans for entire towns was a serious handicap and in this domain Britain lagged well behind Germany even on a theoretical level. Much progress was made in traffic engineering after the turn of the century but only Birmingham was clearly on the way to formulating a coherent transport, housing and planning strategy by 1914. In the capital the high hopes raised by the report of the Royal Commission on London Traffic in 1905 were not sustained; the newly-created London Traffic Branch of the Board of Trade proved a meagre surrogate for what the Commission had envisaged — a single authority to direct all road and rail developments in the London region. In fact, after the municipal renaissance stimulated by the creation of the London County Council in 1889, the progress of environmental reform in the capital began to decelerate once again from the early 1900s. When the Conservatives, in their local guise of the Municipal Reform Party, took over the London County Council from the Progressives (an alliance of Labour and Liberals) in 1907, London lost all pretence to leadership of the planning movement. A comparable effacement occurred in the case of Manchester; Sheffield, on the other hand, rose from near obscurity at the turn of the century to become one of the acknowledged leaders of the municipal town-planning movement by 1914. However, even Birmingham and Sheffield were still far from imposing an acceptable pattern of development on the areas within their boundaries, and the Liberal Party's Land Enquiry Committee could only conclude, a few months before the war, that '... over the vast majority of urban areas the development of building estates continues on the old, unsatisfactory lines' (Land

Enquiry Committee, 1914, II, 149). As for the planning of conurbations and urban regions, Britain had not yet set foot on the path down which Germany was already far advanced, defective though the organization of the Berlin region might have appeared to German critics. Indeed, in all but the detailed design and arrangement of low-density residential areas, Britain still lagged as far behind Germany as she had in the 1890s, before the German *Stadterweiterungen* had even been acknowledged in Britain. Even more surprising, however, was Britain's retardation, in certain areas of planning, in comparison with another country which had rapidly adopted the idea of planning in the early 1900s — the United States.

Four

The United States
Taming the Urban Wilderness

Plan commissions officially connected with the municipal administration did not exist in the United States, and legislation labelled
'City Planning' was not written before 1907. Today there are at least
one hundred such commissions, and planning legislation has been
passed or is now being considered by the legislatures of at least fifteen
states. Before 1900 there were occasional articles on city planning
which increased in volume during the last few years of the nineteenth
century, but by far the greater part of the very considerable body of
American writing on the subject has been brought out since 1905.
The City Plan, vol. I, no. 1, March 1915, foreword

The evolution of urban planning in the United States bears a superficial resem-
blance to its emergence in Britain. A number of developments in the 1890s and
early 1900s converged to produce the idea of 'city planning' and a combination
of events in 1909 suggested that it had come to stay. In terms of achievement
thereafter, city planning was something of a disappointment. In more fundamental respects, however, the American movement was unique.

In the United States planning existed at two levels. One was that of the plans
themselves, the scale and ambition of which were widely recognized, even in
Germany, as surpassing anything produced elsewhere. The other level was that
of physical implementation, which remained flawed, partial or non-existent. A
paradox? Certainly, but its explanation is quite simple. Most American city plans
were propaganda exercises, visions of a shining future designed to emphasize the
defects not only of current environmental policy, but of urban government as a
whole. Thus they were more the product of bad government than the culmination
of decades of municipal progress. However, generalizations such as this can be
highly vulnerable. The quality of urban government varied from state to state,
from town to town within each state, and often from year to year within each
town. The sooner we examine these complexities, the better.

In the United States we encounter an urban phenomenon very different from that of Western Europe, embedded in a unique social system which generated a distinctively suspicious attitude to the activities of government (Warner, 1968, ix—xiii). Until the late eighteenth century European settlement was very largely limited to a narrow strip of land, no more than 200 miles in depth, down the eastern seaboard. The economy of this area was predominantly agrarian and almost the only large towns were the seaports which linked it to its principal market and source of industrial products in Europe. These towns, of which New York, Boston, Philadelphia and Baltimore were the most important, came to be governed on much the same lines as English boroughs, with municipal councils and bodies of commissioners for special tasks. Moreover, in their compact layout and variegated building pattern, most resembled English towns of that period (Bridenbaugh, 1955, 303—29).

By the beginning of the nineteenth century, this homogeneous pattern had begun to break up. Settlement had begun to expand westwards into the huge areas progressively acquired by the Federal government, and new states were coming into being. From the very first, towns were founded in the new territories, most of them created by private promoters on land secured through the official land-grant machinery. Most were, and remained, very small, closely linked to rural society. A minority among them, however, were to be transformed by two massive developments — the generation of a huge export trade in agricultural products, and industrialization. The origins of both could be detected in the early decades of the nineteenth century, but it was the advent of railways, steamships and large-scale European immigration which, from the 1840s, began to generate in the United States the world's most dynamic urban system. By the third quarter of the century a number of mid-western communication centres, with Chicago at their head, were growing, at rates far in excess of any achieved in Europe, to rival the older eastern seaports. Meanwhile, mechanized industry was beginning to spread from its breeding-ground in the East, encouraging a growing proportion of European immigrants to settle in the cities.

This huge urban growth generated fewer problems than might have been anticipated on the basis of European experience. A whole continent, rich in natural resources, was being opened up at a rate and on a scale completely without precedent in the history of the globe. Great resources of capital were drawn into the task, but labour remained more scarce than in Europe, resulting in high productivity and real earnings which, in nearly all classes of employment, were by far the highest in the world. Most urban centres had pockets of poverty, but the problem only reached serious proportions in some of the big northern ports and industrial cities, where immigrants tended to overstock the labour market, and in the South where negroes produced a similar effect. Poverty had its physical expression in central districts of poor and overcrowded housing, which in New York and Boston took the form of tall tenement blocks. Beyond these inner areas, however, the rapidly growing population of the second half of the century was largely accommodated in great tracts of low-density, single-family housing, regulated by large-scale grid networks of streets, built cheaply in wood, and generously served by streetcar and railway lines which developed on a scale unparalleled in Europe (see Warner, 1962). Indeed, outside the East most towns took this low-density form from the start; there were few tenement blocks even in the giant city of Chicago (McKelvey, 1963, 75—7). Normally, the municipalities provided adequate drainage in the new districts. Some even provided water, but in any case, this and other utilities were readily laid on by private enterprise. Thus most of the cities of the United States did not generate the serious physical problems which cried out for ambitious public intervention in Europe. Moreover, the controllers of private wealth had even stronger grounds than in Europe for assuming that the interests of all were best served by the free play of the market. Only in the big cities of the East were conditions more favourable to public enterprise, but here many municipalities were hamstrung by the worst effects of the corruption and inefficiency for which American urban government became notorious after the Civil War.

As the nineteenth century wore on the pattern of urban government became increasingly fragmented (McKelvey, 1963, 86—114). The Federal government, despite its growing willingness to be drawn into matters of domestic policy, still had almost nothing to do with urban government as late as 1917. The state governments, in complete contrast, constantly intervened in urban affairs, not always to good effect. All municipalities were normally empowered by charters which were not only granted by the state legislatures, but were constantly open to amendment by them. The states also had the power to set up other public bodies with competence to act in urban areas. After the Civil War nearly all the state legislatures, and particularly those in the East, were affected by urbanization and the political corruption which so often accompanied it. Their reactions were confusingly diverse. Some, at times, favoured strong, integrated municipal government on European lines. Others preferred a multiplicity of boards and commissions exercising specialized functions. Sometimes strong mayors and weak councils were seen as holding the key to efficiency, but the unbridled corruption of many such mayors generated the contrary view that the councils should keep a tight control over the executive. To prevent such councils acting rashly, bicameral systems were often favoured, with a board of aldermen separate from the common council. Bicameral government, however, often proved slow and clumsy, and by the early twentieth century some of the most respected reformers had come to favour administration by city managers or small, executive commissions.

The overall effect of these multiple changes, some of them imposed by the states and others requested by the municipalities themselves, was no doubt to improve the quality of urban government after the Civil War, in terms of efficiency and the range of tasks undertaken. However, no obvious temporal or spatial pattern emerges and even during the 'Progressive Era' after the turn of the century, when striking progress was made in some cities, the general standard of urban government in the United States remained inferior to that of Britain and

Germany. Moreover, by the turn of the century the suburbs of most of the larger cities had set their face firmly against annexation by the central municipalities, and their splendid isolation, though often combined with high standards of local services, complicated the overall task of administering the urban areas (see e.g. Warner, 1962, 164–5).

It was within this confusing and somewhat discouraging context that public control of the urban environment had to evolve. There are two main ways to approach it. One is to evaluate the various partial, isolated modes of intervention which had developed by the end of the nineteenth century, some of them dating back to the very origins of settlement. These activities may have lacked coherence but they were at least effective. The other is to examine the process by which city planning came to be accepted as a credible improvement tool for American cities, notwithstanding its lack of physical achievement, during the Progressive Era. We shall take each of these approaches in turn, overlap though they do.

ISOLATED DEVELOPMENTS IN THE PUBLIC SHAPING OF THE AMERICAN URBAN ENVIRONMENT

The grid plan
The grid plan has been the mark of the founded town since ancient times. It produces an efficient circulation system and a distribution of equal, rectangular parcels. Most American towns, old and new, were the product of deliberate foundation, and during the nineteenth century most developed on the basis of a single grid or a cluster of them (Nolen, 1916, 5–6; Reps, 1965, 295–324). Beyond the Appalachians, many of the new towns of the westward expansion were based on fragments or multiples of the one-mile squares laid down from 1785 by the national geographical survey and used to order the land grants (Robinson, 1916, 20). In the older towns of the East, peripheral growth occurred in circumstances more comparable to those of Europe, encountering fragmented landownership and a scattering of established farms and villages (Warner, 1962, 67–116). An intermediate form often resulted, with promoters preferring a grid layout, but applying it to small tracts of land. Normally the promoters could be relied upon to ensure adequate communication between their own tracts and the rest of the town, and very often they conformed to the orientation and block size of neighbouring grids (Robinson, 1916, 25). In the bigger cities, however, neither the municipal authorities nor the landowners were entirely happy with an increasingly incoherent pattern of growth which, in the long term, was bound to reduce the value of peripheral land by slowing access to the centre. The problem was exacerbated when building spread into neighbouring municipalities. Even if these were eventually incorporated into the central municipality, by this time much of the damage would have been done. The solution was to establish the street pattern by public boards of survey, securing coordination between neighbouring municipalities where necessary.

The most impressive model of this type of street planning was provided by the city of New York. In 1807, after private owners had encountered difficulty in conveying land for building, the common council of the city persuaded the New York state legislature to set up a board of commissioners which, by 1811, had planned an extensive grid of streets covering the whole of the lower part of Manhattan island. Reservations were made for small parks, public places and markets (Committee on the City Plan, 1914, 13; Ford, 1936, 83–4). New York thus emulated the ambitious street plan for the Federal capital of Washington which had been drawn up by the French engineer, Pierre L'Enfant, in 1791. The Manhattan grid plan was extended later in the century, and similar systems were planned by commissions in the Bronx, Brooklyn and Queens (Committee on the City Plan, 1914, 14–18). At Philadelphia, powers existed under a colonial act of 1721 to appoint 'surveyors and regulators' to fix street and building lines in the city. By 1854 annexations had increased the area of the city to 129 square miles and in that year a consolidation act of the Pennsylvania legislature set up a department of surveys for Philadelphia. Each of the twelve districts of the city was allotted a surveyor-and-regulator, and these twelve officials combined in a board of surveyors under the presidency of the chief engineer and surveyor of the city (Scott, 1969, 5–6).

What prevented this public street planning from spreading beyond a small number of towns was the attitude of the courts. In most states they ruled that property-owners were under no obligation to conform to the plans of streets which as yet had no physical existence. If a municipality wanted to impose its plan it could do so, but only by paying compensation for disturbance to the owners of buildings standing on land required for the streets. In Pennsylvania the state Supreme Court was willing to respect the pre-revolutionary precedent, and the United States District Court upheld the judgment. Indeed, in 1891 the Pennsylvania legislature extended the Philadelphia practice to the whole state by requiring every municipality to have a general plan of its streets and alleys, with no damages payable to infringing properties (Scott, 1969, 5–6). Other towns and states, however, encountered serious difficulties when, in the 1890s, they tried to extend public control over 'platting' (the laying-out of streets and lots) in response to a further acceleration of suburban spread (Scott, 1969, 3). At Boston, for instance, a board of survey was set up in 1891 under the authorization of the Massachusetts state legislature to lay out highways in outlying areas. However, the Massachusetts Supreme Court ruled that the no-damages provision incorporated in the board's powers was illegal. The City of Boston's solution was to put pressure on non-conforming property-owners by withholding water, sewers and lighting. Gradually, Boston banks began to refuse to lend on property which infringed the board-of-survey lines, and violations declined in number (Scott, 1969, 3–4). More typical was the experience of Baltimore, where a topographical survey commission was set up in 1893, under an enabling act of the Maryland legislature, to make a street plan of the entire city. The Maryland

Court of Appeals struck out a clause which would have allowed the city council to refuse to adopt any street which did not conform to the plan, and the property-owners generally managed to ignore the board's proposals (Scott, 1969, 4–5).

Even in those few towns where municipal boards of survey were able to plan the new streets, the grid pattern continued to predominate until the First World War. The boards hesitated to depart from what had long proved acceptable to land developers, builders and purchasers. Consequently, the public control of the planning of new streets did not become a major issue, and it played only a small part in the generation of the idea of city planning. However, the near universality of the grid at least established a basic pattern for the American city which allowed the planning debate to focus on other elements in the urban structure. The most important of these elements was the public park.

Parks

The mid-century urban revolution struck a society which previously had valued its close links with the land and rural life. In the late eighteenth and early nineteenth centuries Thomas Jefferson, Ralph Waldo Emerson, Henry Thoreau and other fathers of American ideology had idealized the countryside as a source of virtue and happiness denied to the teeming inhabitants of Europe's impoverished cities. This love of nature could not stave off urbanization, but it was gradually transmuted into an ambition which in the United States was easier to realize than in Europe — the conservation of natural scenery and rural resources. Land was so cheap that less productive areas could easily be set aside for conservation or recreation. Part of the conservation movement was purely rural, epitomized by the creation of Yellowstone Park, the first of a series of national parks, as early as 1872. However, the urban park movement was not entirely separate, in that its promoters' objective was not so much to create genteel extensions of the private garden on the lines of European parks, as to conserve stretches of wild landscape close to the expanding towns.

The first of these big city projects was New York's Central Park, acquired by a specially-appointed Park Commission and laid out from 1858 to the plans of a young landscape architect, Frederick Law Olmsted (1822–1903). Other cities soon followed suit, and by the end of the 1860s a number were considering the creation, not of one park, but of systems of parks linked by broad, suburban avenues. In Chicago, for instance, the success of the first big park, Lincoln Park, gave rise to demand for a park system which could not be satisfied within the existing boundaries. As early as 1869 the Illinois state legislature was persuaded to resolve the difficulty by setting up three special metropolitan authorities to acquire land outside the city boundaries, well in advance of suburban building (Scott, 1969, 11).

This regional planning of parks was to be emulated on a much larger scale in the Boston area. The huge suburban expansion of Boston from the 1850s had spread into a large number of nearby municipalities which, from around 1880, had begun successfully to resist annexation. Initially, the most serious problem was that of arranging an effective sewerage system for the whole urban area. Eventually, in 1889, the State of Massachusetts helped Boston and the other municipalities to form a regional drainage confederation, the Metropolitan Sewerage Commission. This precedent was seized upon by Charles Eliot, a landscape architect and organizer of a private association, the Trustees of Public Reservations, formed in the later 1880s to acquire beautiful and historic places in Massachusetts. He obtained the appointment of a temporary state commission to report on the need for a metropolitan system of public parks, after he had called together members of the park commissions of the various municipalities in the Boston area in 1891 to consider petitioning the State legislature to create a metropolitan park authority. The commission asked Eliot to suggest a scheme for a park system, and he responded with an imaginative arrangement of extensive linear parks along the rivers, in a conscious effort to combine town and country. As a result, in 1893 the state set up a permanent metropolitan parks commission for Boston. By 1902 the Boston park system contained 15,000 acres (Scott, 1969, 17–23).

Urban park systems multiplied in the 1890s and the early 1900s. So extensive were they that their creators found themselves having to consider, and acquire expertise in, a number of matters germane to urban planning. An articulated programme of land purchase was the first essential, but large-scale forward planning of the parks also required an understanding of the evolution of the built-up area. The linking of the parks by broad avenues (parkways) led the park commissions into street planning, and, because the parkways were prime sites for the most expensive homes, into residential planning as well. The relationship of public transport to the parks also had to be considered if they were to be of any direct use to the poorer residents of the inner districts. Indeed, just as the early park boom had prompted the rise of the American profession of landscape architect to an eminence unrivalled elsewhere in the world, the spread of the park system had, by the end of the century, converted some of the more able landscape architects into potential city planners. In fact, some had already branched out into comprehensive planning, notably by designing rich suburban communities.

Residential communities for the rich
During the second half of the nineteenth century most American cities were transformed by a process of suburbanization whose vigour far surpassed anything experienced in Europe, even in Britain (see Warner, 1962). The spreading street car lines were supplemented by steam railway services and, towards the end of the century, by electric inter-urban (light railway) routes. The rich, who led the outward movement, found that they could reach out beyond the monotonous lines of the urban grid, and the promoters of the more distant suburban communities began to consider more informal styles of layout. They turned to the

growing body of landscape architects whose work in park design had allowed them to acquire experience in planning curvilinear layouts with abundant greenery.

The most prominent of the early romantic suburbs was Llewellyn Park, in South Orange, New Jersey, developed between 1853 and 1868 (Lubove, 1967, 5). In 1870 Frederick Law Olmsted and his associate, Calvert Vaux, designed Riverside, Illinois, a suburb nine miles from the centre of Chicago (Creese, 1966, 153). The success of these schemes, and their emulation elsewhere (Fein, 1972, 32–5), further strengthened the reputation of the landscape architects and generated a mode of residential design which offered a clear alternative to the gridiron, albeit at the cost of restrictions on the individual owner's freedom to make use of his site. By the end of the century curvilinear layouts and provision for greenery were beginning to be found even in land-promotion schemes which did not pretend to cater for the very rich. However, the grid continued to dominate and, in the absence of a strong housing reform movement and efforts by enlightened employers to make the best residential planning available to the working man, the informal, sylvan suburban style failed to impinge on the great mass of the urban population.

Railway planning

As soon as the steam railway was introduced into North America in the 1830s, the Federal government recognized its potential as a stimulus to western settlement. Although it refrained from building the lines itself, it encouraged the railway companies by generous loans, grants and allotments of land. Many towns were founded by the railway companies themselves, while the promoters of others kept a constant eye on railway developments, negotiating with the companies for changes of route or branch lines to enhance the value of their speculations. In the established towns associations of businessmen, with or without the cooperation of the municipal councils, fought to secure good and cheap railway connections which could give their communities the edge over their rivals (see e.g. Goldfield, 1977, 54–6). The bigger the town, the greater was the area affected by these developments, and the state governments often became involved.

In the middle decades of the century towns old and new generally failed to appreciate the disruptive power of the railway. Railway lines were allowed a free run inside the urban areas, often being conceded part of the public highway. Even when they ran on their own land, they were normally allowed to cross the town streets at unguarded level crossings. The big cities of the East controlled the railways better than most, but the smaller and newer the town, the more likely was it to find itself divided, polluted and generally inconvenienced by the railway. As the towns grew and their suburbs spread the railways caused more and more concern. At the same time, urban business interests began to fear the monopoly power of the railways. From the 1870s the state governments, particularly those of the East, began to assume a degree of control over the railway companies in response to urban pressure (McKelvey, 1963, 30–4). As a result, the railway systems within each state were to some extent reorganized at the behest of the towns, which began to pursue a related effort to soften the railways' impact on the urban environment. Much of this activity was on a small scale; for instance, bridges and tunnels replaced level crossings. In many of the larger cities, however, the companies and the municipalities, with state support, undertook a major replanning of the lines. These efforts were epitomized by the construction of union stations to replace a scatter of separate termini. The first were built in the 1890s; St Louis obtained one in 1896 and Boston in 1898. Others followed after the turn of the century; notably at Washington, Philadelphia and Kansas City.

These projects had important implications for the development of urban planning. They disturbed urban property on a much larger scale than ever before, and established a precedent for the sweeping use of compulsory-purchase powers. The adjustment of the railway system within the urban area, which usually included the building of new marshalling yards and goods stations, required considerable study of the structure of the city. Finally, the union stations were usually grandiose buildings which invited the construction of impressive street approaches. Such surroundings were considered a good investment of public money because it was felt that travellers often formed a lightning impression of a city while changing trains. The more palatial the station and the more elegant the view from the threshold, the more likely was it that new business and investment would be attracted to the city (see e.g. Wilson, 1964, 91–119).

By the early 1900s a number of cities were going on to combine the building of new stations and their approaches with an even more ambitious undertaking, the construction of a civic centre (Griffith, 1974, 201–2). This peculiarly American institution was the product of a long-established movement of civic beautification which reached its apogee at the turn of the century.

Civic beautification
While the suburbs increasingly offered the rich an environment in which art and nature could play their part, a widening gulf yawned between these suburbs and the shambles of the central areas. Rapid growth and economic change, in the virtual absence of controls over building, advertising, overhead wires and other causes of ugliness and disorder, created in the newer cities a visual squalor without parallel in the industrializing world. Even in the older cities of the East the core areas, which retained a degree of dignity, were swamped after mid-century by undisciplined development. This contradiction between the wealth and the appearance of the American city gradually drew some of the rich into a variety of efforts to endow the city with beauty and culture.

The motives of the beautifiers were varied. As in Europe, the social conscience of the rich did not normally extend as far as the advocacy of social reform based on a redistribution of income or wealth. However, the poor could be offered beauty and culture which, it was hoped, would imbue them with the values of their social betters and economic masters and persuade them that the best things in life were as open to them as they were to the rich. Indeed, this debased Ruskinism, in the virtual absence of welfare policies conferring material benefits on the poor, was an even stronger reforming force than in Britain. The case in its favour was further reinforced by the presence of so many foreign immigrants in the cities, for it was tempting to view social reform in terms of the *education* of aliens who, once integrated into American culture, would no longer offer any cause for concern.

More selfishly, many rich Americans were simply aware of the stark contrast between their mundane and repetitive cities and the historic towns of Europe. As time passed more and more were able to see Europe for themselves, and their resulting sense of inferiority, so poignantly expressed in the novels of Henry James, was a potent stimulus to investment in culture. Of course, they could have surrounded themselves with private beauty by collecting paintings and statues, and many did so; what drove some of them to create public beauty as well was the extraordinary competitiveness between towns and cities which rapid economic and territorial growth had engendered. With mobility of population and capital considerably higher than in Europe, a pattern of communications which remained fluid until the end of the century, and a multitude of towns competing for prominence, beauty and culture came to be seen as creators of prosperity. With so many nondescript centres in contention, those which could offer a civilized environment would have a better chance of attracting private capital, simply because owners and managers would prefer to live in them.

The earliest efforts to develop urban beauty and culture can be traced to before the Civil War, when a number of New England towns, some of them quite small communities, were the scene of efforts to improve the environment, principally with a view to attracting those wealthy families which left the large cities in the summer. The Laurel Hill Association, founded at Stockbridge, Massachusetts, in 1853, was the prototype. By 1880 Massachusetts had twenty-eight such improvement associations and Connecticut had between fifty and sixty (Peterson, 1976, 422). Then, in 1876, the Philadelphia centennial exhibition, the first full international exhibition (as distinct from trade fairs) ever held in the United States, provided a modest sample of an ordered urban environment. A much bigger stimulus, however, was provided by the World's Columbian Exhibition which was held at Chicago in 1893, to celebrate the four-hundredth anniversary of the discovery of the new continent (see Burg, 1976).

The Federal government, which provided much of the finance for the exhibition, chose to locate it in Chicago in order to pay tribute to the spectacular development of the Mid-West since the Civil War. The Chicago and Illinois authorities, prompted in part by the raw character of their mushrooming metropolis, were determined that the exhibition site and buildings should vie with the best European exhibitions, which had just reached new heights with the Paris exhibition of 1889. In 1890 the exhibition corporation set up by the state of Illinois commissioned Frederick Law Olmsted and his partner, Henry Codman, to examine sites for the exhibition park, and subsequently retained them as consulting landscape architects. Meanwhile, the Chicago partnership of Daniel Burnham (1846–1912) and John Root, arguably the most distinguished practice in the city, were made consulting architects. In the autumn of 1890 the four men jointly produced the first outline plan for the exhibition, and Burnham was appointed chief of construction (later to be called director of works) (Hines, 1974, 77–8).

Burnham drew in distinguished architects and designers from all over the United States. At a series of enthusiastic meetings held to coordinate the work, all showed a willingness to conform not only to the overall plan but also to the chosen style, a grandiose Beaux-Arts manner with long colonnades, shining white surfaces, free-standing statues, and vistas enhanced by long stretches of ornamental water. Even European visitors were very impressed, and most of the Americans had never seen anything like it.

The Chicago exhibition not only reinvigorated the campaign for civic beautification throughout the United States, but generated a new confidence in the American architect. The earliest product of the new mood was the municipal art society. The first was founded at New York in 1893, Cincinnati followed in 1894, and by 1899 societies had been founded at Chicago, Cleveland and Baltimore (Peterson, 1976, 417; Scott, 1969, 44). Composed largely of leading citizens and local architects and designers, these societies discussed a wide range of proposals, from the design of lamp-posts to the layout of parks and cultural buildings. Until the end of the century economic depression held up the execution of most of these schemes, but the movement was encouraged by the creation of municipal art commissions at Boston and New York. In 1899 the art commissions joined the societies in a national conference on the artistic development of cities, convened by the Baltimore society (Scott, 1969, 44). The interest aroused by the conference was further intensified in the following year by events in Washington.

In 1894, Glenn Brown, secretary of the American Institute of Architects, had come across a copy of L'Enfant's plan while writing a history of the Capitol. Appalled by the divergence of modern Washington from the original concept, Brown persuaded the Institute to hold its annual meeting in Washington in 1900. The meeting passed a motion calling on the Senate, which was directly responsible for the administration of the District of Columbia, to appoint a commission to draw up a new plan for the city. The Senate eventually concurred and in 1901 a commission was appointed, principally to report on a system of parks for the District of Columbia. It included Daniel Burnham and Olmsted's son, Frederick Law Olmsted Junior, also a landscape architect. They in turn coopted Charles Follen McKim, the architect, and Augustus St Gaudens, the sculptor, both of whom had been involved in the Chicago exhibition. Burnham persuaded the others (except for the stricken St Gaudens) to join him on a study tour of Europe and in 1902 the commission produced a series of proposals which, in due course, were accepted by the Senate. They included plans for the enhancement of the vistas between the Capitol and the White House, a park system, new government buildings, and a union station (Reps, 1967, 70—138).

The publication of the Washington proposals generated a new wave of interest in beautification throughout the United States, and prompted the preparation of civic centre schemes in a number of cities, notably Cleveland and Philadelphia (Hines, 1974, 158—63; Scott, 1969, 60). However, their main significance for the development of urban planning is to be found in the extension of the commission's considerations to a number of matters which lay outside the aesthetic domain. Indeed, some historians have identified a steady evolution of American planning from the 'City Beautiful' stage of the early 1900s, to the creation of the American City Planning Institute in 1917 (e.g. Reps, 1965, 497—525). However, the grandeur of the Washington vision can easily obscure the weakness of some of the other foundations of American planning. Therefore, before going on to examine the evolution of the American planning movement, we ought to look at its most important weakness, the absence of a strong tradition of housing reform.

Housing

In Britain, we saw how town planning, an amalgam of domestic residential estate planning and German town-extension planning, broadened the perspective of a powerful housing reform movement and complemented the established practice of public regulation of private building. In the United States this fruitful combination could not be so readily achieved.

From the late eighteenth century American towns had introduced various regulations affecting the environment, including the inspection of lodging houses, the removal of dilapidated buildings, the control of fire hazards, and rudimentary public health regulations (Scott, 1969, 6). However, codes of building regulations were slow to emerge, if we exclude the crude requirement to build in brick in the central areas which some municipalities imposed after disastrous fires. When, in 1867, the state of New York passed its first tenement house law, laying down rudimentary building regulations for tenement blocks in the cities of New York and Brooklyn, building codes were virtually unknown anywhere else in the United States (Adrian and Griffith, 1976, 55). Most large towns did not draw up building regulations until the 1880s or 1890s, and even then fire still remained the prime consideration (Lubove, 1962, 142). Height restrictions were very rare, and it was their absence which allowed the commercial skyscraper to make its appearance from the 1880s in step with developments in building techniques and passenger lifts (see e.g. Hines, 1974, 44—72).

Of many cities it could no doubt be said that the lack of regulation was a function of the high quality of most residential building. However, the history of building regulation in New York reveals the underlying strength of the private land and building interests, for which the weak American municipalities and the spasmodic and divided efforts of the reformers were no match. The New York State Tenement House Commission, looking back in 1903 over sixty years of efforts to reform the city's congested, multi-storey housing, concluded that their cumulative effect had been very slight (De Forest and Veiller, 1903, I, 11).

There was, nevertheless, a quickening of concern for the housing of the poor from the 1880s, particularly in New York and Chicago. The close personal and intellectual links between American and British reformers produced an echo of the London housing debate of the early part of the decade, with New York social reformers seeking, and finding, areas of poverty, squalor and overcrowding which appeared comparable to the worst slums of the British capital (Abbott, 1936, 50). Two tenement house commissions sat in New York during the decade, in 1884 and 1887, though they achieved little (Scott, 1969, 10). A more productive import from Britain was the idea of the settlement house. In 1886, after a stay at Samuel Barnett's Toynbee Hall in East London, Stanton Coit, a young college graduate, set up the East Side Neighborhood Guild in New York (Lubove, 1962, 187). In 1889, the year in which the Guild was reorganized as the College Settlement, Jane Addams, a woman of independent means with an interest in social questions, created her own settlement in Hull House, Chicago, having been to see Samuel Barnett during her tour of Europe the year before (Tims, 1961, 39, 43).

The American settlement house movement, which soon attracted great support from socially aware students and teachers in the country's numerous universities and colleges, grew to a scale unparalleled in Britain. By 1900 there were over a hundred settlements, and by 1911, four hundred (Tims, 1961, 48). The movement was especially strong in New York, Chicago, Boston and Pittsburgh (Griffith, 1974, 12), where it came fully into contact with the poor physical conditions of the poorest districts (see e.g. Woods, 1898). Its objectives were, however, too diverse and too centred on the self-regeneration of the individual through participation in an enlightened, balanced community to allow it to become a single-minded promoter of housing reform, even after 1900 when it reached full maturity. Its main interest in the environmental sphere lay in the provision of playgrounds in overcrowded districts. One of Jane Addams's earliest achievements is most instructive in this regard. Her Hull House people used the enthusiastic period of preparations for the Chicago Exhibition to draw attention to poor housing in the city. After they had singled out a particularly decrepit block as an example of poor landlordism, the owner was shamed into giving it to them to see if they could do any better. They soon decided that the houses were beyond improvement and demolished them, in 1892, to lay out Chicago's first public children's playground on the site. Jane Addams admitted later, however, that the residents, who had to be evicted by legal process, had always regretted the loss of their homes (Addams, 1911, 289–91).

Awareness of the slum continued to progress in the 1890s. In 1890 Jacob Riis, a New York reporter, published a widely-read study of the city's immigrant poor, *How the Other Half Lives*. In 1892 Congress made a small grant to the Federal Bureau of Labor, which had become the main government agency for the collection of social statistics, to study slum areas in large cities. The eventual report, covering New York, Philadelphia, Chicago and Baltimore, appeared in 1894. Meanwhile, a number of cities and states were making their own surveys. Inquiries in Boston in 1891 and Buffalo in 1892 were followed in 1894 by New York's third tenement house investigation, which produced some outspoken criticisms (Scott, 1969, 7, 10). Some of the surveys led to rudimentary improvements in public health and building regulations. At Boston, for instance, new regulations were introduced requiring the construction of fireproof tenements. The New York state legislature did rather more, voting powers in 1895 for the compulsory purchase of unfit tenements and the provision of small parks in the slums of New York city (Lubove, 1962, 93; De Forest and Veiller, 1903, I, 174). A number of other cities also took their first steps to provide playgrounds and parks in their crowded districts.

These faltering steps towards slum clearance now began to raise for the first time the question of rehousing. As part of its slum inquiry, the Federal Bureau of Labor had commissioned a study of European model housing from Elgin Gould (1860—1915), a prominent housing reformer. Published in 1895 as *The Housing of the Working People*, Gould's report expressed the hope that private capital could be persuaded to provide model housing at economic rents, on the lines pioneered in London. However, he recognized that, in New York at least, central land was far too expensive to allow workers to be accommodated satisfactorily on it, and he looked forward to the day when rapid transit would reduce the pressure by allowing the better-paid workers to move to the suburbs. In 1896 Gould himself became president of the City and Suburban Homes Co., an initiative of the Better Dwellings Committee of a venerable body, the New York Association for Improving the Condition of the Poor, which had been founded in 1843 on lines inspired by British example. Gould's company built a number of model tenement blocks in Manhattan, but its long-term objective was to encourage suburban living. To this end, it purchased 530 acres in Brooklyn for its 'Homewood' project of single-family houses, 250 of which had been built by 1916 (Lubove, 1962, 101—2, 110—11). Meanwhile, in 1898, the New York Charity Organization Society, which like its British equivalent had become very interested in the role of the environment in creating poverty, set up a Tenement House Committee. Sitting until 1901, it stimulated further interest in the slums which has encouraged Roy Lubove, the leading historian of American housing reform, to conclude that a national housing reform movement was at last in existence by 1903 (Lubove, 1962, 140, 143).

Although slum and housing reform had clearly advanced in the 1890s, it still lagged a long way behind the equivalent British movement. The idea of subsidizing housing, directly or indirectly, was entertained by no one. The labour movement, in any case lesss well organized than in Britain, was largely indifferent to housing. Company towns, though numerous, were for the most part poorly planned and constructed (see Taylor, 1915). The only outstanding exception, the model town of Pullman near Chicago, founded in 1880, was foolishly used by its owners to put pressure on Pullman Company workers (see Buder, 1967). The resulting bitter strike of 1894 discouraged other employers from putting much effort into their housing schemes (but see Garner, 1971). Even in the 1900s, when much employers' housing in Germany and Britain was beginning to observe enhanced standards, little of note was produced. For instance, at Gary, Indiana, where the United States Steel Corporation built a new town for 12,000 people between 1906 and 1909, streets and utilities were planned by the company but most of the housing was left to private interests, with nondescript results (Lubove, 1962, 226). Slum clearance, meanwhile, was still at a rudimentary stage; even in New York city no powers of area clearance were available as late as the war.

As we shall now see, the absence of a strong housing reform movement and effective local regulation of new building did not prevent the emergence of city planning in the United States. Nevertheless, it goes a long way to explain the diversity and instability of the American planning movement.

THE CITY PLANNING MOVEMENT

In Germany and Britain, urban planning was very largely the product of developing municipal government. In the United States the idea of planning emerged almost independently of any institutions of local administration. It did so, nevertheless, in the context of a municipal reform movement which, by achieving a measure of success, greatly encouraged the advocates and practitioners of planning.

Although the greatest advances in municipal government were made after the turn of the century (Griffith, 1974, 10 ff.), their origins are to be found in the 1890s. By the beginning of that decade nearly all the productive territories of the United States had been settled; the Frontier was closed. Although there was still scope for an increase in the rural population, the urbanized proportion of the population of the United States rose rather faster after 1890 than before. By 1910, 45.7 per cent were living in towns (nucleated communities of more than 2,500 people), compared to 35.1 per cent in 1890 (Griffith, 1974, 5). Although promoters and industrialists continued to found new towns after 1890, few achieved any great size (McKelvey, 1963, 32). The urban pattern stabilized and the United States began to conform more clearly to the European mode of development with growth rates tending to rise in proportion to the size of town. The rapid growth of many of the biggest towns was partially obscured in the population statistics by the spread of building into neighbouring districts, but many reacted vigorously by securing their largest-ever annexations of outlying tracts, before suburban resistance began to make itself felt after the turn of the century (Adrian and Griffith, 1976, 104–5).

These developments strengthened the position of the urban reformers. They passed an important milestone in 1894 when they organized, at Philadelphia, a national convention of municipal leagues and similar organizations from twenty-one cities. The convention led to the creation of a National Municipal League, which had 180 branches by 1895, and to a series of Conferences for Good City Government (McKelvey, 1963, 101). Momentum was maintained into the later 1890s when a new phase of prosperity began to make urban residents less tax conscious and reinforced their desire for civic improvements (McKelvey, 1963, 106). It was at this point that the municipal reformers and the embryonic planning movement began to join forces.

During the 1890s news of the new German *Städtebau* had begun to penetrate professional and reforming circles in the United States. In 1893 Joseph Stübben, whose abilities as a linguist were commensurate with his other qualities, went to Chicago during the exhibition to address the International Congress of Engineers on the preparation of town plans (text in Stübben, 1895). In 1895 the municipal reform publicist, Albert Shaw, who systematically sought to demonstrate the superiority of European municipal government to his fellow-countrymen, devoted part of a widely-read book to German town-extension planning and urban transformations (Shaw, 1895). It was not, however, until the end of the decade that an infusion of aesthetics, the product of growing interest in beautification among architects and landscape architects, and the spread of local improvement societies and municipal art societies, made the idea of planning potent enough to be promoted seriously by municipal reformers. The main milestone here was the December 1899 issue of the recently-founded New York reforming journal, *Municipal Affairs*. Devoted entirely to urban improvement, it made much use of an emotive term, 'the City Beautiful', which had now come into common use.

Although aesthetics greatly strengthened the appeal of planning, it nearly swamped it in the process. In the early 1900s schemes for civic centres, park systems and other embellishments were canvassed in numerous towns and set in train in a few, but the motives of their rich supporters were often patently selfish. However, the ideologues of the movement continued to think about its general implications. Outstanding among them was Charles Mulford Robinson (1869–1917), a journalist from Rochester, New York. In 1891 Robinson had become associate editor of the Rochester *Post–Express*, where he developed a strong interest in civic improvement. By 1899 he was achieving a wider audience for his writings and after contributing three articles on civic improvement to the *Atlantic Monthly* he was commissioned by *Harper's Magazine* to write a series on comparable efforts abroad. Already a seasoned European traveller, he made a new tour there and decided to expand his articles into a book. Published in 1901, *The Improvement of Towns and Cities, Or the Practical Basis of Civic Aesthetics* made Robinson an acknowledged leader of the beautification movement. In 1902 he left his editorship in Rochester to travel more widely, lecturing and engaging in freelance writing. In 1903 he produced a new book, *Modern Civic Art, Or the City Made Beautiful*, which was even more widely read than its predecessor.

The main message of Robinson's first book was that the various embellishment schemes which the inhabitants of a city might be tempted to pursue should be seen as part of a general programme of improvement:

> It has seemed well, then, in the great new awakening of enthusiasm and concern for city beauty in a score of directions, at last to grasp them all, to group them logically, in a single volume and show the relative positions. (Robinson, 1901, viii)

However, at many points in the book Robinson went on to discuss the relationship of the embellishment movement with other aspects of urban reform, notably the 'hygienic' (parks and playgrounds). In discussing the regulation of the urban environment, including smoke control and the limitation of building heights, he recognized that aesthetic and material motives were very difficult to distinguish (Robinson, 1901, 55–75).

Robinson returned to this difficulty in 1903. Consistency of thought and clarity of expression were not his strongest points, but his new concept of 'civic art', an improvement strategy embodying both aesthetic and practical objectives, marked a step forward in his thinking:

> This art, which is so utilitarian in its purposes as to be civic first and art afterwards, may be defined, then, as the taking in just the right way of those steps necessary or proper for the comfort of the citizens — as the doing of the necessary or proper civic thing in the right way. (Robinson, 1903, 27–8)

His discussion of the importance of beauty now had a more Ruskinian flavour than in 1901, and he cited William Morris to support his view that art should be for all, and not for the few (1903, 36). However, he also felt free to discuss purely material considerations; early in the book he argued that the most important prerequisite of progress towards better cities was that they should spread over a wider area, and he stressed the importance of rapid transit (ibid., 3–9). Clearly aware of current German practice, he wanted to see cities adopt a radial system of traffic streets, allowing the planning of residential areas with narrower, curved streets (ibid., 189–98). An understanding was required of 'the anatomy of cities' (ibid., 29), and at several points he referred to 'the science of city-building'. The first step in any town was to draw up 'a general plan of development and improvement' (ibid., 34). And finally:

> The total of that [civic art] may now be defined: it is the adjustment of the city to its city needs so fittingly that life will be made easier for a vast and growing proportion of mankind, and the bringing into it of that beauty which is the continual need and rightful heritage of men and which has been their persistent dream. (ibid., 375)

The broader awareness of urban well-being which Robinson helped to generate was reflected, in 1904, in the merger of the American League for Civic Improvement (founded in 1900 as the National League of Improvement Associations) and the American Park and Outdoor Art Association (founded 1897). The title of the new body, the American Civic Association, was intended to suggest concern for the urban community as a whole. In practice, sectional motives still predominated. In the localities, the betterment movement had begun to fall under the leadership of chambers of commerce and businessmen's clubs which had no interest in social reform, and whose primary aim was to increase the prestige of their cities (McKelvey, 1963, 43–4). However, they were able to bring great financial resources to bear and it was under their aegis that the first steps were taken, outside Washington, towards the preparation of the town development plans advocated by Charles Mulford Robinson.

San Francisco provides an instructive example. In 1897, after a long period of poor government, a municipal reform campaign had built up to the point when it secured the election of a rich Progressive, James D. Phelan, as mayor. As so often happened, the reformers could not maintain their enthusiasm in the face of the daily drudge of local administration, while Phelan's personal popularity among the poorer sections of the electorate was sapped when he resisted a wave of strikes among the city's employees in 1901. He decided not to seek re-election in that year, and the reform group's nominee who stood in his place was defeated by the local machine led by the powerful 'boss' Abe Ruef. The new mayor, Eugene F. Schmitz, was a former leader of the local musicians' union. Phelan and his reform group now adopted new tactics, looking round for a rousing crusade issue. With the idea of city planning a matter of moment, thanks to events in Washington, they decided to campaign for a new city plan. They found much support in the business community, which was beginning to worry that the upstart city of Los Angeles might replace San Francisco as a tourist attraction and as a magnet for rich Easterners seeking a home in the sun. In January 1904 Phelan's party and others sympathetic to the cause of civic improvement, most of them businessmen, met at the Merchants' Exchange to form the Association for the Improvement and Adornment of San Francisco (Hines, 1974, 175–8).

The main objects of the Association were 'to promote in every practical way the beautifying of the streets, public buildings, parks, squares and places of San Francisco; to bring to the attention of the officials and the people of the city the best methods for instituting artistic municipal betterments; to stimulate the sentiment of civic pride in the improvement and care of private property, to suggest quasi-public enterprises, and, in short, to make San Francisco a more agreeable city in which to live' (Burnham, 1905, 7). It was soon decided that the best way of demonstrating what could be done with the city would be to commission Daniel H. Burnham, fresh from his successes at Washington and at Cleveland, where he had been involved in a civic centre scheme in 1903, to prepare a plan. Burnham readily agreed and, working quickly from a bungalow high up on the Twin Peaks, he was able to submit his plan and report to the Association in 1905 (Hines, 1974, 179–81).

Burnham's plan was ambitious in its physical scope, for it covered the entire city area, including extensive tracts awaiting development. It also recognized the need to cater for rapid growth. In other respects, however, it was superficial. Burnham proposed the superimposition of a number of new traffic streets on the existing grid, mainly in the outer districts. One was a ring boulevard but most of the others were 'radials' (diagonals) intended to shorten some cross-town journeys and create a number of star junctions (Burnham, 1905, 36). Some of the new streets led to the ambitious park system which Burnham planned for the suburbs, but he also wanted to see small parks and playgrounds distributed uniformly throughout the city (ibid., 145—68). Finally, he suggested a huge new civic centre to the south of the business district. No proposals at all were made for the control of private development, and there was nothing in the plan to suggest that scientific methods had been used in its preparation.

The fate of the plan was thus an apt comment on Burnham's work as well as on the quality of municipal government in San Francisco. On 18 April 1906, large parts of San Francisco were destroyed by an earthquake and the ensuing fire. Burnham, who was in Europe at the time, returned immediately. Not only did the reform party urge him to press for the adoption of his plans, but Mayor Schmitz himself offered him the chance to supervise the reconstruction. After some consideration, Burnham refused the offer, fearing that local bureaucracy would frustrate him (Hines, 1974, 190—4). Left to itself, the municipality allowed the city to be rebuilt on its old plan, and even the chance to widen existing streets was not taken (see *Plan of Proposed Street Changes*, 1906). The parallel with the fate of Wren's plan for London can hardly fail to suggest itself, especially as Wren's vision had been used by William Lindley to inspire the city fathers of Hamburg in an ambitious replanning scheme after their own fire of 1843 (see below, p. 194). Indeed, Burnham faced the same obstacles as Wren; the fire had destroyed the buildings but not the value of the private sites on which they stood. Faced with the need to get the city working again as soon as possible, the municipality was in no position to undertake an expensive expropriation programme. However, Burnham no doubt recognized that his San Francisco plan was too lightweight to be worth fighting for, especially as he had already been offered the chance to prove that he could do better.

Before Burnham finally turned down Schmitz's offer, he had been invited to prepare a plan for Chicago, his home city. This opportunity also sprang from the efforts of businessmen. Ever since the exhibition in 1893 a number of improvement schemes, some of them proposed by Burnham, had been under discussion in business and reforming circles. However, little had come of them and it was partly in frustration that, in 1906, the Merchants' Club set up a Chicago Plan Committee and commissioned Burnham to prepare a complete plan for the city (Hines, 1974, 313—22). Burnham devoted much more time and effort to this plan than he had at San Francisco, and he enjoyed the additional advice of specialist committees set up by the businessmen. It was not until November 1909 that the plan was ready to be conveyed to the mayor as a present to the city.

18 *Burnham's Chicago plan (1909): railway circuits and industrial areas. Burnham aimed to rationalize Chicago's railways by building four interlinking circuits, additional to the existing Loop. The dark-grey areas indicate existing industrial districts while the light-grey indicate probable future industrial growth. (Burnham and Bennett, 1909, plate 73)*

19 *Burnham's Chicago Plan (1909): Twelfth Street Boulevard, looking west. New railway termini front the southern side of the boulevard, in the middle ground. (Burnham and Bennett, 1909, plate 121)*

Burnham's Chicago plan marked a great advance over his San Francisco effort (see Burnham and Bennett, 1909). It covered an area sixty miles in radius from the centre of Chicago, considered by Burnham to be the limit of daily commuting. It anticipated growth. It was a scientific plan, at least in that Burnham maintained that it was based on an attempt to understand the processes at work in the city. Above all, it was an impressive plan, fully able 'to fire men's blood', in Burnham's memorable phrase. The main weaknesses were the virtual absence of proposals for the control of the use of private land, and the lack of any serious consideration of housing. Indeed, Burnham wrote: 'The two prime considerations for every city are, first, adequate means of circulation; and second, a sufficient park area to insure good health and good order' (ibid., 80). In these two areas, Burnham thought on a grand scale. In addition to radials to supplement Chicago's particularly rigid grid, he also proposed four ring roads ('encircling highways'), the longest on a sixty-mile radius, and the improvement of the major highways running out of the city. He planned a big rearrangement of Chicago's railway system, with new stations. His park system combined central schemes, including

20 *Burnham's Chicago plan (1909): monumental perspective of a new north—south boulevard, drawn by Jules Guérin. The French architect's atmospheric views were a big asset to the published report on the plan, not least because of the Parisian flavour which they injected into a vision of superhuman proportions. (RIBA, 1911, 785)*

a lakeshore belt which he had first proposed in the 1890s, and longer-term parks to cater for suburban growth. To crown the new Chicago, he planned a huge civic centre, supplemented by 'suburban civic centers' for the outlying districts (ibid., 34–5).

To his credit, Burnham called for the enactment of powers to plan the suburbs as a whole, on the lines currently being discussed in England (ibid., 34–5). However, he said little of how this planning might be done, or what its objectives should be. More surprisingly still, he managed to avoid referring to the central slums. Chicago, unlike London, had not yet reached the point where people ejected from congested districts needed to be rehoused at public expense, claimed Burnham (ibid., 109). Instead, he implied, people would move painlessly to the planned suburbs as civic and private interests remodelled the centre.

Through the work of Burnham, American planning had graduated beyond mere beautification. By 1909, the idea of comprehensive planning had been adumbrated. Burnham's work, however, has to be understood as an advertisement for city planning rather than a blueprint. Serious consideration of residential planning was not to be expected from him. For progress in this area, we have to look to New York and the unusually influential housing reform movement which its unique problems were beginning to generate.

After several years of discussions, the New York state legislature decided in 1897 to amalgamate the municipal governments of New York, Brooklyn and other authorities in the area to form a Greater New York covering 315 square miles. As in London, a two-tier system was set up, with functions shared between five boroughs (Manhattan, Brooklyn, the Bronx, Queens and Richmond) and the City of New York. Nearly three and a half million people, out of a total of four and a half million in the New York metropolitan district, lived in the enlarged New York City (Scott, 1969, 26–30). Coming into effect in 1898, the new charter reinvigorated public efforts to secure an efficient water supply and communications system for the whole of New York. The housing reformers welcomed the new charter, and Elgin Gould redoubled his efforts to secure the rapid-transit system which, he hoped, would break down the pattern of high-density housing in Manhattan and parts of the other boroughs (see Lubove, 1962, 111). However, the new tenement building code which the new authority applied to the enlarged New York in 1899 failed to secure the approval of the reformers, and in the following year the Tenement House Committee of the Charity Organization Society put on a tenement house exhibition to stir public opinion. The exhibition was largely based on the work of Lawrence Veiller (1872–1959), a young social reformer who had developed a special interest in housing. It included a comprehensive, block-by-block survey, complete with disease and poverty maps. Also displayed were American and European examples of model tenements and suburban housing, and an architectural competition for model tenement designs was held in connection with the exhibition (De Forest and Veiller, 1903, I, 111–12).

The exhibition and the associated agitation led to the appointment of a new tenement house commission by the governor of New York, Theodore Roosevelt. Veiller was its secretary, under the chairmanship of Robert W. De Forest, a rich social reformer. The work of the commission, which included a full study of European housing conditions and regulation, resulted in the New York State Tenement House Law of 1901, which applied to 'all cities of the first class', of which New York and Buffalo were the only two in the state. The commission also proposed the creation of a Tenement House Department for New York City, and this was incorporated in a new charter which came into effect in January 1902. The newly-elected reforming mayor of New York, Seth Low, appointed De Forest as tenement house commissioner and Veiller as his deputy. The leading reformers thus found themselves administering the new law, which banned the airless 'dumbbell' tenement and replaced it with the 'new law tenement' incorporating large interior courtyards, its height related to the width of the street onto which it faced. The effect of the new regulations was to reduce the maximum number of households which could be accommodated on the standard New York building lot of 25 X 100 feet from twenty-six to twenty-two (De Forest and Veiller, 1903, I, xiii–xv). However, the new law provided neither for extensive slum demolition nor for public replacement housing, and the Tenement House Department concentrated on improving existing dwellings (De Forest and Veiller, 1903, I, xvii–xviii).

In New York, as in Germany, city-wide building regulations designed to control the excesses of the tenement block created problems for building in the outer districts. The new law came into force at a time when rapid progress was being made, thanks partly to the enlargement of New York City, towards the creation of an efficient rapid-transit system for the whole urban area (see Committee on the City Plan, 1914, 38–51). The main agent of change was the subway, construction of which began in 1900. In the following year the Queensborough and Manhattan bridges were built, and in 1902 the subway reached Brooklyn. Within a few years access to the suburbs had been transformed, bringing the housing reformers closer to their dream of a mass decentralization of population from Manhattan (Ford, 1936, 213–14). Lawrence Veiller, writing in 1903, keenly appreciated the implications:

> One of the chief problems of any tenement house law is in adapting it to the differing conditions of different parts of our cities, which vary all the way from crowded sections in which land values are so high that only tall buildings can be profitable, to country districts in which land is so cheap that it is only adapted to the two or three story frame house. The law must necessarily affect all parts of a city alike, but the degree and extent of regulation should vary according as it is to affect such dissimilar conditions... This difficulty is inherent; it is not entirely surmountable. Its nearest solution in tenement house law lies in the adoption of the principle of height as the determining factor. (De Forest and Veiller, 1903, I, xxvii)

Veiller meant by this last remark that the taller the building, the more stringent the regulations should be. Indeed, a number of amendments were made to the original tenement house bill, as a result of representations from the suburbs, to make it more relevant to less densely constructed areas on the outskirts. However, the commission had rejected the idea of more radical distinctions. A proposal that two building codes should be drawn up, one for (poor) tenements and the other for (rich) apartments had been turned down as implying 'a class distinction obnoxious to the democratic policy of our state'. Another suggestion, that the building of tenement houses should be completely prohibited in certain outer areas, was judged to involve too many complicated issues to be seriously considered (De Forest and Veiller, 1903, I, xxvii, 37–8, 42).

In the first years of the new century, however, it looked as though time might remove these weaknesses. A Board of Public Improvements had been set up for the enlarged city in 1898. It was making some progress towards a coordinated strategy of works when the Washington proposals rekindled City-Beautiful enthusiasms in New York. In 1902 the New York Municipal Art Society, in association with other reform groups and big-business interests, began to campaign for the adoption of an ambitious plan of embellishments and improvements. To reinforce its case, it prepared a list of specific projects, many of which were of practical as well as aesthetic value (Kantor, 1973, 153–7). With Seth Low as mayor, an integrated public works and housing strategy looked on the cards. However, Low and his supporters had underestimated the powers of recovery of the Tammany Hall machine, and in 1904 Low was replaced at City Hall by George B. McClellan, the Tammany candidate. Veiller and De Forest soon detected the new administration's indifference to housing reform, and resigned from the Tenement House Department. As a patrician and art-lover, McClellan was not unsympathetic to the aims of the Municipal Art Society, and in 1904 he went ahead with the creation of the New York City Improvement Commission which Low had been planning towards the end of his term. However, most of his appointees were nonentities, and in the absence of support from the administration they worked with little urgency. They did not present their final report until 1907, by which time even the civic improvement party had largely lost interest in them (Kantor, 1973, 160–71). In fact, their report contained some interesting proposals, including new highways, bridges and parks, and a civic centre. However, most of these schemes were located within the built-up area, and would have been very expensive to carry out. Not surprisingly, the report was virtually ignored by the New York authorities (Committee on the City Plan, 1914, 22–6; Lubove, 1962, 155–6; Adams, 1927, 32).

Veiller returned from 1904 to his efforts to influence public opinion. He agreed to become the secretary of the City Club, an association of rich, reforming businessmen, and he led the Club in a number of campaigns for civic improvement, including better traffic regulation and the extension of the rapid-transit system. Meanwhile, in 1907, the leaders of the New York settlement house movement, supported by a wide range of philanthropic and reforming bodies, set up the Committee on Congestion of Population in New York. This new organization appointed as its secretary Benjamin C. Marsh (1877—1952), a recent college graduate and professional social worker whose initial practical experience had been gained as assistant state secretary of the YMCA in Iowa. In the early 1900s he had studied political economy at the University of Chicago and had toured Europe to study vagrancy control. At the time of his appointment in New York he was secretary of the Pennsylvania Society to Protect Children from Cruelty (Lubove, 1962, 231—2; Kantor, 1974, 422—3). Marsh soon applied himself to the study of the urban environment and its reform. He planned a large exhibition in an attempt to rekindle some of the enthusiasm that had surrounded the tenement house exhibition of 1900, and he spent much of the summer of 1907 gathering material for it in Europe (Scott, 1969, 83—6).

The exhibition opened in March 1908. It included contributions from a number of New York reforming bodies and from the Tenement House Department, and much of it was devoted to the exposure of slum conditions. However, thanks largely to Marsh, it put forward a strong case for the adoption of planning and zoning on German lines as the only effective solution (Lubove, 1962, 231; Scott, 1969, 83—6). Supported by Marsh's direct lobbying, the exhibition persuaded the Governor of New York and the municipal authorities to set up a new inquiry. This was the City Commission on Congestion of Population, set up in 1910 with a membership of nine New York aldermen and eight private citizens, with Marsh as its secretary (*Proceedings of the Third National Conference*, 1911, 38—9). Meanwhile, however, Marsh had risen to prominence in the national housing reform movement and his knowledge of German planning had made some impact even in architectural and engineering circles. In 1909, Marsh persuaded the Committee on Congestion of Population to convene a conference in Washington with a view to establishing a national city planning association. Marsh put to the conference an urban planning programme which included a strong element of land reform, including land taxation on the lines proposed by Henry George, and municipal land purchase similar to the German practice (Lubove, 1962, 232—4). In the same year he published a book, *An Introduction to City Planning*, and helped organize a city planning exhibition in New York under the joint aegis of the Committee on Congestion of Population and the Municipal Art Society of New York (Scott, 1969, 91).

The work of Marsh and his associates, combined with that of Burnham and his fellow urban designers, had by the end of 1909 firmly rooted the idea of planning in the consciousness of American politicians, professionals and the general public. The first university course in city planning, at Harvard, was launched during the year by James Sturgis Pray (Adams and Hodge, 1965, 47). The Washington conference did not generate a national association but it inaugurated an annual series of national conferences on city planning which grew visibly in influence and expertise as the years went by (see *Proceedings of the Third*

National Conference, 1911, 4, 261–2). Marsh's book, which was widely read, was sufficiently imbued with his knowledge of German *Städtebau* to ensure that no aspect of planning, except perhaps the aesthetic, was neglected therein. In its extensive coverage of European practice it included whole sections on the Frankfurt policies and English garden cities and garden suburbs (Marsh, 1909, 46–61, 113–22). It advocated building and use zoning (which Marsh claimed was the most important part of city planning), the rational planning of the street network, separating traffic streets from residential streets, cheap transport, the reservation of land for parks, playgrounds and public buildings, the public planning of port areas, municipal acquisition of land, and the annexation of independent suburbs (Marsh, 1909, 28–39). Linking the whole of this programme to the continuing campaign for municipal reform, Marsh ended by urging his readers to press for a city plan in their own localities, together with an efficient administration to carry it out.

CITY PLANNING PROGRESS IN THE UNITED STATES, 1909–17

In the United States, as in Britain, the high hopes raised in 1909 were to be largely disappointed in the remaining years of peace. The first permanent city planning commission had been set up at Hartford, Connecticut, in 1907. By 1915 ninety-seven were believed to be in existence (Nolen, 1916, xxvi). Most, however, were the products of citizen reform initiatives and were purely advisory. Indeed, in many cases their supporters did not want them to be tied too closely to the execution of municipal policy as this would restrict their freedom to produce alluring plans and so reduce their value as a stimulus to a fundamental regeneration of city government (see e.g. Committee on Town Planning, 1917, 1–3). Most produced a superficial but glossily presented plan or improvement scheme, often the work of a consultant architect, and then sank into inactivity (see Robinson, 1916, 294). When the commissions were allotted a defined role in local administration on the lines pioneered at Hartford, they were usually given no control over the use of private land and they did little more than fix street lines and approve street plans submitted by the landowners. As much had been done, and was still being done, by the older boards of survey (Scott, 1969, 80). Moreover, most commissions were allowed no control over municipal or state resources, so that investment in the entire range of civic improvements remained in the hands of established boards and committees.

Apart from passing the charter amendments under which the city planning commissions were set up, nearly all the state legislatures remained indifferent to the needs of planning, and particularly to the German type of comprehensive planning advocated by Marsh. No state went so far as to *require* its larger towns to set up planning boards until Massachusetts did so in 1913, and no other state followed this example before the war (Robinson, 1916, 243). In 1914 Pennsylvania was still the only state in which property-owners could be forced to comply with municipal plans for new streets without obtaining damages (Scott, 1969, 135). No progress was made anywhere towards municipal purchase of building land, for which state authorization was required. Even the Massachusetts state legislature, which had once helped in the creation of regional machinery to plan a park system in the Boston area, baulked at the idea of a Boston metropolitan planning board in 1912, after some of the outlying areas had objected (Scott, 1969, 110–16).

Although the days of the purely selfish beautification scheme were now past, there continued to be a correlation between the areas in which planning controls progressed, and the interests of the richer citizens. Nowhere was this connection more apparent than in zoning. In 1885 the town of Modesto, California, had restricted laundries to one small district, partly in order to keep the Chinese, who ran the laundries, out of the better residential areas (Scott, 1969, 75). For some years this example was not emulated, even in California, but in the early 1900s, in the context of the swelling discussion on city planning, zoning ordinances began to be more widely adopted (see Heights of Buildings Commission, 1913, 32–47). One of the most ambitious was the Los Angeles zoning ordinance of 1909–10, which restricted industry to certain districts and designated most of the rest of the city as a residential area. The main intention here was to preserve the value of land and buildings in potentially desirable residential suburbs against intrusions by noisy or noxious industries and the people who worked in them, and the property interests were among the strongest supporters of the zoning scheme. Not all towns possessed the economic and social structure, and pattern of growth, which could generate such a consensus, and the landowners and sub-dividers were generally suspicious at first (*City Plan*, II, 1, 1916, 3–8). However, as the German zoning advocated by Marsh was more widely debated after 1909, it began to make converts, not as a means of combating high land values in the centre, but of maintaining them in the suburbs (see Cheney, 1917). By 1917 a number of state legislatures had passed general laws to permit some or all of their towns to establish purely residential districts, and zoning ordinances were in force in hundreds of towns (Lubove, 1967, 13). With the courts now more favourable to restrictions which applied only to certain districts of towns, and land- and house-owners more easily convinced (see e.g. Nolen, 1916, 81–5), the United States had leaped ahead of both Britain and France in the practice of zoning. They had done so, however, not in response to a reforming impulse to improve the housing of the poor, but in order to protect the environment of better-off citizens, and the property values which it sustained, against the alarms and shocks which sprang from North America's extraordinarily dynamic process of urban change (see e.g. Cheney, 1917). In short, American zoning was not designed primarily to help the poor; it was more to keep them in their place (see Mancuso, 1978).

This association between the distortion of zoning and its rapid adoption was also present in New York, where the introduction of city-wide zoning in 1916 helped overcome the last objections to the idea throughout the country. However, the New York system, which combined use zones with differential building regulations on lines previously attempted only in Germany, was basically a genuine effort to solve the city's extraordinary congestion problems. Indeed, it was arguably the most impressive achievement of American city planning before the war. We have already seen that the debates surrounding the introduction of the new tenement house law in 1901 had raised the question of the applicability of a standard building code to the whole city. However, it was not New York but Boston which, having adopted a tenement house building code in 1899 and encountered much the same difficulties as its fellow seaport, went on in 1904 to impose differential regulations distinguishing between the centre and the rest of the city. A maximum height of 125 feet (depending on street width) was fixed in the centre, and 80 feet elsewhere (Scott, 1969, 75). Property interests in the city objected, and began a legal process which lasted until 1909, when the United States Supreme Court ruled that the Boston height zones were legal (Robinson, 1916, 279).

The Boston judgement aroused great interest in New York, and the idea of building zones was one of the innovations discussed and advocated by Marsh's Commission on Congestion of Population. However, by the time the Commission reported in 1911 Marsh had acquired a lurid reputation as a land reform fanatic. The inclusion of proposals for land taxation in the report helped to ensure that it was virtually ignored by the New York authorities, while splitting the housing reform and planning movements (Ford, 1936, 227; Kantor, 1974, 426). However, it was clearly only a matter of time before the great variations in the building fabric of New York forced the authorities to follow a German example with which most American urban experts were now familiar.

As early as the 1880s the larger American cities, led by New York and Chicago, had begun to generate a building form that was completely unknown in Europe. The skyscraper was the product of massively inflated land values in the central business districts of cities that were growing far faster than any in Europe, and the absence of the height restrictions which had been introduced almost everywhere on the continent of Europe to control the tenement block. From the 1890s the widespread use of frame construction allowed even greater heights. Until the turn of the century the most adventurous skyscrapers were in Chicago, not New York, but thereafter the uncrowned capital began to outshine its midwestern rival. By 1913 there were more than fifty buildings of over twenty storeys in Manhattan, and nine of over thirty storeys. The highest had fifty-five storeys (Delafons, 1962, 20). Owing partly to the eclipse of Marsh, further action was not prompted primarily by the housing reformers but by business interests in Manhattan. For some years department stores and merchants in Fifth Avenue had been complaining about the northward movement of clothing manufacture in the nearby sidestreets. They claimed that the extra traffic congestion, the reconstruction of the district for industrial uses, and the flooding of the fashionable streets at midday by poor workers from the Lower East Side, were driving away their clientele. In 1911 the Fifth Avenue Association, which represented these interests, launched a campaign for public regulation of industry in the vicinity. The campaign was welcomed by George McAneny, a progressive New York politician with a background in law and journalism, and a former president of the City Club, who served as president of the borough of Manhattan between 1910 and 1913. Sympathetic to the housing reformers, McAneny saw in the Fifth Avenue issue a chance to open up the question of zoning for the whole city (Hays, 1965, 6–8; Heights of Buildings Commission, 1913, 51).

In the winter of 1911–12, McAneny appointed the Fifth Avenue Commission, an advisory body composed largely of business representatives, which he invited to investigate the possibility of preserving Fifth Avenue as an exclusive shopping district. It recommended in 1912 that a maximum height of 125 feet should be fixed for all buildings on the Avenue and within 300 feet of it on either side (Heights of Buildings Commission, 1913, 51). This restriction, it was hoped, would discourage the redevelopment of the Avenue and its sidestreets with 'lofts' (multi-storey factories) which thanks to their intensive use of their sites could outbid retail uses even in the downtown area. McAneny put the proposal to the Board of Estimate and Apportionment of New York City in May 1912. It was not adopted, but by this time the planning debate in New York had moved into a new phase which ensured that the idea would not pass into oblivion.

In 1911 and 1912 the New York business community had built up an enthusiasm for general city planning comparable to that which had produced the Burnham plan for Chicago a couple of years before. Indeed, two of the businessmen involved in this wave of interest, Charles D. Norton and Frederic A. Delano, had been associated with the Chicago plan before moving to New York (Hays, 1965, 6–8). In 1911 the two men had begun to discuss the possibility of promoting a private plan to galvanize the authorities (Adams, 1927, 31–2). McAneny drew on this groundswell of opinion in persuading the Board of Estimate and Apportionment to set up two committees to examine the coordination of environmental policies over the whole city. The first of these was the Committee on the Height, Size and Arrangement of Buildings, which was set up in February 1913 and on which sat the borough presidents of Manhattan, Brooklyn and the Bronx (Heights of Buildings Commission, 1913, 1–2). In the following year it set up a standing Committee on the City Plan, to consider 'all larger questions of public improvements' (Committee on the City Plan, 1914, 7). The bulk of the committee was constituted by the presidents of all five boroughs, and its chairman was McAneny, now president of the New York Board of Aldermen (Committee on the City Plan, 1914, 2).

Although these two committees had more potential power to plan than any previously established in New York, their membership lacked time and expertise. Both were therefore willing, once again at the advice of McAneny, to set up advisory commissions. The Committee on the Height, Size and Arrangement of Buildings set up the Heights of Buildings Commission, and the Committee on the City Plan created the Advisory Commission on City Plan. Both commissions were well staffed. The Heights of Buildings Commission consisted of twenty experts and representatives of New York interests, including Lawrence Veiller. The chairman was a lawyer, Edward M. Bassett, and George B. Ford, the architect and planning consultant, was secretary and director of investigations. Frank Backus Williams, another lawyer and expert on building codes, was employed specifically to write a report on building regulations and zoning in Europe (Heights of Buildings Commission, 1913, ii). The Advisory Commission on City Plan numbered twenty-four, most of them businessmen or architects. It included Edward M. Bassett, and was chaired by Charles D. Norton. George B. Ford was actively involved in this side of the work as well, as consultant to the parent committee (Committee on the City Plan, 1914, 2; Adams, 1927, 33).

Unfortunately, the Committee on the City Plan soon encountered the problem of inter-borough jealousy. By 1915 it had virtually fallen to pieces and its advisory commission was eventually reduced to discussing the possibility of organizing a citizens' group to finance and draw up an independent city plan (Adams, 1927, 33—4). What dissuaded Norton and his friends from such a course, however, was the considerable progress achieved in the sphere of building regulation. The remit of the Committee on the Height, Size and Arrangement of Buildings had included a specific instruction to consider the division of New York into building districts, and the Heights of Buildings Commission, which was instructed to work quickly, focused its attention on this solution. Reporting as early as December 1913, the commission outlined a scheme of differential building regulations which was comparable to the most advanced of the German *Staffelbauordnungen*, on which it was directly based (Heights of Buildings Commission, 1913, 56—76, 94—119). With property-owning interests generally favourable to the idea, the City obtained a charter amendment in 1914 allowing the Board of Estimate and Apportionment to introduce differential building regulations (Commission on Building Districts, 1916, 1, 45—6). In June of that year the Board set up a new body, the Commission on Building Districts and Restrictions, to prepare a detailed scheme. The chairman was again Edward M. Bassett, and George B. Ford was consultant. Most of the seventeen members were representatives of architectural, business and property interests.

The new commission worked for two years. In that time it developed a keen awareness of the implications of dividing the city into building districts, particularly in terms of future employment location and transit provision. It undertook extensive studies of commuter flows and developed a strategy of suburban employment centres to reduce pressure on the subway lines into Manhattan (Commission on Building Districts, 1916, 8). It urged that public improvements and the development of private land should in future be planned together: 'New York City has reached a point beyond which continued unplanned growth cannot take place without inviting social and economic disaster' (ibid., 6). Though the hope of an overall plan had been frustrated for the time being by the failure of the Committee on the City Plan, the commission's recommendations clearly looked ahead to a day when fully comprehensive, scientific planning would be a reality in New York. It proposed to divide the 327 square miles which the city now covered into four types of use-district (residence, business, unrestricted and undetermined). All streets were distributed between five types of height-district, in which maximum facade heights were determined by multiples of the street width, ranging from one to two-and-a-half. Finally, the city was further divided into five classes of area-district, in which stipulations varied as to the area of courts and yards and the proportions of the total lot to be left unoccupied (ibid., 15—41).

21 *New York zoning ordinance, 1916: part of the height-district map. The maximum height on the street frontage was calculated by multiplying the width of the street by the figures shown on the plan. Note that these multiples were in excess of those applied in most European cities, where the maximum permitted height did not normally exceed the street width. (Commission on Building Districts and Restrictions, 1916, figure 34)*

The content of these proposals was not revolutionary. They consecrated the existing pattern of building densities in New York, thus securing wide support from the property interests. Even in the outer districts there was no ban on the building of tenements, though it was hoped that other stipulations would discourage their construction in the suburbs. Over most of the city it remained possible to build up to at least four or five storeys. Skyscrapers could rise to any height as long as they did not occupy more than one-quarter of their plots, and commercial buildings were allowed to reach heights well above the normal maxima by a progressive stepping-back of the upper storeys (see *City Plan*, II, 3, 1916, 2–7; Ford, 1936, 232). Indeed, George B. Ford commented somewhat ruefully:

> It would be most unfortunate if the law were applied as it stands to other cities for it is full of unduly liberal provisions in the way of height and size that tend strongly to defeat the object of the law but which were necessitated by the exceptional economic conditions of New York. (*City Plan*, II, 3, 1916, 3)

In many other respects, however, the commission's proposals, which, with minor modifications, were enforced by the Board of Estimate and Apportionment in 1916, marked an advance over the best German practice, particularly in view of the great area which they covered. They were generally welcomed by health and housing reformers and, in the absence of a full city development plan, they immediately began to act as the principal regulator of the physical evolution of New York. Thomas Adams, the expatriate British planner, provided a fair assessment a decade later: 'Although the Zoning Resolution was not in the nature of a comprehensive plan, it has proved to be the most effective piece of planning work which has ever been carried out in New York' (Adams, 1927, 32).

The New York zoning scheme, limited in its aims but effective, helps to put in proper perspective the superficially attractive and sometimes quite well prepared plans which issued in even greater numbers from the city planning commissions and improvement societies of various sorts after Burnham's Chicago plan had won such wide acclaim. The Newark, New Jersey, plan of 1913, for which George B. Ford was the most influential consultant, was one of the better ones. It was even suggested later, admittedly by a potentially biased commentator, that the Newark plan had inaugurated a new era of scientific planning in the United States (Ford, 1936, 236). However, the plan report dwelt at great length on the street system, proposing a number of central improvements, before going on to civic art. There was some interesting discussion of 'the zone system', which for the authors meant the replacement of the normal grid by special local street networks designed to cater for the functions envisaged for each district. However, there was no detailed analysis of how this might be done and, surprisingly, there was no mention of differential building regulations. Then there followed sections on the harbour, markets and transport, and recreation crept in at the end. There was no mention at all of housing and the report's main claim to a scientific approach seemed to rest on the inclusion of a traffic engineer among the consultants (City Plan Commission, Newark, 1913). In any case the plan, which had been commissioned by a City Plan Commission set up by the municipality in 1911, produced few practical results.

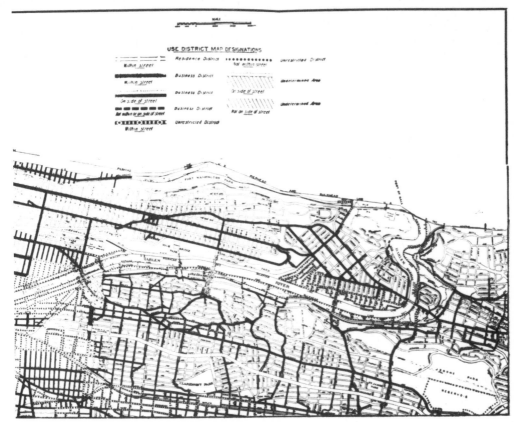

22 *New York zoning ordinance, 1916: part of a map showing use-districts for Manhattan. Streets are shown allocated to one of three types of district: residence, business, and unrestricted (i.e. available for industry). These controls may appear crude, but they were based on a scientific inquiry which rivalled and even outshone the best of German planning research. (Commission on Building Districts and Restrictions, 1916, figure 123)*

For a plan which broke firmly away from aesthetic preoccupations and established a mode of intervention which might fairly be described as comprehensive, we have to look to the plan for the neighbouring towns of Oakland and Berkeley, California, which their municipalities published jointly in 1915. Its author emphasized that the prime aim of planning was to promote economic efficiency and social utility. Beauty was a secondary consideration and, in any case, it could not be achieved by a town which lacked an efficient productive base. In a long section on housing, the need to conserve and enhance the existing system of low-density suburbs was stressed. Parks, civic art and civic centres were deliberately placed at the very end of the report. The whole of the author's approach to planning was summed up in the statement which headed the report:

CITY PLANNING IS INSURANCE AGAINST WASTE OF PUBLIC AND PRIVATE
FUNDS

City-planning means co-ordination of the activities that make for the growth of the
city, especially the activities of railroad and harbor engineers, landscape architects,
street-building and civil engineers, builders of factories, of offices, of public buildings
and dwelling houses. Without this pre-planning co-ordination, clashes between these
different activities, unsatisfactory results and most expensive rearrangements, become
unavoidable. City-planning therefore does not mean additional expenditure of money,
but it means an INSURANCE AGAINST INEFFICIENT EXPENDITURE of the
enormous sums that go − in the regular course of events − into the development of a
progressive city. (Hegemann, 1915, inside cover)

This indeed suggested scientific planning, comparable with the best of German
practice, and George B. Ford hailed it as 'one of the most studious city planning
reports which America has produced' (Committee on Town Planning, 1917, 15).
However, the Berkeley and Oakland plan *was* German practice. It was the work
of Werner Hegemann who, after his brilliant contribution to the Berlin planning
exhibition, had been invited to the United States in 1913, as a lecturer and
planning consultant, by the People's Institute of New York (Hegemann, 1915,
1−2). No stranger to North America, having already been director of the division
of city planning at the Boston exhibition of 1909, Hegemann had quickly settled
down into an environment which was more congenial to his liberal inclinations
than that on offer in his home country. Almost completely Americanized, he
decided to stay on after the outbreak of war in Europe, and soon built a reputation as one of the most brilliant figures in North American planning.

Although the United States produced few fully-rounded planners of Hegemann's
stature, the plethora of superficial and partial plans and reports at least generated
a large class of professionals who had come into contact with aspects of city
planning. Widespread demand for their expertise encouraged many architects and
landscape architects, and smaller numbers of engineers, economists and housing
reformers, to try their hand at planning after 1909. Some of the big names
travelled widely, producing plan after plan, often on the basis of a very brief
acquaintance with the towns concerned. However, the smaller the town, the more
likely was it that local professionals would be called upon, and such people usually
did most of the detailed work on those plans which finally appeared under the
names of famous consultants. In addition, professionals were now called upon
more frequently by industrialists to design factory communities (Lubove, 1962,
226). Although landscape architects continued to dominate the scene, participation by non-architectural professions, sustained by a growing number of university
courses in city planning, eventually became important enough to stimulate the
creation of a distinct professional organization, the American City Planning
Institute, in 1917.

Even that biggest vacuum of all, residential planning, was on the way to being
filled by 1917, at least in the suburbs. Central to this development was the idea of

the 'neighbourhood' which had originally been generated by the settlement movement in the 1890s. Following much the same path of evolution as in Britain, the idea was extended from the revitalization of a poor district by the injection of a settlement house full of middle-class social workers to the generation of a socially-balanced community which would centre on a set of communal facilities maintained by the generality of the residents. However, in the United States the neighbourhood concept attracted additional support from the municipal reformers, who saw it as a means of replacing the ward as the basic political unit and so undermining the bosses (Guttenberg, 1977, 5–6). By 1902 Jacob Riis had developed the idea of a city composed of neighbourhoods using their own public schools as social centres, and to a large extent governing themselves, with city-wide government organized by a federation of neighbourhoods (Scott, 1969, 72). Scientific developments, not entirely unconnected with the university branch of the municipal reform movement, added plausibility to the idea. In 1902 the pioneer social psychologist, Charles Horton Cooley, published an influential study, *Human Nature and the Social Order*, which argued that the health of the personality depended on contact with two primary groups, the family and the neighbourhood (Guttenberg, 1977, 2–3).

Cooley's work helped to reinforce the view, which had already made great progress in the 1890s, that social problems were the products of environment rather than of the innate defects of the individual (see Riis, 1902, 140–3). Indeed, by the early 1900s it had begun to be expressed in municipal policy at Cleveland under Tom L. Johnson, a reforming mayor (1901–9) who leaned more strongly towards municipal socialism than any other leading civic figure in the United States (Griffith, 1974, 11, 146). Johnson's municipal renaissance in Cleveland was publicised and explained by Frederic C. Howe, a local attorney and leading member of the reform movement which had helped put Johnson in power (Hines, 1974, 159). In 1905 Howe published a widely-read book, *The City, The Hope of Democracy*, which put forward a programme for the eradication of poverty and other social problems by an extension of the activities of reformed municipalities. Although the agent of change for Howe was the city as a whole, and his main inspiration lay in the land reforms of Henry George, he laid heavy stress on a combination of housing improvement and militant democracy which indirectly supported the neighbourhood idea (see Howe, 1905, esp. 300–13).

New support, however, tended to undermine the original emphasis on the central, slum district. The concept of a neighbourhood remained as distant as ever from the more pressing needs of the poor, but it appealed to expanding ranks of middle-class suburbanites who wanted more local facilities and feared the spread of bossism into their districts. This transition was symbolized by the suburbanization of the civic centre idea. In 1907 the Committee on Civic Centers of the St Louis Civic League proposed the division of that city into neighbourhoods, each with its own centre (Scott, 1969, 72), and suburban civic centres were one of the few elements of detailed planning for the suburbs to appear in Burnham's Chicago plan of 1909. In 1911 the proceedings of the First National Conference on Social Center Development had a heavy suburban emphasis (Ward, 1913, 155–6), and by now the idea of grouping all local services, including education, in a single building was being defended on grounds of economy alone (see e.g. Guttenberg, 1977, 7–8). Slums were hardly mentioned at all in *The Social Center*, a book which the new leader of the movement, Edward J. Ward, published in 1913; his main emphasis was on 'the self-organization of the voting body into a deliberative body to supplant party divisions' (Ward, 1913, v–vii).

This new form of the neighbourhood idea did at least contribute more effectively than its predecessor to the development of physical planning. Broad-brush planning of the Burnham type naturally generated an interest in what could be achieved by conscious design in the new suburbs which would clearly spring up when the envisaged transport improvements were carried out. Chicago, appropriately enough, took the lead. In 1913 the City Club sponsored a competition for the design of a suburban district which produced an entry, by William Drummond, which in grouping housing and open space round communal facilities foreshadowed the mature neighbourhood-unit concept of the 1920s (Guttenberg, 1977, 8). Walter Burley Griffin did much the same in his plan for the New Trier Neighborhood Center in suburban Chicago (Peisch, 1964, 99–102). Private promoters, aware of changes in purchaser demand, also began to lay out their tracts on neighbourhood principles and to provide certain communal facilities.

It has nevertheless to be recognized that as residential planning became an aspect of good business, and as transit improvements and suburban planning were put forward with growing plausibility as solutions to the housing problem, the question of how to provide decent housing cheaply in the inner districts sank once again into neglect. Having reached its peak at the turn of the century, the tenement house reform movement was outshone thereafter by the new craze of city planning. By 1912, thirty-eight towns claimed to have a housing association or committee (Lubove, 1967, 144), but this was far fewer than the number which had city-plan commissions. Admittedly, a number of states had now followed the example of New York and enacted housing codes, but the idea of public support for housing remained anathema until the United States entered the war. In 1910 the National Housing Association was set up on the initiative of Lawrence Veiller, with the support of the Russell Sage Foundation and De Forest as its president, but its existence, which Marsh regretted, tended to reinforce the split between the housing and planning movements (Lubove, 1962, 144; McKelvey, 1963, 262). It even encouraged the authors of city plans to ignore housing completely, as an area requiring arcane expertise; this is, for instance, what Arnold W. Brunner and Frederick Law Olmsted Jr, architect and landscape architect respectively, did in their Rochester, New York, plan of 1911 (Brunner *et al.*, 1911, 7–8). And so did the two commissions on building regulations in New York between 1913 and 1916 (see Heights of Buildings Commission, 1913, iii).

On the eve of the entry of the United States into the war, American city planning had clearly passed through its cosmetic phase and had generated a guiding theory comparable in some respects to German orthodoxy. The literature of planning now exuded a degree of maturity. Since 1915 the National Conference on City Planning had published a quarterly journal, *The City Plan*. Nelson P. Lewis's *The Planning of the Modern City*, published in 1916, was a full manual, written by an engineer (see Schultz and McShane, 1978). In the same year John Nolen brought together articles by a variety of specialists in his *City Planning: A Series of Papers Presenting the Essential Elements of a City Plan*. Nine universities and colleges were offering city-planning courses by 1916 (*City Plan*, 1916, II, 1, 12). The foundation of the American City Planning Institute in 1917 clearly marked the end of the foundation phase of American urban planning. Yet it was Charles Mulford Robinson, the planning pioneer, who had the last word. Writing in 1916 of all that had been achieved so far in terms of commissions, reports and plans, he coolly remarked that the next step would have to be to provide 'a continuously directing power' (Robinson, 1916, 294). In other words, he recognized that planning was still a collection of ideas, that it had no real administrative existence. Indeed, it would be many years yet before that existence could be firmly established.

Five

France
The Reluctant Planner

In the field of civic improvement, our French towns have sunk to un-believable depths of stagnation. Our smaller, older towns are shrivelling away, all hope gone. On the rare occasions when they rouse themselves to action, it is only to destroy the last remnants of their former charm. Our thriving urban centres, from Paris at one extreme to the tiniest fashionable resort at the other, are being sucked down into a deadly slough of negligence by their own ignorance and improvidence, buttres-sed by a blind confidence in the inevitability of progress... The future of our towns is being choked off by chaotic outward growth. Not a trace of an overall plan! No attempt to complete or even to respect the fine work of our eighteenth-century Intendants! Our most recent tradition, Haussmann's, was shabby enough, but even that has not been continued...

We did not need to go to London, in the first two weeks of October 1910, to realize that French municipal enterprise had been completely outstripped by foreign countries, and especially by the United States, Great Britain, Sweden, Germany and Austria. But we had no inkling of the depth and breadth of this new urban science, and of the extent to which it was being generally applied... At the Royal Academy, fifteen rooms were packed with schemes and plans for urban improvement; ...Fifteen rooms! Of the fifteen, six and a half were occupied by the Germans and one and a half by the French — or, to be more accurate, by the Parisians. But when one compared the plans exhibited in the German rooms with those in the single [*sic*] French room, our pitiful stagnation and the reasons for it stood out for all to see. All that we had to display was the past, the sixty-year-old past of Haussmann; the foreigners put on show the vigorous achievements of their present — a present based on completely different principles.

Robert de Souza, *Nice: capitale d'hiver* (1913), pp. ix–x, 377–8

Count Robert de Souza wrote this lament in support of a town-planning campaign which in its timing and objectives had much in common with the agitation which culminated in Britain in the 1909 Town Planning Act. In France, however, there were no legislative results before the First World War. Admittedly, many of the campaigners expected very little from parliament and concentrated on trying to generate support for planning in the localities. In this respect the French movement resembled the American, yet very little was achieved at local level either. In fact, urban planning, in the sense in which it was understood in Germany, Britain and the United States, simply failed to take root in France before 1914. It was only under the impact of wartime destruction that a planning bill was pushed through parliament, to become law in 1919. Yet even this belated statute, though supported by subsequent enactments, had virtually no effect on French urban development before war broke out again in 1939.

Before we accept De Souza's gloomy diagnosis, we have to consider the possibility that new methods were shunned because older ones remained adequate. The environmental policies in force in the larger towns at the turn of the century were largely an inheritance from the phase of massive urban reconstruction in the 1850s and 1860s which had been the wonder of the world. This was a respectable tradition, and one to which we shall devote some attention. Nevertheless, underlying the general unwillingness to progress beyond it we can detect a widespread malaise in French urban life, consideration of which will take up much of this chapter.

FRENCH TOWNS AND ENVIRONMENTAL CONTROL BEFORE THE MID-NINETEENTH CENTURY

In each of the three countries studied so far the urban phenomenon of the nineteenth and early twentieth centuries was largely the product of recent developments. Sweeping industrialization had blotted out much of a weak pre-industrial urban tradition. In France matters were very different. A rich, varied agriculture, thriving trade, and the development of strong, centralized rule had promoted the growth of an urban system which by the seventeenth century had reached a degree of development unrivalled in Europe outside Northern Italy and the Low Countries. During the eighteenth century, it is true, most French towns grew more slowly than their English counterparts and the larger ones suffered heavy losses of population in the troubles of the 1790s. As the nineteenth century opened only about one-fifth of the population of France was urbanized, compared to nearly one-third in England. However, much of England's seventeenth- and eighteenth-century urban growth had occurred in small towns. Although London was nearly twice as populous as Paris in 1801, Lyons, Marseilles and Bordeaux, each of which had about 100,000 residents, were still larger than any provincial city in England (see Sutcliffe, 1976).

Thanks to their long-established importance and prosperity, Paris and the leading regional centres were solidly built and well-appointed towns. From the sixteenth century a great deal of construction and reconstruction took place, much of it using the good building stone which abounded in many parts of France. In some of the more important towns the Crown or its agents undertook ambitious schemes of extension and embellishment. This work began in Paris at the end of the sixteenth century and was extended to the provinces in the seventeenth when the power of the monarchy reached its peak. In some cases, as at Nancy (Lavedan, 1959, 106–10, 315–19) and Marseilles (Baratier, 1973, 163–5), completely new districts were laid out. Nearly all the schemes, large and small, observed the classical principles of urban design which had been revived and refined in the Renaissance. Order, symmetry and vista became the ideal.

Royal powers did not stretch to the reconstruction of the medieval cores, but municipal efforts to stop buildings encroaching on public streets were reinforced by the crude *alignement* (building line) procedure established by an edict of Henri IV in 1607 (Bergel, 1973, 4–5). In principle, this enactment required owners to obtain permission before erecting a new house on a main thoroughfare. It thus encouraged the emergence, from the seventeenth century, of rudimentary supervision of the fire safety of new buildings in the larger towns. In Paris, the dual growth of building congestion and administrative expertise culminated shortly before the Revolution in the introduction of the most comprehensive building code in Europe. In a royal declaration of 1783 a minimum width of nine metres was fixed for new streets, and all new houses were subjected to height maxima related to the method of construction and the width of the streets onto which they faced. The declaration also provided for the progressive widening of established streets by the enforcement of new *alignements* when rebuilding occurred (Jourdan, 1900, 20 ff.).

Although these controls were the product of arbitrary royal power (the streets of Paris were legally part of the royal domain), they were too useful to be abandoned at the Revolution. Provisionally confirmed in Paris by a law of 1791, they or variants of them began to be adopted by other big cities under the new, two-tier system of local government based on district authorities (*communes*) and *départements* (Jourdan, 1890, 6). The *alignement* powers were finally codified in a typical piece of Napoleonic legislation, the law of 16 September 1807 on the drainage of marshlands. Based on an order of 1796 relating to Paris only (Rouleau, 1967, 88–9), its urban clauses empowered all towns to draw up plans showing the desired *alignements* of all their streets and other public places, including those not yet in existence. After approval of the plans by the prefect of the *département* and the central government, the mayors were empowered to require all new building to conform to the *alignement*. Lands ceded to the highway in execution of the *alignement* were to be compensated at their assessed value only, with no indemnity paid for disturbance. General powers of compulsory purchase were also clarified. Moreover, where public works increased the value of adjacent lands, the owners were to be liable to taxation on the betterment value (Des Cilleuls,

1877, 153, 243, 346).

In principle, the 1807 law permitted urban authorities to draw up fully articulated plans for all public spaces in their existing built-up areas and outside, and to carry out ambitious improvement programmes in execution of them. This was certainly the result sought by Napoleon, whose ambitious programme of public works and *alignement* revisions in Paris indicated what he envisaged for the rest of France (Lavedan, 1952, 8–30). Germany also benefited, in that the example of the 1807 powers contributed to the successful regularization of the arbitrary urban controls of the princes in many of the states reformed under French influence in the early 1800s. Ironically, however, the most important feature of German practice, the power to plan new streets in unbuilt areas, never took root in France. After some early decisions in favour of the principle, the courts began to rule (much as they did in the United States) that restrictions could not rightfully be enforced on landowners in respect of streets which were not yet in existence. This principle was confirmed beyond all further dispute by a decision of the court of appeal in 1837 (Hottenger, 1913, 22). The ruling meant that if urban authorities wanted to lay out new streets they had to use compulsory-purchase powers to acquire the necessary land, incurring heavy indemnities for disturbance. As a result, most continued to leave it to the landowners to lay out new peripheral streets. Even those towns such as Lyons, which had been planning new street systems as recently as the late-eighteenth century, desisted from the practice in the early nineteenth (Latreille, 1975, 273).

The emasculation of the 1807 powers meant that when French towns began once again to expand, in the 1820s, they did so largely at the initiative of the landowners. However, as in Britain, a modicum of order was imposed by established roadways. In addition to the national and departmental roads, the width and line of which were laid down, ultimately, by the central government, *alignements* were also fixed, by the general council of each *département*, for roads, lanes and even tracks of purely local interest. Under the *ancien régime* and the Empire the widths allotted, particularly to royal and imperial (later, national) roads, had been very generous (e.g. Rouleau, 1967, 69–70). During the nineteenth century the authorities maintained this tradition, often with an eye to the needs of expanding urban areas.

The municipal authorities, for their part, did their best to persuade owners to observe basic standards of width, paving and drainage in their new streets by refusing, or threatening to refuse, adoption of defective thoroughfares. In most of France, landownership near the towns was not as fragmented as it had come to be in much of western Germany. Despite the reforms of the revolutionary period much of the land in the vicinity of towns was divided into substantial estates owned by townspeople and worked by tenants (Mollat, 1971, 450–3; Zeldin, 1973, 152). These estates passed easily into building use. Sometimes, even, developers would bring together a number of parcels and promote them as a distinct suburban community. In the Paris area, the most notable examples were

Grenelle and the Batignolles, both launched in the 1820s, and Le Vésinet, founded in 1856 (Mollat, 1971, 466–7; Lavedan, 1975, 375).

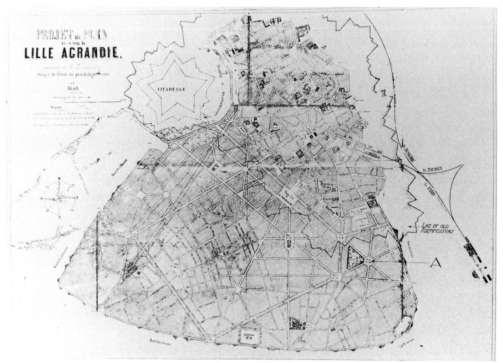

23   *Extension plan for Lille, 1859. The refortification of this frontier town allowed an extension plan, comparable to the best German practice, to be applied to an area outside the old ramparts. It was, however, entirely untypical of the French approach to the peripheral planning of towns.* (TPR, *1914, plate 75*)

However, such coordinated promotions were not representative of the overall growth of Paris, and they played an even smaller part in the provinces (*Aperçu*, 130–9; Gaillard, 1977, 102). More typical was the Paris suburb of Belleville, which evolved during the century from a collection of villages and hamlets outside the *octroi* (municipal customs) wall into one of the best-known working-class districts in Paris. At Belleville, the basic network of main roads, linked by old-established lanes and tracks, was gradually filled out by new residential streets, cul-de-sacs and courts (see Lépidis and Jacomin, 1975). The result was by no means chaotic, but there was nevertheless a marked decline from the generally solid, ordered development along the main streets, through the more variegated building on the new sidestreets, to the often rickety and unhealthy housing lying off the streets in disordered courts, linked by narrow and tortuous tunnels and passages. In refusing to adopt such courts, as they usually did, the authorities contributed to their rapid deterioration once the houses had passed the first flush of youth.

URBAN RECONSTRUCTION, 1850–70

The years between the Restoration and the fall of the July Monarchy in 1848 saw very little development in environmental policy. The cholera outbreak of 1832 generated much the same panic as in Britain but the associated good intentions proved even more ephemeral (see Chevalier, 1958). The only major piece of general legislation, the law on municipal organization of 1837, broke little new ground. It confirmed the power of local authorities to fix *alignements*, but it turned a blind eye to the obstacles that had arisen to their enforcement on the urban periphery. It also failed to reiterate the requirement, which had been implicit in the 1807 law, that towns should maintain a general improvement plan for their streets.

Underlying this complacency was the slow rate of urban growth in France, the product of uneven economic development and a nearly stagnant population. Even in the great provincial seaports and in the growing, coal-based, industrial regions of the north, east and the Rhône valley, urban populations expanded more slowly than in comparable districts in Britain. The urbanized proportion of the population tended to increase overall, but only slowly; as late as 1851 only one Frenchman in four lived in a town (Carrière and Pinchemel, 1963, 86). France thus failed to join the urban revolution which by now was well under way in Britain. Consequently, although the municipal authorities of Paris, Lyons, Bordeaux, Marseilles, Lille and a number of smaller industrial towns were aware of an accumulation of environmental problems, the legislature, dominated by rural representatives, remained largely indifferent to them. The leading towns did what they could, and some made solid progress in improving drainage and water supplies. In Paris, which in contrast to London was already growing as fast or faster than its main provincial satellites, growing congestion, a rising death rate, and fear of public disorder prompted the government to initiate a modest programme of street improvements and other works in the 1840s (Sutcliffe, 1970, 14–19). However, these efforts pale into insignificance in comparison with those of the following two decades.

In 1848, at a time of acute economic depression, the monarchy of Louis-Philippe was overthrown, partly as a result of disorder in the streets of Paris. A new republic, France's second, replaced it. Universal male suffrage was established and a presidential election was held. The man chosen, by a large majority, was Louis-Napoleon, nephew of the late emperor and the official Bonapartist pretender. His democratic credentials were convincing enough at first, but towards the end of his four-year term he began to dig himself in. He assumed personal powers with his *coup d'état* of December 1851, and proclaimed himself emperor a year later. Thereafter his regime had its ups and downs, but it was not seriously threatened until defeat by Prussia brought it down in 1870.

Louis-Napoleon's overriding domestic ambition was to modernize French economic institutions so that the country might resume the European hegemony which it had enjoyed during the First Empire. His main model was England, where he had spent some time in exile, but he also drew on a much older French tradition, recently updated by Saint-Simon and his followers, of centrally-directed public investment. In the long run, however, his ambition was to stimulate private investment and he chose to concentrate State efforts on improvements in communications. Fortunately, the building of long-distance railways had begun in the 1840s and was already attracting substantial private funds. Louis-Napoleon acted to stimulate it further, but it also proved possible from the early 1850s to devote major public funds to a secondary objective, the improvement of communications within the big cities (see Girard, 1952).

The immediate stimulus to the building of new streets was the need to provide access to the new railway stations, but there were such important related advantages that it amounted almost to an urban panacea. New sewerage and water-distribution systems could be built more cheaply in association with street improvements. Some of the worst slum districts could be decimated, to the advantage of both public health and public order. Visual order, too, could be imposed on districts old and new in accordance with the royal and imperial traditions beloved of even the most republican of Frenchmen. Above all, the authorities recognized that urban public works directly stimulated the building industry and so reduced unemployment more effectively than any other form of contrived stimulus. The multiplier effects of a building boom were not unappreciated, being summed up in the businessman's saw, 'when the building industry does well, everything does well'.

It took much prodding and encouragement by the central government to make the larger urban authorities see the advantages of ambitious improvement programmes, but after the early 1850s many of them became enthusiastic agents of a programme of urban reconstruction unrivalled in the world. Paris, Lyons and Marseilles were the towns most affected. More modest works were undertaken in Bordeaux, Lille, Le Havre, Toulon, Montpellier, Toulouse, Rouen and Brest (Leonard, 1961, 2–3). In Paris and some of the other towns the initial investment was supported by government capital grants. From the later 1850s the national assembly refused to approve further subsidies, but momentum was sustained by local borrowing and a wave of private investment which shifted into building after the completion of the main railway network.

The scale of public investment (over £100 million was spent on capital schemes in Paris during the Second Empire) called out for a coherent programme. The guiding strategy was worked out in the first instance for Paris, and diffused almost unmodified to the other towns. In Paris the strategy was the product of three major contributions – Louis-Napoleon's aspirations to modernize the city, the expertise of Georges Haussmann, the Prefect of the Seine whom he appointed to direct the works in 1853, and the experience accumulated by the municipal and departmental authorities from the more hesitant modernization efforts of the 1840s.

The main emphasis was on the improvement of street communications within the congested medieval core, and between the core and the outskirts. The resulting easier movement would allow the city's main institutions to remain at the most accessible point, the city centre, and would reduce building congestion by encouraging residential development on the periphery (Haussmann, 1890, II, 33–4). To these ends, a network of radial and ring streets was planned, with the biggest effort devoted to the central areas. A number of new arteries were planned to open up under-built peripheral districts, but the division of virgin land into building sites by sidestreets was left almost entirely to private developers, except in the fashionable north-western suburbs. Sewer and water improvements were planned in conjunction with the new streets, as were a number of public buildings, and a few new parks in the outer districts (see Pinkney, 1958; Leonard, 1961).

As a strategy for public investment the Parisian programme was comprehensive and, according to the lights of the time, well thought out. It fell short of comprehensive urban planning, however, in its approach to private development. Most of the land in the city remained in private hands throughout the modernization process, and in its development or redevelopment it was subject only to the normal building regulations. To acquire more land than was needed for the streets themselves was difficult and expensive. The compulsory purchase powers of 1807 had been modified by the law of 3 May 1841, but this was a classic railway-building instrument which, when used in towns, revealed the normal defects. Louis-Napoleon made early use of his personal powers to supplement it by the decree-law of 25 March 1852. This allowed the Paris authorities to expropriate sites affected by street-improvement schemes in their entirety if the remnants lying off the new streets were unsuitable in size or shape for the construction of healthy buildings.

During the 1850s the courts smiled on these new powers, and Haussmann used them to carry out a number of schemes which amounted to area clearance, notably on the island of the Cité. The decree-law was also adopted, as its final clause permitted, by most of the other towns engaged in public works. In the following decade, however, a sullen opposition began to make itself felt at all levels of French society to the emperor's constant political and legal *leger-de-main*. The courts began to favour a more restrictive interpretation of the compulsory-purchase powers while compensation, which was fixed by panels of property-owners, rapidly inflated. Now the authorities were able to acquire no more than narrow strips of backland along the new thoroughfares. They were sufficient to bear the continuous four- to six-storey apartment houses which proliferated during the Second Empire, but the result was nearly always a narrow corridor of redevelopment virtually unrelated to the urban fabric on either side. Consequently, the new thoroughfares did very little to bring about the reconstruction of older districts or to shape the development of new ones. On the contrary, by displacing numerous poor tenants they tended to increase overcrowding and physical deterioration in slums nearby. In theory, powers were available under the Melun law of 13 April 1850 (named after its promoter, the Vicomte de Melun) to inspect, improve and, if necessary, to demolish unhealthy dwellings (text in Guerrand, 1967, 316—18). However, the Melun law was not the product of government initiative and its clumsy procedures were unsuitable for the ambitious intervention desired by the imperial authorities (Guerrand, 1967, 12—13, 72—3; Des Cilleuls, 1877, 135—226). Consequently, very little use was made of it during the Second Empire, or indeed thereafter.

The authorities' basic unwillingness to disturb private interests was also reflected in the building regulations. During the first half of the nineteenth century there had been very little development, in Paris or anywhere else, of the late-eighteenth-century codes. In anticipation of a building boom, the decree-law of 25 March 1852 allowed the Parisian authorities (and those of any other town which adopted it) to draw up regulations in the interests of public safety and health. However, no change was effected in the Paris regulations until 1859 when an effort was made to restrict high building. The maximum facade-height of houses facing wide streets was reduced from 20 to 17.55 metres, and height controls were extended to buildings facing interior courts and passages. For the first time a minimum height for ceilings was laid down, at 2.60 metres. These new controls generated such criticism that they were modified in 1864 to allow facades to rise up to twenty metres in streets twenty metres or more in width, thus restoring the maximum of 1783 (Sutcliffe, 1970, 262—3). In sum, new building in Second Empire Paris was not substantially more restricted than under Louis XVI. The result, in a period of publicly-stimulated property boom, was the multiplication of tall, densely-packed blocks even in the outer districts of the city. As for the other towns which adopted the 1852 decree-law, most based their building regulations on those in force in Paris. Thus they encouraged more intensive development than their lower land values might otherwise have required.

THE QUIET YEARS, 1870—c.1900

By the end of the 1860s the urban reconstruction programme was grinding to a halt throughout France. Once the first, most urgently needed streets had been built, usually to great public acclaim, there was nothing to do but build more and more of them. Diminishing returns set in, costs rose, and the public began to react against high taxes and constant disruption. In 1870 Napoleon III, under pressure on a number of fronts, dismissed Haussmann. Before the end of the year the disastrous war with Prussia brought the work to a complete halt. Then followed a change of constitution, the Paris Commune of 1871, and the world economic crisis of 1873. Not until the middle and later 1870s was there any question of resuming urban improvements and by this time the full cost of the imperial approach had sunk in on the municipal authorities. In Paris and Lyons elected councils had replaced the compliant nominated commissions of the Second

Empire. Heavy, new borrowing, government subsidies, and concealed financing were now out of the question. In fact, the time was ripe for a full reappraisal of the imperial strategy.

24 *Rue St Martin, Paris. Haussmann's failure to push his widening scheme beyond the first junction north of the Rue de Rivoli symbolizes the obstacles which massive renewal schemes can generate in the absence of control over land values. (Photo: the author)*

That no such reappraisal occurred was largely the result of the massive inertia generated before 1870, which the depressed economic conditions of the 1870s paradoxically reinforced. The fall in property values convinced the Parisian authorities that the more important of the streets left unfinished by Haussmann could be completed without incurring excessive debts. The inexperienced city council concurred and it proved possible to complete one of the grandest of the imperial thoroughfares, the Avenue de l'Opéra, in time for the Paris exhibition of 1878. Thus renewed, the strategy survived into the 1880s and the 1890s, encountering much the same problems as under the Second Empire, but not on a scale sufficient to force radical re-thinking. As before, the provincial towns largely followed the Parisian example, with rather less physical achievement. Only in the later 1890s, when the Paris authorities began to build an underground railway system, nearly forty years after the first underground line had opened in London, was there any clear sign of new thinking.

Admittedly, there were some areas of environmental policy in which progress was made between 1870 and the end of the century. Medical knowledge greatly advanced, under the leadership of Pasteur. Understanding of the relationship between public health and the physical environment improved, much as it did in Germany. More and more towns adopted the decree-law of 25 March 1852 and drew up building regulations — over 200 had done so by the early 1900s (*DPC*, 28 May 1915, 784). Building codes tended to become more severe, particularly with regard to the ventilation and lighting of interior rooms via courts and airshafts. The problem of pulmonary tuberculosis, more acute in the larger French cities than almost anywhere else in Europe, was increasingly recognized as other infectious diseases were brought under control. Water supplies were improved and there was a distinct spread of waterborne sewerage systems from the mid-1880s (Guerrand, 1967, 214).

None of these achievements, however, can mask the underlying malaise of French urban environmental policy. There was no progress towards area slum clearance and rehousing. The planning of suburban areas, and the encouragement of rapid transport to them, were virtually unconsidered. Hardly any new parks were added to those created under the Second Empire. As for differential building regulations and zoning, they do not appear to have entered into the heads of French urban administrators even in the 1890s, apart from the rudimentary banning of noxious industries from populous districts. Even civic beautification no longer warmed the municipal heart. Not only in Germany, but in Britain and the United States as well, we have detected *some* progress towards comprehensive planning by the end of the century. But in France — almost nothing.

How are we to account for these slumbers? Much of the answer lies in the French urbanization process. After about 1870 France resumed the low rate of population growth which it had experienced in the first half of the nineteenth century. Between the censuses of 1872 and 1911 the national population increased by a mere 10 per cent, from thirty-six million to thirty-nine and a half million people. Economic development proceeded at a respectable rate, and the urbanized proportion of the population, which had risen from 25 to 30 per cent during the Second Empire, reached 44 per cent in 1911. This was well below the German Empire's 60 per cent, but not sufficiently so to suggest a markedly retarded economy. The real contrast with Germany emerges from the absolute numbers involved. The urban population of France rose by six and a quarter million people between 1872 and 1911. In the German Empire, during a similar period, it increased by twenty-four millions. As in Germany, and for much the same reasons, the increase was concentrated in the larger towns, but even these grew at a placid rate. The Paris conurbation, which was still the fastest-growing urban centre in France, increased its population by only 66 per cent between 1872 and 1911, slightly less than the increase which it had registered between

1851 and 1866 (Carrière and Pinchemel, 1963, 119). The population of Lyons, already 384,000 in 1876, was still only 465,000 twenty years later (Latreille, 1975, 389). In short, the years after 1870 were an anti-climax. Building coped quite well with demand, and the acute land speculation which rapid urban growth generated in Germany was not reproduced in France. Even political disorder faded under the Third Republic, and the threat of revolution made in the streets of Paris and other cities dwindled. Urban death rates, which had been reduced in the modernized cities during the Second Empire, continued to fall after 1870. No really new challenges emerged to face the urban administrations. Indeed, the massive urban investment under the Second Empire, which for reasons of national policy had taken place well in advance of local demand, had to a large extent provided for the needs of a number of years to come, and the administrations could safely rest on their laurels. Moreover, the great expertise generated by the efforts of the 1850s and 1860s tended to live on, especially through the paid administrators, who persisted in the methods which had apparently worked in the past. At Paris, for instance, Jean Alphand, who had planned the Paris parks under Haussmann, became director of works after the latter's fall and retained the post until his death in 1892. Though a competent and widely-respected official, he remained faithful to the methods of the Second Empire and was largely responsible for the efforts to complete Haussmann's street plan (Sutcliffe, 1970, 220).

Of course, new approaches were difficult to generate under legislation which was principally appropriate to the Haussmannic strategy. And hardly any new legislation emerged between 1870 and the early 1900s. Partly to blame was the lack of demand for new powers from Paris and the other leading cities. However, parliament itself was a serious obstacle to progress. With the urban population of France still in a distinct minority, and an electoral system which overrepresented the countryside, the Chamber of Deputies remained dominated by rural representatives (Zeldin, 1973, 574–6). The close control which parliament liked to exercise over the executive meant that few governments came to power with a clear programme of domestic legislation and most social reform measures were promoted by private members. Some were fortunate enough to secure government support, which could shorten the tortuous parliamentary procedures, but the frequent changes of administration killed many such measures. Moreover, the indifference of many deputies to any but the interests of their own constituencies, a product of the electoral system, was a serious discouragement to all reform legislation. If a bill passed through the Chamber it usually met further trouble in the Senate, a body with all the negative characteristics of the Chamber plus a fine eye for legal niceties and administrative precedent (Zeldin, 1973, 591–2). One example will suffice. In 1886 Jules Siegfried, the former mayor of Le Havre, who had just been elected to the Chamber, deposited a bill requiring all towns of more than moderate size to draw up and enforce public health regulations, including powers to inspect, and where necessary to demolish, insanitary housing. The measure had much in common with the English public health statutes of the early 1870s. After various adventures, including several visits to the Senate, the bill finally became law, in a much amended form, on 15 February 1902. It was the first important measure affecting unhealthy dwellings since the Melun law of 1850! (Guerrand, 1967, 227).

A CHANGING CLIMATE: THE TURN OF THE CENTURY

The public health law of 1902 was the first big sign of a change in the general climate of French opinion in regard to the urban environment. For the first time parliament had been persuaded to accept the principle that all towns should maintain certain minimum environmental standards. In thus bruising the counter-principle of local autonomy which had largely held sway since 1870, the law paved the way for further efforts to achieve environmental improvement through parliament. With the help of hindsight, it can be identified as the first real achievement of an environmental reform campaign which was to culminate in 1919 in the passing of a town-planning law comparable to the British statute of 1909. The parallel with Britain would be less striking if we examined the nature of the campaign (as we shall shortly proceed to do) and the impact of the 1919 legislation (analysis of which, as a virtual failure, we shall not attempt). Nevertheless, in the early 1900s a new breeze began to blow through the cities of France.

The breeze was generated by a combination of changed realities and new perceptions. At the root of it all lay a slight but perceptible acceleration of the urbanization process from the mid-1890s. With a higher rate of economic growth generally sustained from then until the war (Dupeux, 1974, 156), a new wave of social-overhead investment took place in the towns. In addition to house-building, public transport attracted considerable funds now that electric tramway traction was available. The total length of tramlines and the annual number of passengers both increased roughly threefold between 1895 and 1914 (McKay, 1976, 82). These developments accelerated the outward expansion of urban areas, and particularly of Paris and the large provincial cities, which absorbed most of the new growth of urban population (Sorlin, 1969, 111). Faster economic growth and transport improvements also encouraged the expansion of tertiary activities in the central areas and of highly-mechanized industries on the outskirts. For the first time, a really clear segregation of functions began to emerge in the larger French cities and the process of suburbanization became something to be reckoned with.

The economic revival contributed to a reinvigoration of municipal enterprise from the later 1890s. This was further stimulated by an important Leftward shift in the urban vote during the decade, and the increasing attention claimed by questions of social policy (Anderson, 1977, 5, 15–16). At national level a realignment of the Centre and Right produced a series of moderate governments in the

1890s, but in the city councils (which since 1870 had been elected by full manhood suffrage) the socialists and radicals achieved considerable influence. From the turn of the century, after the upheavals of the Dreyfus affair, the Left generally strengthened its position at all levels. Growing concern with clerical issues up to 1905 and with defence thereafter, and the vagaries of the French parliamentary system, continued to obstruct the passage of sweeping social reform legislation, even during Clemenceau's radical government of 1906–9 (Anderson, 1977, 26; Zeldin, 1973, 698). However, in the cities an atmosphere favourable to municipal activity continued to develop. Although French municipal enterprise lagged well behind that of Britain and Germany, the 'municipal socialism' debate of the early 1900s had its echoes in France, and a definite tendency towards greater municipalization of services is visible between 1900 and 1914 (see e.g. *CM*, 1911, 51; Bellet and Darvillé, 1914).

Although these new circumstances certainly created a climate more favourable to the emergence of urban planning than had existed before 1900, many of the key elements of the conjunctures within which planning was perfected in Germany and adopted in Britain were missing in France. The informed public had no equivalent of the Boer War to concentrate its attention on the harmful effects of the urban environment. Admittedly, fear of German might was on the increase but its urban implications were slight; the majority of conscripts were still of peasant stock. There was not much depopulation of the countryside to worry about – there had been nearly twenty-five million rustics in France in 1872 and there were still twenty-three million in 1901 and twenty-two million ten years later (see e.g. Guillou, 1905). Strikes and civil disturbances grew in number in the early 1900s, but the ultimate stability of French society was doubted by few. The French housing reform movement was a pitiful shadow of its British equivalent. The creation of park systems was not a gripping issue in a country where traditional landscapes could still be found not far from the heart of most towns. The most sedate, well-fed and bookish middle class in Europe was largely indifferent to sportsfields and playgrounds.

How, then, did the idea of town planning emerge in France? There were two main sources, neither of them especially prolific. In Paris, a socially-aware minority among the intelligentsia, equipped by education and inclination to draw on foreign experience, gradually distilled the idea of planning out of various disparate and even selfish preoccupations. In some of the leading provincial cities, notably Lyons and Nancy, the growth of municipal enterprise slowly drew official thinking in the same direction. The Parisian was the more important source of the two, and the capital's concerns dominated the parliamentary discussions on planning which began in 1908.

During the 1890s Paris reinforced its position as the most dynamic urban area in France. A new generation of mechanized industries, with the growth areas of engineering, electricals and chemicals especially prominent, established itself in the suburbs (Lavedan, 1975, 487; Bastié, 1964, 147–60). Confirmation of the city's position as the main money market on the continent of Europe produced an important extension and consolidation of the principal business district, between the Bank of France and the Gare Saint-Lazare. The huge success of the 1889 exhibition strengthened the already considerable role of Paris as a world pleasure centre. The ensuing *belle époque* was crowned by the even more brilliant exhibition of 1900, which marked the first maturity of mass international middle-class tourism.

The Parisian authorities responded to these new opportunities with some vigour. From the later 1890s an energetic but diplomatic new Prefect of the Seine, Justin de Selves (1896—1911) struck up a productive partnership with the city council. He helped remove the remaining obstacles, both local and national, to the construction of the underground railway system which had been under intermittent discussion since the early 1870s. The first line was opened in 1900 to serve the exhibition, and construction proceeded rapidly over the next few years, with the bulk of the network complete by 1910. Rightly hailed by contemporaries as the first really new contribution to the physical organization of Paris since Haussmann, the *Métropolitain* was both a symbol of, and a stimulus to, a general civic renaissance. Even the extraordinary municipal election of 1900, in which a wave of anti-Dreyfusard feeling among the Parisian middle classes brought a cohort of inexperienced men onto the council on an *ad hoc* Nationalist ticket, made a positive contribution. A little of the council's stultifying pettiness went out with the defeated councillors, and some of the new members proved to be men of great ability. Outstanding was the firebrand schoolteacher, Louis Dausset. Elected president of the council as early as the 1901—2 municipal year, Dausset went on, as chairman of the budget committee, to become the most active and influential councillor Paris had seen since the opening of the Third Republic. If the city had been allowed an elected mayor, Dausset would certainly have attained that office; as it was, he had to content himself with his profound understanding of the city's affairs and a close working relationship with Prefect De Selves (Sutcliffe, 1970, 220—1).

Thanks partly to Dausset's enthusiasm, the momentum towards the modernization of Paris was sustained into the early 1900s. In 1902, largely in response to pressure from property-owners and architects, a new building code was introduced. The first major departure from the Haussmannic regulations, it sought to encourage adventurous building by allowing enhanced heights and freer treatment of attics, and offering various inducements to builders to set back part or all of their facades from the street. To promote good taste under the new regulations, the authorities institutionalized their annual competition for new facades, descendant of the 1897 architectural competition in the Rue Réaumur (Sutcliffe, 1970, 194). In 1903 the *Société du Nouveau Paris* (Society for a New Paris) was set up to represent a wide range of private interests eager to further the city's modernization. Ambitious architects and engineers were drawn into the society and one of them, the versatile municipal architect-cum-engineer, Eugène Hénard

(1849–1923), produced a series of proposals, 'Les transformations de Paris', for new public works in the city (Wolf, 1968, 20–1; Hénard, 1903–6). Hénard's eight studies, published at intervals between 1903 and 1906, caught the public imagination and were seriously considered by the authorities which, partly under Dausset's influence, were beginning to consider a broad strategy of above-ground improvements to maintain the momentum of the *Métropolitain.*

Hénard's proposals marked some advance over the urban-improvement strategy pursued during the Second Empire. However, in their emphasis on expensive central works they lay securely within the Haussmannic tradition. They contained no hint of decentralization, and even a scheme for a belt of parks on the line of the fortifications (to which we shall return) was presented by Hénard as a gain for the city rather than for the suburbs. Underlying this serious limitation was the general indifference to the suburbs which pervaded much Parisian thought, both official and unofficial. In 1860 the government had extended the city boundaries as far as the fortification ring which Thiers had built in the early 1840s, taking in nearly all the suburbs which had grown up outside the old *octroi* wall since the Napoleonic wars. It had encountered serious opposition in doing so and in the more democratic circumstances of the Third Republic there was no question of further annexations, even though little open building land remained in the city after 1870 and a growing proportion of the total population increase of the Paris agglomeration occurred in a new ring of suburbs outside the fortifications (Mollat, 1971, 466).

These areas were by no means deprived of government. The suburban communities had no difficulty in retaining or obtaining incorporation as independent *communes* and as most lay within the *département* of the Seine they enjoyed the supervision of the same prefectoral administration as did the City of Paris. Their elected representatives sat with the Parisian councillors in the general council of the Seine. However, while successfully postponing the need for radical reform, these arrangements produced a quality of local administration which, in all but a few of the rich, western suburbs, fell well below Parisian standards. Sewerage and water arrangements were generally poor, new building was virtually unregulated, and public amenities were almost non-existent (*Considérations*, 1913, 81). For the increasingly working- and lower-middle-class suburban populations these disadvantages were largely outweighed by low living costs, and the last thing they wanted was a Parisian annexation which would immediately subject them to the dreaded *octroi*. As for the increasingly middle- and upper-class population of Paris, it had no desire to face the extra taxation which the adhesion of poor and ill-equipped suburbs would have made necessary.

As the suburbs deteriorated, a process which accelerated from the 1890s as heavy industry spread to form an almost continuous girdle around the city (see Mollat, 1971, 493), the Parisian upper and middle classes increasingly turned in on themselves. Far from copying their British and American counterparts by seeking solace in the suburbs, they took growing pleasure in the urbane atmosphere of the city centre and the western apartment districts near the Bois de Boulogne which combined increasingly dense building with fashionable appeal. To escape the stifling summer heat more and more of the rich took advantage of improved railway services to migrate to villas or apartments in mushrooming spas and resorts such as Vichy and Nice which offered an echo of Parisian elegance (Zeldin, 1973, 17; Mollat, 1971, 505). As humbler members of the middle classes followed their example, second homes in the Paris environs were abandoned to the pullulating suburbanites and the estates which surrounded the larger of them were freely sold for building (*Aperçu*, 1913, 232—3). By the end of the nineteenth century Paris and its suburbs were well on the way to forming two distinct societies (*Aperçu*, 1913, 235—8), a state of affairs which was epitomized by the city council's refusal to allow any of the *Métro* lines to leave the city or to link up with suburban railways, in case they encouraged taxpayers to migrate outside the boundaries.

Clearly, this neglect of the suburbs was inimical to the generation of serious thinking about comprehensive urban planning. However, a growing minority of the Parisian intelligentsia began around 1900 to develop a critique of the city's development which was largely prompted by the circumstances of suburban growth. Aristocrats and others with pretentions to nobility were very thick on the ground in the Paris region, where they resided on their estates and divided their time between the stuffy social life of Versailles, Fontainebleau and similar small towns, and the delights of Paris. A number were also active politically in central or local government. As the suburbs spread some of these nobles copied the Parisian rich and sold their estates, but others resented the intrusion and sought to control or arrest it. They found ready allies in a Parisian upper-class element which continued to value the arcadian retreats of the Paris environs, or disliked the ugliness (and low social tone) of the new suburbs. What crystallized public opinion was the desecration of a number of cherished views by new houses and factories in the suburban boom of the 1890s, and 1901 saw the creation of a Paris-based society, the *Société pour la Protection des Paysages de France* (Society for the protection of French landscapes).

The society's main promoter and first president was a respected Radical deputy, Charles Beauquier (1833—1919). Although he represented the Doubs, Beauquier had long lived in Paris where he engaged in part-time journalism in the fashionable press and dabbled in local history. His society generated strong, mainly upper-class support, and soon set to work to prepare a private bill for Beauquier to deposit in the Chamber. The bill was designed to empower the departmental authorities to classify beautiful or historic pieces of countryside in much the same way as historic monuments could be listed, under legislation dating back to 1837. It included powers to purchase land compulsorily where the owner refused his consent to the listing. Thanks to Beauquier's parliamentary expertise, and his fortuitous position as chairman of the committee which examined the bill, his measure became law on 21 April 1906. Like much private members' legislation, the new law proved weak and difficult to enforce, but it represented an important extension of the principle that restrictions could be imposed in the public interest on the free use of private land. As such, it was to be much cited in later years by advocates of general town-planning controls.

25 *Post-1902 apartment block, Paris. This upper-class residence, built on part of the Champ de Mars sold off for development by the City of Paris after the 1900 Exhibition, provides an extreme example of the overbuilding which could be achieved under the 1902 building regulations. (Photo: Russell Walden)*

Meanwhile, Beauquier's society had formed a close working alliance with a number of interests campaigning for the provision of more open space within the Paris built-up area. Although open space was by no means the most burning issue of the day, it definitely aroused more concern in the early years of the twentieth century than it had done previously. No new parks had been provided in the city of Paris since Haussmann, and there were hardly any public parks or gardens in the suburbs. Growing pressure on land rapidly reduced the number of private gardens in the city in the 1890s. Matters came to a head in 1900 when, in a curious episode, the city authorities introduced a tax on gardens and unbuilt sites. The intention was to reduce part of the regressive *octroi* taxation by a levy which would fall almost exclusively on rich owners of mansions and on land speculators. However, the tax encouraged many humble owners to sell their gardens for building. Within a year or two, public opinion had swung round to condemn the tax as an *encouragement* to speculation and overbuilding. This sudden reaction against building congestion was reinforced by growing experience of the 1902 building regulations, which were used (or mis-used) by many builders to achieve unaccustomed heights, sometimes combined with an even more intensive site usage than had previously been tolerated. The biggest scandal of all surrounded the building of tall apartment blocks on the Champ de Mars, the large parade ground in western Paris, part of which the authorities had decided to sell after the 1900 exhibition. By 1904, what had at first been accepted as a sensible sale of a dusty waste had come to be regarded as a short-sighted sacrifice of valuable open space. For many of the intellectuals and artists who so dominated Parisian opinion, the Champ de Mars symbolized a sell-out to selfish interests which were destroying the true beauty of Paris, and a potent alliance emerged between the advocates of open space and the more venerable campaign for the protection of Old Paris (Sutcliffe, 1970, 179—212).

However, more was involved in the open-space campaign than the rarefied interests of the upper classes. Since the early 1890s there had been a considerable improvement in the quality of Parisian social statistics, and progress in medical knowledge, thanks largely to the discoveries of Koch, had helped draw attention to the extraordinarily high Parisian incidence of pulmonary tuberculosis. In the early 1900s, Ambroise Rendu led a campaign in the city council for the demolition of the main tubercular districts, a course of action which was generally recognized by 1905 as the only means of eradicating the disease. In one of the less glorious episodes of Parisian municipal history, virtually nothing was done to clear the slums but, as a *pis aller*, Rendu was gradually able to arouse interest in his schemes for small public parks and playgrounds in the congested districts.

These medical considerations helped strengthen a growing feeling among social reformers that gardens, allotments and playgrounds, and indeed a general contact with nature, were essential to the full well-being of workers and their families. Although this sentiment did not appeal to the French mind as readily as to the British or American, a number of developments in the early 1900s indicated that it was gaining ground. A movement for the creation of allotment gardens (*jardins ouvriers*) sprang up almost from nothing in the later 1890s, and its leaders organized the first international congress on allotment gardens at Paris in 1903 (*CM*, 1903—4, 69; Rivière, 1904, 30—60). Eight hundred people attended, mostly from France (*MSA*, 1903, 325—9). The creation of more green areas in towns, both public and private, was also one of the most important objectives of the French garden city movement. Set up in 1903 largely on the initiative of Georges Benoît-Lévy, a leisured Parisian reformer who acknowledged Le Play, Ruskin, Morris and Tolstoy as his major inspirations, the *Association des Cités-Jardins de France* attracted a numerically small but influential support among the Parisian intelligentsia, before going on to found a number of provincial branches. Benoît-Lévy himself described his association as part of the same general movement which had produced the conference on allotment gardens

(Benoît-Lévy, 1904, v—vii). In 1904 Benoît-Lévy published the first of a series of books on garden cities. Based on extensive foreign travel, they employed a somewhat lax definition of the term 'garden city' and in *Cités-jardins d'Amérique*, published in 1905, Benoît-Lévy devoted much of his attention to the parks and gardens of established towns.

Benoît-Lévy certainly saw more in the garden city than a means of creating open space, but this aspect of his advocacy soon aroused more public interest than the principles of cooperative production and redemption through beauty which he also espoused. Indeed, in 1906 it was crystallized in a single-minded call for the systematic creation of open space in and around towns, J. C. N. Forestier's *Grandes villes et systèmes de parcs.* Writing in the immediate aftermath of the liberal economist Jules Méline's *Le retour à la terre* (1905), which had advocated a wholesale dismantling of large cities and a return to agriculture and artisan production, Forestier acknowledged the social dangers of large and congested urban areas. Perhaps, he mused, the French people might one day return to the land, but in the meantime society could not work without big cities. In the immediate future all that could be hoped for was the eradication of some of the worst defects of the large agglomerations, and this could most effectively be achieved by the provision of open space. Forestier went on to describe in glowing terms the planned open spaces of Adelaide, Letchworth ('la Garden-City d'Angleterre'), Vienna, Cologne, Boston and other American cities. He was particularly impressed with the park-system technique pioneered in the USA and this example was clearly uppermost in his mind when he came to his major recommendation: 'Parks and schemes for new parks ought to be *included in an overall plan (programme d'ensemble)* in the preparation of which towns, *communes, départements* and provinces ought to work together' (Forestier, 1906, 53).

Hindsight might identify Forestier's book as the first blow in a French town-planning campaign. It was, however, a thin, disjointed piece and it took its place in a Parisian open-space debate which was now beginning to revolve around one issue, the future of the fortifications. In the early 1900s the unusually friendly relations between the city council, the departmental authorities, and the central government had generated the expectation, which was supported by informal discussions, that the State would soon hand over to the city the sixty-year old fortification ring and the field of fire, roughly 250 metres deep, which lay outside it. These defences no longer served any military purpose, and the State's only remaining concern was to secure attractive financial terms for the transfer. At the Hôtel de Ville they at first thought of selling most of the land off for building, but the sudden revulsion of public opinion against congestion generated the view that it should be laid out as a park belt. Eugène Hénard's scheme for such a belt, published in 1903, caught the public imagination, and Hénard's proposals played a big part in a lively debate on the fortifications which flared up in 1905 when a number of rival projects were accorded generous publicity in the Paris press.

The matter might have come to a head there and then if the city authorities and the State could have agreed terms, but the more the transfer was discussed, the more complicated it became. Consequently the debate dragged on into 1906 and 1907 in an atmosphere of growing frustration. As it did so, the use of the fortifications came to be regarded more and more as the key to the problems of the Paris area. The housing reformers saw the zone as a windfall of cheap building land for public utility societies (see Benoît-Lévy, 1905, 425, 442). Councillor Rendu and the other advocates of slum clearance wanted to see displaced residents relocated there, possibly in municipally-built housing. Other councillors and officials had in mind the needs of hospitals, asylums, colleges and other public institutions, increasingly cramped in the densely built city. Hénard and other interested architects delighted in their chance to show how these needs might be reconciled within a single scheme, and the issue evolved from one merely of open space to one of comprehensive development.

Of course, to lay out an area of public land, however extensive, was a far cry from the general urban planning already practised in Germany. Some contributors to the fortifications debate showed an awareness of foreign experience, but it was nearly always vague and limited to the field of open space. The vital extra steps were taken by Jules Siegfried within the social reform institution which he had set up in 1894, the *Musée social*. To understand these developments fully, we must glance briefly at Siegfried's career up to this point.

Jules Siegfried (1837–1922) was born at Mulhouse into a family of cotton textile manufacturers. His upbringing gave him the strong Protestant faith and paternalistic social conscience which were the mark of the Alsatian business elite. After early training in the manufacturing side of the business he went on to gain experience in the cotton import trade with stays at Le Havre and Liverpool. In 1863 he struck out on his own, setting up as a cotton merchant in Bombay and making a huge fortune out of exporting Indian cotton while American supplies were held up by the Civil War. In 1866, with Indian cotton in less demand, he established himself at Le Havre, retaining his Bombay office and setting up new branches in the United States. Although he retained an active interest in the business until 1880, he devoted more and more time to public service, especially after his marriage in 1869 to the daughter of a Mulhouse pastor. In 1870 he was elected to the municipal council of Le Havre and almost immediately became a deputy mayor (*maire-adjoint*). He was elected mayor himself in 1878, and held the office until 1886 (Siegfried, 1946, 5–38; Zeldin, 1973, 68).

The most famous creation of Mulhousian enlightened paternalism was the *Cité ouvrière*, a model settlement of small workers' houses started in 1853 by one of the earliest French housing associations, the *Société mulhousienne des Cités ouvrières*. To encourage thrift, the occupants were allowed to purchase their houses by a system of annual payments, but a variety of communal facilities were provided by the society. By 1867 there were 800 houses and 6,000 residents in the *Cité ouvrière*, and similar colonies had been founded in the nearby towns of Guebwiller, Beaucourt and Colmar (Guerrand, 1967, 122—4). This achievement far outshone the modest activities of housing associations elsewhere in France, which had stagnated after the initial enthusiasm of the early 1850s when Louis-Napoleon had granted them a generous subsidy. Jules Siegfried had been active in the housing associations before he left Mulhouse, and after the German annexation of Alsace prevented his return he promoted a strongly Mulhousean brand of social reform in Le Havre. He believed that happiness and progress rested on a healthy and welcoming home and a secure family life. Consequently he became involved in the foundation of housing associations and grew interested in the design of workers' housing. He maintained a related interest in leisure facilities of an improving type and in 1874 he founded at Le Havre the Cercle Franklin, a suite of meeting rooms for working men. Though his fundamental inclination was to self-help, he greatly extended municipal activity in Le Havre. Having nearly succumbed to typhoid fever in 1879, he became an expert on sanitary matters and in 1882 he founded the first municipal office of hygiene (*bureau d'hygiène*) in France. He planned a network of new streets and boulevards, a waterborne sewerage system, and a slum clearance programme, and drew up an outline plan of *alignements* for the suburbs in anticipation of a boundary extension (Siegfried, 1946, 44—70).

By 1885 Siegfried had made Le Havre into one of France's most admired cities, and it was at this point that he switched his attention to the national stage. Elected as a Republican (i.e., moderate) deputy for Seine-Inférieure, he immediately moved his home to Paris, giving up the mayoralty in the following year. Although he thus fulfilled a long-standing ambition (he had stood unsuccessfully for parliament in 1877), his face never really fitted in the highest political circles. His moderate republicanism and obvious ability should have qualified him to serve in most of the governments of the 1890s and early 1900s, but he took a portfolio only once, in the Ribot administration of 1892—3. His son and biographer, André, blamed this relative failure on his Alsatian background, fortified by periods of residence abroad, which had given him an eclectic, practical outlook similar to that of many Englishmen. Certainly, as a Protestant and free-trader he stood outside the mainstream of French politics and his freedom from executive responsibilities no doubt contributed to the determination with which he pursued a large number of social reform objectives. In addition to public health, he developed interests in friendly societies (*mutualisme*), cooperation, employment insurance, old-age pensions, and the abatement of unemployment (Siegfried, 1946, 7, 100—35).

In 1889 Siegfried helped to organize the 'social economy' and workers' housing displays at the Paris exhibition, under the aegis of the Ministry of Commerce and Industry. In June an international congress of low-cost housing (*habitations à bon marché*) was held in the exhibition premises. Siegfried was active throughout the summer both at the exhibition and in his own *salon*, where many French and foreign reformers congregated. In December, in execution of a decision of the housing congress, Siegfried convened a meeting of a number of people who had participated in the housing exhibit. The assembly constituted itself as the *Société française des Habitations à bon marché*, which held its first full meeting in February 1890. Though intended purely as a disseminator of information, the society soon identified the need for new legislation to encourage housing associations. In March 1892 Siegfried deposited a bill designed to encourage working-class owner-occupation by tax concessions and deferred repayments, and to stimulate housing association building by further tax concessions and borrowing from charitable trusts and public savings banks. After various adventures in the Senate the bill became law in November 1894 (text in Guerrand, 1967, 319–24). By French standards this was a rapid passage, but the legislation was too weak to have much effect. Meanwhile, Siegfried had completed his four months as Minister of Commerce and, somewhat chastened, was prepared to throw himself into the biggest social reform enterprise of his whole career (Guerrand, 1967, 283–305; Siegfried, 1946, 111, 123).

Since the middle of the nineteenth century many French middle- and upper-class social reformers had revealed a strong positivistic streak, in the sense that they believed that fundamental problems could be resolved by the accumulation of *knowledge*. This idea, which had its origins in the French Enlightenment and had been present in the work of Saint-Simon and other social strategists in the first half of the nineteenth century, was given institutional form in 1856 when Frédéric Le Play founded the *Société internationale d'Economie sociale*. The society published a journal, *La Réforme Sociale*, and organized an important 'social economy' section at the Paris exhibition of 1867. The precedent was followed and enhanced at the exhibitions of 1878 and 1889, and advantage was taken of these occasions to convene national and international meetings on a variety of social questions.

Siegfried was by no means the only individual to be caught up in the excitement of the 1889 programme, which was by far the most brilliant of the series. It attracted a wealthy, retired parliamentarian, the Comte de Chambrun, who later approached Siegfried for advice on social reform bodies to which he might make large donations. After an initial gift to the *Société française des Habitations à bon marché*, Chambrun made others to a variety of causes. Finally, he told Siegfried that he would like to devote a very large amount to the establishment of a new institution, the aim of which would be to develop 'the intellectual, moral and material well-being of the working population'. After consulting two fellow-organizers of the 1889 exhibit, Charles Robert and Emile Cheysson, Siegfried came up with the idea of what amounted to a permanent exhibition and venue for meetings and conferences. Chambrun agreed to provide the necessary funds, which were substantial, and the *Musée social* opened in Paris in November 1894. It was housed in a large building incorporating a library, display space, and meeting rooms (*MSMD*, 1905, no. 1, 5–11).

Under Siegfried's imaginative presidency, the *Musée social* was a great success, at any rate as a debating chamber. Despite his original intention that it should act purely as a source of information, without intruding on the work of the existing reform associations, it developed a programme of regular, plenary meetings which soon generated specialized working groups (*sections*). Quite quickly, it became a large and brilliant *salon* for the more socially aware of the Parisian upper class and aspiring young professionals. Foreign travel was encouraged by generous study-grants, and the resulting reports often stimulated new discussions within the *Musée*. Housing was an important interest but in the late 1890s and early 1900s labour matters took up most of the *Musée*'s attention, reflecting the main political concerns of the period. The only area of interest within which concern was expressed for the environment as a whole was that of 'social hygiene'.

The concept of 'social hygiene', which implied the combination of a healthy environment with correct behaviour by the individual, lay firmly within the French positivistic tradition. Interest in it had been reinforced by progress in sanitary and medical knowledge in the 1890s, and the eventual passage in 1902 of Siegfried's public health bill. Discussion of this belated measure had revealed, at least to some of the members of the *Musée*, that France lagged behind certain other countries in coordinating the various aspects of public policy and private initiative that were relevant to 'social hygiene', and it was in 1902 that the *Musée* sent one of its members, Edouard Fuster, to Germany to report on 'social hygiene' there. On his return, Fuster lectured at a plenary session of the *Musée* on the 'energetic and successful campaign against unhealthy housing, alcoholism and tuberculosis' which he claimed to have discovered in Germany. In the ensuing debate, several leading members of the *Musée*, including Jules Siegfried and Emile Cheysson (at that time president of the League Against Alcoholism), had called for the establishment of 'a federation between the main social-hygiene associations' to promote such a concerted approach in France (*MSA*, 1903, 1–2). The result was yet another body, the *Alliance d'Hygiène sociale*, which started to hold annual conferences from 1904, some of them in provincial centres. In consequence the initiative moved somewhat away from the *Musée*, but it was in 1904 that the *Musée* attached itself to a new aspect of 'social hygiene', the garden city idea. It did so by agreeing to send Georges Benoît-Lévy on a mission to England. Benoît-Lévy, who already had some knowledge of English garden suburbs and model settlements as a result of earlier visits, ensured that his advocacy of the principle conformed to the general objectives of the *Musée*. Early in 1904, for instance, he wrote in an essay on Port Sunlight which the *Musée* published:

> Given that the social question is to a large extent merely a question of hygiene, and given that the happy community is above all (or so it would appear) one whose inhabitants are directed by the laws of social hygiene, we believe that it is impossible to overestimate the social significance of the garden cities whose recent creation in England merits the full attention of the sociologist. (*MSMD*, 1904, no. 1, 1)

Benoît-Lévy's main objective in 1904 was to study Letchworth, which he had only just heard about in a lecture on 'social hygiene' by Charles Gide, France's leading advocate of cooperation and a professor at the Paris Law Faculty. According to Benoît-Lévy, Gide had inspired him with his evocation of a model town which would outshine all the previous utopian visions of Fourier and other idealists (*MSA*, 1904, 67; Benoît-Lévy, 1904, 8—10). Later in the year the *Musée* sponsored Benoît-Lévy's American visit. Admittedly, the *Musée* disbursed such sponsorships fairly freely, but in July 1904 André Lichtenberger, associate director of the *Musée*, joined Benoît-Lévy in London at the first international garden city congress and made a speech affirming the *Musée*'s strong interest in the garden city idea (*MSA*, 1904, 464—7). Thereafter Benoît-Lévy, whose individualistic personality belied his interest in cooperation, began to plough his own furrow as president of his own association, the pretensions of which far outran its real influence. However, news of British developments now reached the *Musée* more readily than in the past and their significance was particularly plain to Jules Siegfried.

THE CAMPAIGN FOR PLANNING LEGISLATION

It was at the very beginning of 1908 that Siegfried took his crucial decision to set up a new section of the *Musée social* to study the environment. For some time he had been aware of German achievements in extension planning and the developing English enthusiasm for the idea. It was, however, a new wave of concern over the future of the Paris fortifications that finally prompted him to action. On the last day of December 1907, the City Council had decided to invite the Prefect of the Seine to begin negotiations with the State authorities for the transfer of an initial section of the fortification ring. Hopes for an early agreement were high, and the thoughts of many in Paris turned once more to the use that would be made of the land. By coincidence, Benoît-Lévy was due to address the *Musée* on 'Open spaces in Paris' on 14 January 1908. About a week earlier, Siegfried wrote to a couple of dozen members of the *Musée* and other interested individuals to suggest that they take advantage of the occasion to hold the inaugural meeting of an 'Urban and Rural Hygiene Section'. This distinguished group duly met and Siegfried, expanding on a letter of invitation which had referred to a number of matters of environmental concern, remarked:

> Of all these questions, that of open spaces currently dominates everyone's attention. One thing is definite: towns urgently need extension plans. Many French *communes* hardly even have a set of by-laws to regulate their thoroughfares. (*MSA*, 1908, 56—8)

In the discussion, several members dwelt on the problem of the Paris fortifications, and it was agreed to devote the second meeting of the section, later in January, entirely to this issue. This second meeting largely dictated the course of a third, in March, by which time the section had agreed to mount a concerted campaign to influence public opinion in favour of the urgent conversion of the fortifications into a park belt much on the lines suggested by Hénard, who was a founder member of the section (*MSA*, 1908, 58–61, 118–25). Many contributors were preoccupied by the needs of the city of Paris and Siegfried had to fight hard to maintain a broader perspective. However, he won some support for his view that the adoption of 'a general plan for the suburbs' need not conflict with the provision of open spaces within Paris. Augustin Rey, the architect and housing reformer, told the section that Councillor Rendu favoured the idea, and that an extension-planning measure was under discussion in England. Eventually, it was agreed to set up two sub-committees, one to study the planning of open spaces on both sides of the Paris municipal boundary, and the other to investigate the legislative and administrative implications of the idea.

Two further meetings in April dwelt almost exclusively on the fortifications and on the conservation of existing open spaces in the Paris region, and Siegfried's suggestion that they consider the general future of Paris aroused no immediate response. However, a characteristic complaint from Forestier, who bemoaned the lack of visually impressive road exits from Paris, bore unexpected fruit in that it encouraged the legislative sub-committee to come to the section in May with proposals which extended beyond the provision of open space (*MSA*, 1908, 184–92). It wanted to see the creation around Paris of a network of radial and ring roads, and the preparation of twenty-year development plans for large cities, with powers to purchase land compulsorily at the original value. The section approved these proposals, thus encouraging the dominant figure in the sub-committee, Georges Risler (another retired industrialist and housing reformer of Mulhousean ancestry), to pursue a growing interest in extension planning which would soon rival that of Siegfried himself.

In June the success of a public meeting on the open-space question, which the *Musée* organized at the Sorbonne, convinced Siegfried that the time was ripe to seek legislation. On 1 July 1908 he and fifty-one fellow deputies, including Charles Beauquier, deposited a bill relating to the fortifications and the open spaces of the Paris conurbation (*DoPC*, so, 1908, 637–8). It included, in modified form, a proposal originally generated by Risler's sub-committee, that a general planning committee (*commission supérieure d'aménagement*) should be established for the Paris conurbation, under the chairmanship of the Minister of the Interior:

> This committee will be required to draw up, in consultation with the City of Paris and the suburban municipalities, an extension plan for the city. The plan will include all thoroughfares to be created or widened, and all lands to be designated as open space. The commission would also give attention to the conservation and enhancement of the State forests and to the regulations of public hygiene which might apply to private properties. Its authority will extend over a zone ten kilometres in depth around the present fortifications. (*DoPC*, se, 1912, 112)

In the mythology of the French planning movement, Siegfried's action has come to be regarded as the first blow in a parliamentary campaign for planning powers which first bore fruit in 1919. However, 'campaign' is a misleading term if it suggests the accumulation of irresistible momentum. Until the war the advocates of planning in the Chamber did little more than keep the idea in the air in the hope that a surge of backbench opinion, or government favour, would secure the necessary parliamentary time and drafting expertise. In the continuing absence of both they had no need to put much study into their bills, and the somewhat effete forum of the *Musée social*, sometimes in association with other Paris-based pressure groups, remained the principal locus of the planning debate until 1914. The war earned planning more serious consideration, but the fundamental frustrations and weaknesses remained.

Some brief account of the parliamentary events of these years is nevertheless necessary. Despite a lively debate in the Chamber in January 1909 the fortifications issue did not survive the continued failure of the State and the City of Paris to secure a financial agreement, and Siegfried's Paris planning bill never even reached committee (*MSA*, 1909, 54–60). To keep the whole question alive, Charles Beauquier brought forward, in January 1909, a bill of five brief articles requiring all towns of more than 10,000 inhabitants to draw up 'extension and embellishment plans' (*DoPC*, so, 1909, 80–2). Such plans would 'establish the location of public gardens, planted squares, parks and open spaces, lay down the width and direction of the thoroughfares and the way in which the houses are to be built, and, in a general way, impose a variety of hygienic and artistic restrictions with a view to the embellishment of the town and the improvement of sanitary conditions within it'. Although the exact provenance of this bill is unclear, it was almost certainly the product of largely informal discussions between Risler and his sub-committee, Benoît-Lévy and his garden cities association, and Beauquier's countryside preservationists, conducted in a number of Paris salons (see De Souza, 1913, 225). Beauquier doubtless agreed to present it because he was still chairman of the committee of the Chamber which studied all legislation affecting local government, and could therefore hope to repeat his memorable success of 1906. Indeed, the bill emerged from Beauquier's committee, in slightly amended form, as early as December 1909 (*DoPC*, se, 1909, 254–5). However, it was still a crude and sketchy piece of work and it quickly sank into oblivion when parliament was dissolved early in 1910.

In July 1910, after the general election, Beauquier, Siegfried and eighteen other deputies requested the reprise of the Beauquier bill (*DPC*, 5 July 1910, 2419–20). Once again it was sent to Beauquier's committee, but Beauquier soon recognized its deficiencies and took it to Risler's sub-committee at the *Musée social*. After some delay it re-emerged as a 'bill for town development and extension plans', which Siegfried brought to the Chamber in November 1912 (*DPC*, 28 November 1912, 2856; *DoPC*, se, 1912, 112–13). Now a more impressive text, it was sent to Beauquier's committee where it was joined, early in 1913, by a bill for the establishment of road and open-space plans by the prefectoral authorities in each *département* (*DoPC*, so, 1913, 7). This bill had been presented by Amédée Chenal, a deputy from the Paris area.

It was in June 1913 that the local government committee reported on the Siegfried and Chenal bills, together with the original Beauquier bill. Now under the chairmanship of Joseph Cornudet, a liberal (Progressive Republican) deputy from the Paris region, it had produced a composite bill based largely on the Siegfried proposals (*DoPC*, so, 1913, 916–21). Encouraging though these developments were, the Cornudet bill went into limbo for lack of parliamentary time until it fell victim to a new dissolution of parliament. Its reprise was agreed by the new parliament in June 1914 (*DPC*, 23 June 1914, 2566–7), but the war then threw the legislative programme into complete disorder. It re-emerged from Cornudet's committee in May 1915, by which time it had secured government support (*DoPC*, so, 1915, 233–9). Debated in late May and early June, it was at last passed by the Chamber and sent up to the Senate (*DPC*, 28 May 1915, 1 June 1915, 782–821). The Senate immediately sent it to committee. Unfortunately, all the papers were then lost, ostensibly as a result of the death of the chairman, and the Senate appears to have forgotten about the bill until March 1918, when it received an urgent reminder from the Chamber (*DPC*, so, 14 March 1918, 919–20). When the war ended the Senate found itself under government pressure and it at last passed the bill, with amendments, in December 1918 (*Sénat*, so, 27 December 1918, 875–8). The text returned to the Chamber where it was passed in February 1919, becoming law immediately thereafter.

No detailed analysis of the Cornudet law is necessary (*Bulletin*, nouvelle série, IX, 1919, 558–63). For all this effort and delay, it marked very little advance over the Beauquier bill of 1909. It was a general injunction to towns of more than 10,000 people to draw up, within three years, 'a development, embellishment and extension project'. This plan was to include streets, open spaces, and sites for public buildings, together with building and public health regulations, and arrangements for water supply and sewerage. The financial aspects and relationships with the landowners were virtually ignored – a procedure for the compulsory purchase of land during a thirty-year plan period at its original value, which Siegfried had included in his 1912 bill, had been deleted in committee almost immediately owing to its controversial character. Admittedly, it was normal French procedure to fill in the gaps in legislation such as this by issuing a detailed set of administrative regulations prepared by the Ministry of the Interior, but neither this nor a supporting law passed in 1924 could rescue the Cornudet measure (Besson, 1971, 16–17). The government, recognizing its impracticality, refrained from enforcing the three-year deadline and the law remained virtually a dead letter. The inter-war years witnessed a deterioration of environmental quality in many new suburban districts (see e.g. Bastié, 1964, 264–77) and French local authorities continued to lack an effective legal basis for town planning until the Vichy regime provided one in 1943.

For all their eventual goodwill, the Chamber and the Senate never really grasped the essentials of the Beauquier and Siegfried proposals. The debates in the Chamber in 1915, and in the Senate in 1918, concentrated on aesthetics, which appealed particularly to the representatives of the Paris region who were consistently the principal supporters of the idea. Open space, parks and playgrounds emerged as a secondary cause of concern, but housing and transport were scarcely mentioned. Admittedly, there was some recognition, especially on the Left, of the need to limit the existing freedom of the landowner to create districts of defective suburban housing. Moreover, wartime destruction prompted parliament to vote a bill allowing the compulsory purchase of whole areas which had originally been deposited by Siegfried in 1910 with a view to permitting slum clearance in Paris on the lines pioneered in Britain since 1875. This new legislation, which reached the statute book in 1917, was widely regarded as complementary to the Cornudet law. However, very little use was ever made of the area clearance powers once the wartime atmosphere of urgency had been dispelled. Even Cornudet himself, an aristocrat of some pedigree (full name: Joseph, Vicomte Cornudet des Chaumettes), who lived on his estates near Paris and had built up a distinguished political career after his initial training in law, never appeared to appreciate fully the implications and potential of town planning, for all his impressive references to the achievements of Germany and Britain.

FRENCH URBAN PLANNING: BRILLIANCE AND FRUSTRATION

The virtual inconsequentiality of over a decade of parliamentary proceedings may prompt us to wonder whether we have not been seeking the emergence of French planning in the wrong place. Might not a more positive picture emerge from an examination of extra-parliamentary activity, in particular of local policy, and of the techniques of urban design and layout developed by French architects and engineers?

At first sight, this looks a promising line of enquiry. Between the turn of the century and the outbreak of war a number of French urban designers acquired world reputations largely through their success in planning competitions. In 1899 André Bérard won the competition for a master plan for the University of California campus at Berkeley. In 1904 Léon Jaussely won first prize in a competition for a new extension plan for Barcelona (De Souza, 1913, 410–23). Most impressive of all was the French success in the Antwerp extension-plan competition of 1910. First prize went to Henri Prost (1874–1959) and another Frenchman was runner-up (De Souza, 1913, 399–407). Indeed, so high was the stock of French designers that some surprise was expressed, and not only in France, when Alfred Agache's entry was placed no higher than third in the Canberra competition of 1912 (*TPR*, 1912, 164).

Not only were all these prize-winners architects, they had also trained at the

Paris Ecole des Beaux-Arts, which was generally recognized as the most distinguished school of architecture in the world. The Ecole's normal syllabus included urban design, but several of the leading figures of the period had received a further stimulus in the form of a lengthy stay in the Italian capital after winning the Ecole's most coveted architectural prize, the Prix de Rome (*TPR*, 1912, 306; Wolf, 1968, 85n). During the early 1900s, in particular, the Rome award scheme produced a whole cohort of young architects who were thrilled by the thought of planning entire towns as unified architectural creations. With planning competitions now beginning to spread beyond the boundaries of German-speaking Europe, which French architects had generally shunned for both cultural and nationalistic reasons, these young artists had a chance to show their paces. French architecture and urban design were never more respected than on the eve of the First World War.

Some of the competition juries, it is true, may have been dazzled by the visual *éclat* of the Beaux-Arts style. However, some of the leading designers of the period mastered a sufficiently wide range of skills to qualify them as town planners. Jaussely's Barcelona scheme incorporated a system of building zones. Eugène Hénard (1849–1923) developed an interest in vehicle movements which won him a reputation as Europe's most distinguished traffic-engineering theorist (*TPR*, 1910, 169). Augustin Rey, like Hénard, was honoured with an invitation to address the RIBA town-planning conference in London in 1910; he chose to speak 'On the development and extension of towns' (RIBA, 1911, 266–73). Most important of all, the attentions of the young Lyonnese architect, Tony Garnier (1869–1948), were already beginning to concentrate on the planning of an ideal industrial town which would strongly influence many architects and planners of the Modern Movement after the war (see Wiebenson, 1970). Increasingly aware of their distinctive contribution, these urban designers eventually founded, in 1913, the *Société Française des Architectes Urbanistes*, precursor of the *Société Française des Urbanistes* of today. Far from being a catholic, integrative institution like the British Town Planning Institute, the *Société* recruited its members by invitation, and, as its title suggests, it was dominated by architects in its early years. Its first president was Eugène Hénard (Wolf, 1968, 105, 105n).

It is, nevertheless, not entirely gratuitous to point out that the theoretical achievements of French urban designers, and their successes in foreign competitions, were partly the result of their frustrations within France. Quite simply, very little practical planning activity was going on in France even in the last few years before the war. The construction of housing by public utility societies was on the increase, and employers continued to build workers' colonies, but none of these developments was of a scale or quality sufficient to set a striking example comparable to Bournville or Letchworth. There were no municipal housing estates, no large-scale slum redevelopment schemes, not even any coherent upper-class residential enclaves. In their absence, it was hardly surprising that the parliamentary proceedings should have been so divorced from practicality. Even in Lyons, where Garnier worked as city architect under a reforming mayor, Edouard Herriot (1872—1957), no significant departures from the Haussmannic tradition were made. When Herriot became mayor, in 1905, there had been no extension of the municipal boundaries for over half a century. While the city's population was virtually static, chaotic development went on apace in Villeurbanne and other industrial suburbs (Association française, 1926, 2). Herriot's socialist predecessor, Victor Augagneur, had made a big effort to extend the boundaries but had been defeated by the opposition of the suburbs, the national authorities, and many of the better-off citizens of Lyons itself, who feared the swamping of the council by proletarian votes (Latreille, 1975, 310). Herriot was no more successful. Even within the city, where he pursued a public health strategy without equal in France, he was unable to undertake major physical transformations. Lack of area clearance powers restricted his renovation effort to just part of one slum district (Latreille, 1975, 392). Without powers to initiate a municipal house-building programme, he could do no more than encourage a few small-scale housing schemes undertaken by public utility societies and companies. His street improvements were few and modest, and little different in concept from those carried out in the nineteenth century (Association française, 1926, 356).

Herriot resented these limitations. He travelled widely, and was well aware of the exciting developments in Britain and Germany. He even spoke German, a rare gift among Frenchmen outside Alsace, and his successful effort to develop Lyons as a river port was directly inspired by the example of Frankfurt (Herriot, 1948, 173). Finally, in October 1912, he decided to contribute to the campaign for the Siegfried planning bill by setting up a special committee to prepare an extension plan for the Lyons conurbation. In addition to city councillors and officials, the committee included outside experts and representatives of the suburban districts. In the following year he decided to hold France's first big international urban exhibition, similar to those which had proliferated in Germany since the early 1900s (Soulié, 1962, 41). The first draft of the extension plan was ready in time for the exhibition, which opened briefly in the summer of 1914 (Association française, 1926, 356). Yet even this pioneering and speculative effort, intended mainly to stimulate parliamentary and public opinion, was still far from the comprehensive planning practised in Germany. It was little more than a road scheme, incorporating some new avenues across the conurbation, and a ring boulevard (Latreille, 1975, 392). As much had been done in Haussmann's time.

Nancy, the other planning pioneer of the French provinces, provides a similar picture. Royal attentions in the eighteenth century had made it one of the grandest towns in France; by the end of the nineteenth century the Place Stanislas and its adjacent avenues were a tiny islet in a sea of sprawling industrial suburbs. Yet Nancy entered the new century with a buoyant confidence born of its recovery from the crippling loss of Alsace-Lorraine in 1871. With Strasbourg gone, Nancy had gradually warmed to its new role of capital of the East. Commercial and cultural links made it unusually open, by French standards, to influence from Germany and the Low Countries. Already at the turn of the century its architects were breaking away from the Beaux-Arts to indulge in the Art Nouveau craze to an extent unparalleled elsewhere in France, their inspiration drawn mainly from Belgium (see Ville de Nancy, 1977). In 1909 Nancy celebrated its renaissance with an exhibition, the success of which set in train the idea of holding a further, urban exhibition to support the parliamentary campaign for planning (Exposition, 1913, 237–8). The motive force behind this new exhibition was a group of local industrialists who, inspired by the nearby tradition of Alsatian paternalism, and directly invigorated by an influx of emigré employers from the occupied provinces, had been endeavouring for some years to improve housing and communal facilities in Nancy (Exposition, 1913, 15). Using tactics highly reminiscent of those adopted in the United States, they persuaded the Nancy Chamber of Commerce and the regional employers' association, the *Société Industrielle de l'Est*, to promote an exhibition under the title of 'The Modern City' at Nancy in 1913. The *Société des Architectes de l'Est de la France* gladly agreed to draw up an extension plan for Nancy in time for the exhibition, and exhibits were obtained from some of the other French towns which were beginning to show an interest in planning. The whole enterprise, which was complemented by lectures by leading figures in the French planning movement (e.g. Hottenger, 1913), was a most convincing demonstration of the will to plan in an enlightened industrial community, and frustration at the parliamentary delays in Paris was frequently manifest. Moreover, the aesthetic aspects of planning received little attention; economic development and housing were at the centre of the Nancy debate.

Visitors to the Nancy exhibition would have been convinced that planning was at last on the move in France, but they could not have failed to notice the fragmentary nature of the achievement so far. Only two extension plans were on display, apart from the Nancy scheme. One was for the small town of Agen, where the municipal architect had prepared a plan in about 1910 in anticipation of the passage of Beauquier's bill (Exposition, 1913, 39–40; CMRD, 1910, no. 91, 190). The other was for Dunkirk. Here, the stimulus had been the classic one of an impending removal of the fortifications, which was fortuitously announced around the time that Siegfried presented his 1912 planning bill. As at Nancy the local elite, in the shape of the *Société dunkerquoise*, had taken a hand by organizing a private extension-plan competition, which was won by Alfred Agache (*MSA*, 1913, 115–17; Exposition, 1913, 41). There was also some suggestion that certain large cities, notably Marseilles and Lille, had developed coordinated schemes for the reconstruction of their slums. But this was all very limited. Moreover, there was a notable absentee — the city of Paris.

In 1908 the Paris City Council had begun, almost for the first time, to consider the idea of extension planning. Rendu, stimulated by his membership of the new section of the *Musée social*, constantly urged that the fortification zone should be devoted mainly to open space, in the context of a general scheme for the creation of more parks and playgrounds inside the city. His efforts culminated, in June 1908, with an extraordinary Council speech, in which he completely misinterpreted recent events in England in support of his case that more open space was the key priority:

> We should remember, in this connection, that John Burns has recently brought in a 'town playing' [*sic*] bill on behalf of the English government. If the urban authorities fail in their duty, this bill will allow the State to intervene, in the interests of public hygiene, to create parks – 'play grounds'. (*CMPV*, 29 June 1908, 1277)

In July, negotiations were broken off, but by this time Louis Dausset had the bit in his teeth and in November 1908 he came to the Council with a scheme for the takeover of the whole of the fortifications and the field of fire outside them, and an extension of the city boundaries to include the whole area (*CMPV*, 4 November 1908, 65–72). He wanted to use the fortifications for a ring boulevard with some building development, and to lay out the field of fire as open space. This scheme, which owed much to Hénard's proposals and to discussions in the *Musée social*, was an impressive one, typical of Dausset. It was in his supporting report, designed to meet objections from within his own council, that the shadows appeared (*CMRD*, 1908, no. 91). Some councillors, apparently, thought the scheme too ambitious. Others were worried about its effects on the exodus of population to the suburbs, which they claimed was already reducing property values within the city. Representatives of the inner *arrondissements* felt that their electors would derive little benefit from it. Finally, Dausset had to devote serious attention to an objection which, ludicrous though it may seem, epitomizes the extraordinary limitations within which French municipal administrators had to operate. This objection arose from the city's continuing dependence for part of its revenues on *octroi* duties which were still imposed at customs posts at the gates of the city (see Veber, 1899). The fortifications, though virtually useless in a modern war, at least hindered smuggling and a number of councillors argued that, if they were demolished, it would be necessary to erect an expensive fence to replace them. Apparently in all seriousness, Dausset proposed a cheaper solution – a pathway, three metres in width, on the *octroi* boundary: '...with a circular path, electric floodlights, and night patrols, we'll have all that we need and more to keep the smugglers under control'.

In 1909 the fortifications issue went off the boil owing to the continuing intransigence of the State. Dausset, however, in consultation with his friends in the *Musée social* and other pressure groups, continued to think big. In 1910 he used his budget report to propose the urgent drafting of an extension plan for the whole of the Parisian agglomeration (*CMRD*, 1910, no. 91, 183–92). There was nothing startling in his suggestion that the plan should concentrate

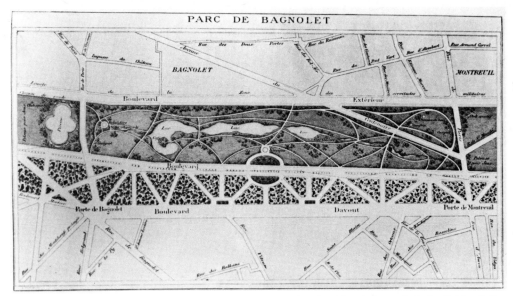

26 *Paris: proposal for the use of land vacated by the fortifications and their field of fire,*
presented by Louis Dausset to the City Council in 1908. (RIBA, 1911, 630–1)

on open space and road communications, but his concern for the future of the
suburbs was an astounding departure from the Parisian norm. In a brave attempt
to jolt his colleagues out of their parochialism, he outlined the German concep-
tion of development plans, including building zones, and urged the Council to
take note of events abroad in that year, including the Greater Berlin planning
competition and the RIBA conference in London. Finally, he called on the
Prefect of the Seine to set up a special committee including outside experts,
to draw up a brief for a Paris extension-plan competition, in the hope that the
result could be executed under the Beauquier powers, once they had been passed.

The Council approved Dausset's proposal, and in June 1911 the Prefect set up
the Extension of Paris Committee much on the lines that he had suggested. However, it did not even meet until February 1912, and the idea of a competition
was postponed indefinitely. In 1913 it produced two reports which, apart from
a large quantity of textual matter, much of it historical, included two outline plans
for the Paris area, one for roads and the other for open space (*Considérations*,
1913, 50–8, 93–103, Plate 8). Though skilfully prepared, and showing sufficient
awareness of the potential of planning to advocate the introduction of special
building regulations in the suburbs to secure lower-density development there
(*Considérations*, 1913, 76–84), the reports were largely of academic interest in
the absence of legislation, and by 1913, with Siegfried's new bill sinking into
the parliamentary morass, there seemed no need for urgency. In this depressing
atmosphere there was no question of discussing a big boundary extension, which
Dausset clearly favoured. The *Musée social* tried to maintain interest into 1914,

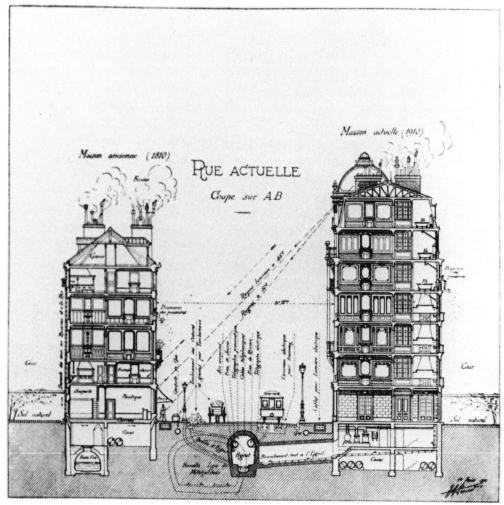

27 *Eugène Hénard: comparison of the existing (Paris) street (above) with two technically superior models incorporating more than one level of traffic flow. Hénard had a rich sense of humour and these designs should not be taken entirely seriously. However, they will not mislead us if they suggest that Hénard, as a good Parisian, saw the planned city primarily in terms of concentration, rather than of dispersal. (RIBA, 1911, 346, 349, 351)*

holding meetings to discuss the new Paris proposals and even securing Stübben to address a well-attended meeting on extension planning a few months before the war (*MSA*, 1914, 125, 205–12, 251–2). However, as France drifted towards war the likelihood of effective action in Paris receded. The proposed competition was not held until 1919 when, owing to the short period allowed to the competitors, it produced little of value, even though the winning entry was the work of Jaussely (Lavedan, 1975, 519). So Paris had nothing to contribute to the Nancy exhibition.

In the light of the experiences of Berlin and London, the failure of yet another national metropolis to set an example in urban planning might not appear to merit special comment. In France, however, the absence of a positive lead from the capital could not be shrugged off as easily as in Britain or Germany. In so politically and culturally centralized a state even the largest provincial centre could not break away from the shackles of Parisian practice; Lyons, even under Herriot, was a pale shadow of Frankfurt or even Birmingham, despite its aspirations to comparable status as capital of the liberal, enlightened provinces. French urban policy thus continued to evolve, much as it had always done, closely in step with Parisian developments.

Yet there is a paradox here. Judged on any but the dispassionate grounds chosen in this chapter, the Paris of 1900 would emerge clearly as the world's leading city, in terms of the quality of its urban life. Its intellectual and artistic

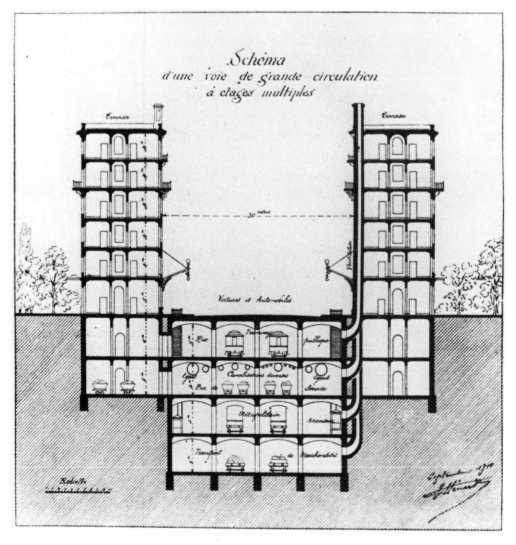

Schéma
d'une voie de grande circulation
à étages multiples

vitality, combined with its position as the vortex of international tourism, made it the unrivalled cultural capital of the advanced world. The defects of its urban planning did not prevent its becoming the main focus of the burgeoning movement of international contact which distinguished the late nineteenth and early twentieth centuries. Thus our discussion of the international aspects of the urban planning movement, which now follows, will quickly bring us back to Paris.

Six

Planning as an International Movement

Man is every day becoming more cosmopolitan, and perhaps a significant indication of this is to be seen in the number of Congresses, both National and International, that have recently been held.
S. D. Adshead, in *Town Planning Review*, 4(3), 1913, p. 234

So far we have looked at the rise of urban planning as a national phenomenon. And with good reason, no doubt. No urban area was under international control before 1914, if we exclude oddities such as the Vatican City, the Peking embassy compound, and a few small protectorates. All effective planning rested on political authority vested in the national state-systems. However, a nagging doubt remains. If we approach the problem from a national perspective, we are very likely to filter out non-conforming indications. Industrialization and the urbanization which accompanied it were, after all, international phenomena. Even our national studies have suggested a general leap forward in planning theory and practice, accompanied by considerable international cross-fertilization, between the 1890s and the First World War. Might not the whole development of urban environmental policy be usefully approached as a world movement, on which each country drew according to its own needs and possibilities?

THE INTERNATIONAL IDEA AND THE URBAN PROBLEM

In Chapter 1 we examined the consolidation of the national state-system in the nineteenth-century advanced world, an evolution which culminated in the First World War. It was complemented and counter-balanced by a massive growth of international organization at a variety of formal and informal levels. However, it was from the 1890s that the most rapid and spectacular progress was made, coinciding with the great leap forward in urban planning.

International organization rested on two principal foundations. One was the internationalist ideal, which had waned in the later Middle Ages but had revived in the eighteenth-century Enlightenment. After the Napoleonic Wars it was greatly reinforced by the new economic ideas of *laisser-faire* and free trade, which emanated principally from Britain. This ideal had a great unifying force in a Europe which had apparently been reorganized on peaceful lines by the Congress of Vienna, and which was in any case being knitted more closely together by the ties of economic development (see Ashworth, 1975, 191–226). Even the nationalist movements of the first half of the nineteenth century, and the imperialism of the second half, could plausibly be regarded as destroying outmoded institutions and preparing the way for efficient and harmonious world organization.

The other foundation was the piecemeal growth of international bodies, a process which did not get firmly underway until after 1815 but which thereafter tended to accelerate exponentially (see *The 1,978 International Organizations*, 1957). These international bodies, sustained by improvements in communications and the expansion of the professional classes, created a world-wide plane of debate on which a variety of practical issues, including the urban environment, could be elevated above their purely local and national contexts. They also stimulated the growth of an international class of creative and influential individuals, people who saw themselves to a greater or lesser degree as world citizens. Urban reformers were very prominent in this class, and the concerns of some of them extended so far beyond the parochial that they became actively involved in the Peace Movement and other efforts to secure world government. This link between urban and world affairs was by no means a tenuous one, especially in the context of the organic, evolutionary ideology of human development which came to influence so many in the later decades of the nineteenth century. The planning of a better urban environment could be seen as part of a general creation of human harmony within which individual potential could be fully realized, thus eliminating the causes of wars. This view was developed to its fullest by an outstanding international figure of the immediate pre-1914 period, Patrick Geddes. It was also linked to the idea that revitalized and reorganized cities, as the obvious centres of economic and social dynamism, could replace the nation-state as the basic political unit, allowing regional and world government to be secured by federations of cities. This prospect was visualized clearly by many of the promoters of the International Union of Local Authorities founded at Ghent in 1913.

Even in the first half of the nineteenth century, the urban problem had figured prominently in the growth of international organization. Efforts to establish quarantine practices which could cope with the growth of trade and migration were given an unpleasant fillip by the arrival of cholera from Asia in the early 1830s. However, the rapid spread of the disease inland soon suggested that its propagation was more a function of overcrowded, insanitary urban areas than of the random movements of infected ships. The vigorous return of cholera in 1848 prompted the organization of the international sanitary congress of 1851, the first of many such meetings. Two years later, the first International Statistical

Congress inaugurated an increasingly fruitful international collaboration in the gathering and interpretation of health statistics (Luard, 1977, 153).

Fear was not, however, the only factor. The great health gatherings of mid-century were enriched by the presence of independent experts and even laymen, as well as officials. In this respect they formed part of a general surge of international meetings designed to exchange scientific information or to discuss issues of general social reform which occurred from the early 1850s. Such congresses had been rare events until the 1840s, when seventeen of them were held, but they multiplied thereafter, with twenty-five in the 1850s and ninety-five in the 1860s (*Les congrès internationaux*, 1960). This growth was sustained by the creation of a rudimentary railway network in Europe in the 1840s and 1850s, and the conversion to steam of transatlantic passenger shipping in the 1850s and 1860s, together with the associated improvement in mail services. For urgent messages, the telegraph linked the major cities of Europe from the 1850s, and Europe and North America from 1866 (Ashworth, 1975, 74–5). Meanwhile, the economic expansion of the 1850s and 1860s contributed to a growth in the numbers engaged in administration and the professions.

A further stimulus to international meetings was provided by the phenomenon of the international exhibition. The first, London's Great Exhibition of 1851, was emulated in Paris in 1855. In both cities it became customary to hold an exhibition in each decade, but Paris's next exhibition, in 1867, established it as the leader in the field, thanks partly to the attractions of the city itself. The practice soon built up of organizing meetings in association with the exhibitions in order to take advantage of the presence of numerous foreigners. Some were put on by the exhibition organizers in connection with the displays, while others were unofficial events which made use of exhibition premises or accommodation elsewhere in the city. The first exhibition to stimulate a large number of congresses was the Paris event of 1867, and thereafter the Paris exhibitions generated considerably more congresses than those held in other cities. In 1878, for instance, sixty-three international congresses were held, most of them in Paris.

The exhibitions, and the meetings held in connection with them, were by no means limited to industrial or even to technical matters. One of the features which distinguished international exhibitions from mere trade fairs (which also were increasing in size and frequency) was the determination of their organizers to reflect all aspects of human endeavour. Space was usually allotted for the social sciences and social reform. Housing reform had been prominent at the London exhibition of 1851, where a complete block of model tenements had been displayed. However, it was the Paris exhibition of 1867 which really secured a prominent place for social reform in the international exhibitions, thanks to the work of Le Play and his Positivist supporters (Guerrand, 1967, 117). Later, Patrick Geddes was to claim that 1867 had been the first example of the 'civic exhibition' which he advocated as a powerful stimulus to urban reform in the early 1900s (Geddes, 1915, 249). It subsequently became normal for social questions to figure prominently in international exhibitions, and especially in those held at Paris. This orientation was, of course, reflected in the meetings held in connection with the exhibitions.

As the century wore on, international organizations concerned with the environment became more specialized. The *Association internationale d'Economie sociale*, founded in 1856 by Le Play, and the *Association internationale pour le progrès des Sciences sociales*, founded in 1862 at Brussels, impressed more by the scope of their proceedings than their practical impact. More directly helpful in spreading practical knowledge was the series of *Congrès internationaux d'Hygiène et de Démographie* inaugurated at Brussels in 1876. This departure both reflected and encouraged the great leap forward in public health achieved throughout the Continent in the 1870s. Housing took longer to emerge as a distinct field of discussion, and the first international housing congress was not held until 1889, at the Paris exhibition (Guerrand, 1967, 283–4). Thereafter, however, meetings were repeated every two years, and in 1900, at the next Paris exhibition, a permanent committee was set up (Hartmann, 1976, 45, 140n).

As the new century opened, international contacts moved briskly into a new, even more exciting phase. Between 1900 and 1913 inclusive, no less than 2,271 international congresses were held, compared to only 853 in the preceding period of fourteen years. Even sharper was the increase in the rate of foundation of international organizations, many of which emerged from the congresses. Between 1900 and 1914 inclusive, 304 international non-governmental organizations were founded, nearly twice the total (163) created in the whole previous history of international organizations since 1693. Exhibitions continued to play their role of midwife. The century was given a rousing send-off by the Paris exhibition of 1900. With 83,000 exhibitors and fifty million visitors, the exhibition was twice as large as any of the thirty-two exhibitions which had preceded it since 1851 (*Les congrès internationaux*, 1964, 5). Paris was the venue for most of the unprecedented number of 232 international congresses held in that year, and the impetus created by the exhibition may account for much of the subsequent frequency of international meetings. However, more fundamental forces were clearly at work. Between 1901 and 1903 the annual total of international congresses dropped again into two figures, and it was from 1904 that a sustained growth occurred. From 125 in that year the annual totals tended to rise until 1909, and in 1910, the year of the Brussels exhibition, 258 congresses were held. Although this figure was not reached again, the annual total did not drop below 200 until 1914, when many congresses were cancelled owing to the outbreak of war.

This growth of international contact was partly underpinned by the widespread revival of the Peace Movement which had begun in the 1890s. Albeit against a background of growing inter-governmental tension, it appeared that the first practical steps were at last being taken towards world government. In 1899 twenty-six nations answered Czar Nicholas II's invitation to a peace conference at The Hague. The main achievement of the conference was to set up an intern-national court of arbitration at The Hague. By 1907 the court had dealt with four cases, and forty-five bilateral treaties had been signed between countries willing to submit their disputes to the court (Hemleben, 1943, 130). In that year a second peace conference was held at The Hague. One of its proposals, that all countries should participate in building an international palace of peace, comple-mented the call made by the Interparliamentary Union (a world-wide association of members of parliament, founded in 1889) in 1905, for a permanent inter-national parliament (Bliss, 1908, 644—5). These years of hope were crowned in 1909 by the publication in London of *Europe's Optical Illusion* by the leading British internationalist, Norman Angell. Angell maintained that economic develop-ment had made the main rival states so interdependent that war had become virtually impossible to contemplate. Republished in 1910 in a revised edition as *The Great Illusion*, Angell's work quickly passed into a number of languages and, until 1914, offered a persuasive vision of a fully integrated world.

The international discussion of urban affairs flourished in this atmosphere. Almost everywhere, the Peace Movement acted as a focus for a variety of issues of domestic reform. In the United States, where the Peace Movement appears to have been stronger after 1900 than anywhere else in the world, strong support came from big-city business interests similar to those which backed the City Beautiful movement. The leading historian of this episode has suggested that the vision of world peace mirrored and sustained the hopes of domestic harmony which were entertained by both reforming and conservative elements (Marchand, 1972, 381—8). The cause of peace, which all could support, helped create the illusion of a national consensus which could not fail to stimulate the different branches of the domestic reform movement. Similar euphoric effects can be detected in relations between the Peace Movement and social reform in Britain and France (see e.g. Schou, 1963, 338—55). The only major exception was Germany, where rampant nationalism kept the Peace Movement weak and dis-couraged many of the leading social reformers from associating themselves with it (Chickering, 1975, xii). In Germany, Rudolf Virchow, the hygienist, was almost the only urban reformer openly to support the Peace Movement, and that principally in the 1880s (Chickering, 1975, 42—3). In the United States, however, Jane Addams was merely the most prominent of an important group of urban reformers who campaigned actively for the advancement of world government, and in Britain Patrick Geddes was by no means alone in this category; W. T. Stead, for instance, the slum campaigner of the 1880s, was a leader of the British Peace Movement in the early 1900s. In France, close ties existed between the peace and garden city movements, and Charles Beauquier published extensively in internationalist journals in the early 1900s (Chickering, 1975, 337—8).

The surge of the Peace Movement even stimulated some early exercises in international urban planning, in the shape of architectural schemes for world capitals or palaces of peace. Such projects became quite common exercises in schools of architecture and the results were occasionally publicized by the Peace Movement. In 1912, for instance, H. C. Andersen and E. M. Hébrard, of the Ecole des Beaux-Arts, published a project for a 'world centre of communication'. Reminiscent of Burnham's plan for Chicago of 1909, though on an even grander scale, this ideal city even included a sports stadium and centre as a permanent home for the Olympic Games, which since their revival in 1896 had become one of the key symbols of the new international spirit (*TPR*, 1914, 14–30).

More realistic, perhaps, was the brand of international planning proposed by Robert de Souza for Nice, which he wanted to see develop as a European as well as a French winter capital:

> People come here not to find a 'town' but an 'urban region'. As an 'urban region' it is all the more refreshing for being rooted in its health-giving qualities and its cosmo-politan pleasures. That cosmopolitanism, moreover, is of fundamental importance in that a regional plan must carefully conserve the existing variety of the area. We know that French people are too easily satisfied with the terrace of a cafe and movement in the sunlit street, with occasionally a few steps along the pavement to the sounds of a distant band. The Italians, however, like to wander through dense banks of flowers heavy with scents and birdsong. The British want broad open spaces for their sports and for long walks and horse-rides – yet nowhere have we provided them. The Germans love woods and thickets, where they can enjoy a long, quiet smoke or drink at some alfresco hostelry, nestling in the undergrowth. The Russians prefer the seaside and the shaded gardens of some lonely restaurant, humming with the timeless strains of gypsy music. Yet all of them want fine roads to take them wherever the splendour of the horizon attracts them, and footpaths through the rocks, the olive groves, and the pine forests. (De Souza, 1913, 233–4)

As for Paris, we have already seen (p. 140) how similar touristic considerations began to bear on the city authorities in the early 1900s, and even London was urged by John Burns in 1910 to stimulate tourist revenue by beauteous planning (RIBA, 1911, 73).

Touristic planning, of course, had only slight relevance to the basic urban issues. Much more important was the big development of the international housing debate which occurred in the new century. As late as the 1890s variations in housing conditions and in public policies had hampered the emergence of inter-national discussion. However, the garden city idea, which swept the urbanized world in the early 1900s, provided much more common ground. Its strongly idealistic character tolerated national variations in practical policy, and, as we have already seen, it particularly appealed to reformers with broader inter-nationalist objectives. It was to acknowledge and further encourage the international appeal of the garden city that the British Garden City Association convened the first International Garden City Congress in London in July 1904. It was quite a modest affair, the main non-British speakers being Georges Benoît-Lévy and Josiah Strong, president of the Institute of Social Service in New York (*Garden*

City, 1904–5, 6). However, much internationalist fervour was generated. Benoît-Lévy went out of his way to link the garden city and peace movements, suggesting that 'garden cities of social peace', as he called them, should also be 'cities of peace between nations'. Indeed, he continued, they already fulfilled this role in that harmonious relations existed between the various national garden city associations, and the French association had reinforced the point by choosing as its president 'the leader of world Peace', D'Estournelles de Constant, the member of parliament and leading French peace campaigner. Ultimately, the congress unanimously voted a resolution inviting the *Fondation Rothschild*, a housing trust recently set up by the French branch of the banking family, to found a garden city in France (*MSA*, 1904, 464–5; *CM*, 1904, 480).

This attempt to bring international pressure to bear on one of the world's biggest financial dynasties produced no immediate result, but the London meeting led on to a series of garden city congresses. Although some of the radical ideals of the early movement were soon watered down, these occasions enjoyed increasing attendances. A highlight of the 1904 meeting had been a lengthy tour of Letchworth, the LCC suburban housing estates, Port Sunlight, Bournville and other examples of low-density housing, and as the years passed there was more and more to see on the ground. Finally, in 1913, the garden city congress set up an International Garden Cities and Town Planning Association at Scheveningen, Netherlands.

By this time, the diffusion of the garden city idea, albeit in a debased form, had done much to invigorate the whole of the international housing reform movement. The international housing congress held at Liège in 1905 far outshone its predecessors in terms of scope and attendance, and subsequent meetings were all very well attended; 2,000 people from both Europe and the United States attended the Vienna congress in 1910, for instance (*TPR*, 1910, 166–7). Henrietta Barnett addressed the Liège meeting on Hampstead Garden Suburb, and Britain's acknowledged lead in residential planning and cottage design allowed British representatives to figure prominently in subsequent proceedings. The Germans, however, were even more prominent, thanks not only to their linguistic ability and their unrivalled stamina in sitting through meetings, but also to the prestige which the refinement of German *Städtebau* afforded them.

As time passed, it became increasingly difficult to consider housing in isolation. The scope of international discussions on public health had greatly broadened since the 1870s under the influence of the 'social hygiene' concept. In 1903 the *Congrès Internationaux d'Hygiène et de Démographie* set up a permanent international committee, and in 1904 the housing and hygiene movements were linked by the creation, in Paris, of the *Commission permanente des Congrès internationaux d'Hygiène de l'Habitation*. Also heavily involved with housing was the *Association internationale contre la Tuberculose*, set up appropriately enough in Berlin, the home of Koch and the *Mietskasernen*, in 1902. This association was the product of a series of international congresses on tuberculosis which

continued at frequent intervals until the war. Meanwhile, public health administration at both local and central government level had produced an additional
potential for international cooperation, which was reflected in the foundation,
at Paris in 1905, of the General Association of Municipal Health and Technical
Experts, and of the *Office international d'Hygiène publique*, an inter-governmental
organization, at Rome in 1907. Clearly, the broadcasting of information on
health continued to offer the most scope for international exchange, but the
desire to disseminate social reform ideas was expressed in the foundation of the
Institut international de Bibliographie sociale at Brussels in 1905 (*The 1,978
International Organizations*, 1957).

The final piece in the mosaic of the international urban debate was provided
by the designers. A Permanent International Committee of Architects had been
set up at Paris as early as 1867, but it had mainly been concerned with questions
of professional equivalence. International discussion of urban design did not
begin in an organized fashion until the 1890s, when Camillo Sitte's rejection of
pompous, rectilinear planning struck chords in many parts of Europe. Charles
Buls (1837–1914), mayor of Brussels between 1881 and 1899, who was already
heavily involved in the conservation of the Grand' Place and other historic parts
of the city, suddenly found himself the coordinator of a European movement
of 'public art'. At first the movement was purely preservationist. The first international congress on the protection of historic monuments had been held in
Paris, largely at the instigation of the French government, in 1889, and a scheme
was launched there to set up an architectural 'Red Cross' to guard historic buildings in wartime (*BSAMP*, 1889, 53–4, 91). These meetings became annual events,
but in the 1890s the pure preservationist concept was complemented by Arts
and Crafts ideas of creative design, and there was also some influence from the
American City Beautiful movement. The result was a series of international congresses on Public Art, the first of which took place in Brussels in 1898 (Piccinato,
1974, 54, 167). Further meetings followed in Paris in 1900, at Liège in 1905,
and at Brussels again in 1910. They were brilliant affairs, in which the French
were able to shine. In 1905 they were consecrated by the foundation of the
Institut international d'Art public, at Liège. Moreover, the same congress set up
the International Federation of Building and Public Works, a body designed to
ensure high standards of design in both private and public construction (*The
1,978 International Organizations*, 1957).

This accretion of organizations and meetings might have been purely confusing.
What increasingly focused the attention of the participants, however, was the
idea of urban planning. Certainly, the idea was not generated in these international discussions; it came directly from Germany and Austria. However, once
Städtebau became prominent in the debates as a comprehensive organizing
principle for cities, the strengths of other countries could be called upon to
fill the various weaknesses and blindspots in German practice. Conference participants thus found themselves able to visualize an ideal mode of planning,

incorporating, among other elements, British garden suburbs, French monumental grandeur and elegance, and the expansiveness of American park systems.

Architects remained the principal guardians of this inspiring vision until the very eve of the First World War. The aestheticist concerns of the Public Art congresses proved too restrictive to allow the incorporation of the complete planning idea, and general meetings of architects began to make the running after 1905. The Seventh International Congress of Architects was held in 1906 in London, just as the RIBA was becoming interested in planning, and urban design was prominent in the proceedings. It was at this meeting that Eugène Hénard made his first appearance outside France, explaining his unique method of traffic-flow analysis (Wolf, 1968, 47; Piccinato, 1974, 54). Much of the subsequent discussion of traffic engineering was carried on at the International Road Congresses, the first of which was held in Paris in 1908, but Hénard nevertheless reappeared at an even more important architectural meeting, the RIBA's Town Planning Conference in London in 1910.

The London conference, which the RIBA claimed to be the first international conference on town planning ever held, attracted over 1,250 people. Few of the numerous foreign delegates were fully aware of the RIBA's ulterior motive of cornering the practice of town planning in Britain now that the Housing, Town Planning, Etc. Act was on the statute book, and most were genuinely impressed and even moved by a magnificently set international occasion. Daniel Burnham, for instance, agreed to attend despite his failing health and told the conference that it was the proudest moment of his life (Hines, 1974, 349–52). Notable among the foreign organizations represented there were the National Conference on City Planning (by Charles Mulford Robinson), the American Institute of Architects, the Chicago Architectural Club, the City of Paris (by Louis Dausset and Louis Bonnier), the *Ligue pour les Espaces libres* (by Georges Benoît-Lévy), the *Société pour la Protection des Paysages de France* (by Count Robert de Souza), the *Band deutscher Architekten* (by Hans von Berlepsch-Valendàs), and the *Verband deutscher Architekten- und Ingenieur-Vereine* (by J Stübben) (RIBA, 1911, 16–29). In such company, Burnham's reply to a toast at the conference banquet caught exactly the right note:

> The history of the present movement of town planning is very short; it goes back less than ten years... The work, however, up to the present time has been done in a disjointed manner, because the best that any one nation can do for itself cannot be equal to that done by them all working together and interchanging their ideas; and those who have been the most deeply engaged in this work, and most earnest in the prosecution of it, have constantly felt that they need a sort of university which they may attend; and it does not surprise us that London has become such a university. (RIBA, 1911, 106)

S. D. Adshead, since the previous year Professor of Town Planning in the newly-established Department of Civic Design at Liverpool University, responded in kind during the conference when he remarked:

> In an age of constant international communication the barriers which separate nations in the direction of their arts are the first to be broken down. At a time when England and Germany are exchanging ideas by the frequent visits of their societies and deputations, by international congresses and exhibitions — when cities like New York are built up in a decade entirely from *motifs* borrowed from European models of the past — at such times it is imperative that we look abroad, and in doing so comparisons must necessarily be made...Year by year the architecture of the civilised world will become more cosmopolitan and international. We should not resist, but should welcome such a result. (RIBA, 1911, 499, 504)

It needs to be said that the significance of the London conference as a planning forum was not quite as great as the RIBA claimed. Chairmen were formally advised to discourage floor speeches on 'questions of hygiene, housing of the poor, administration, traffic, ground values, and the like...as being outside the scope of the Conference' (RIBA, 1911, 8). Some of these matters were discussed in the formal papers, but Rudolf Eberstadt expressed what was probably a quite widely-felt unease among the non-architects present when, in a banquet speech, he remarked that, as a man who viewed planning as a *science*, he was outnumbered on this occasion by those who saw it as an art. The planning exhibition held as an adjunct of the conference was impressive enough, but much of its impact was based on the contributions from Germany, where planning exhibits were technically far superior to anything so far achieved in Britain. In fact, it could plausibly be claimed that Germany, still the main focus of world attention, was the effective centre of the international planning debate between 1910 and 1914.

There can be no doubt, however, that progress towards the international organization of planning accelerated from 1910. In 1911 Patrick Abercrombie, another member of the Department of Civic Design at Liverpool, suggested that the growing frequency of conferences, all attended by much the same people, had revealed the need for an International Federation of Town Planners:

> There is no subject which benefits by international comparison more than Town Planning: we are frequently sending deputations over to Germany, and they are as frequently sending them over here. Each country can learn something from the excellencies [*sic*] and faults of another; and with a new subject like town planning, a systematic interchange would save a great deal of time and effort. (*TPR*, 1911, 138)

Abercrombie was almost certainly the author, too, of an enthusiastic editorial comment in the *Town Planning Review* on a proposal for 'a sort of central exhibition bureau' which was said to be under discussion in the planning world. The aim would be to stop the same material appearing at one exhibtion after another in Europe and the United States: '...the expert has usually seen the rather limited number of exhibits, which appear everywhere, many times before' (*TPR*, 1911, 240—1).

By 1913 S. D. Adshead, on his return from the Third International Road Congress, was ready to express the view that these international meetings, though most valuable, were beginning to encounter diminishing returns. It was imperative, he said, that a limit be set to their frequency (*TPR*, 1913, 234). This weariness, which was not limited to Adshead, contributed to a growing ambition to found some kind of universal forum of urban policy. With rivalries between the great powers now worrying even the most optimistic of internationalists, these hopes centred on the International Congress of Cities which the Belgians planned to hold in connection with the Ghent international exhibition of 1913. The big international exhibition was in fact already on the wane; the French had broken half a century of tradition by not holding one in Paris in 1911, and the modest Ghent affair was the only one available to recreate past enthusiasm.

The Ghent congress, when finally held in July and August 1913, went under the ambitious title of First International Congress of Town Planning and City Life. It was attended by representatives of twenty-two governments and 150 towns. It set up a permanent committee to plan further conferences, but more interesting to many, including Patrick Abercrombie, was a scheme for a permanent international headquarters of town planning and urban affairs. Another committee was set up to discuss this possibility, with Brussels regarded as a strong candidate owing to the presence there already of the secretariats of the road and housing congresses (*TPR*, 1913, 205—18). In fact, by the time war broke out Brussels had been agreed, and an embryonic International Union of Cities was in being. The Union's claims as a means of world government, which were being quite seriously discussed as war clouds gathered in Europe, would perhaps have been put forward more forcefully at the planned San Francisco congress in 1915. Political events moved too quickly, however, and the congress was never held (*TPR*, 1914, 244—6).

PLANNERS AND INTERNATIONAL EXCHANGE

Although Charles Mulford Robinson could refer in 1916 to the existence of an 'international town planning movement' (Robinson, 1916, 229), we still have to assess to what extent truly international tendencies overrode the national ones. The planning movement, of course, was never more than a collection of individuals and the most enlightening way to approach the problem is to distinguish the varying levels of international consciousness visible in those individuals. Four basic types stand out: the fully cosmopolitan planner; the intermediary; the home-based planner with a willingness to look abroad; and the xenophobe.

Cosmopolitan planners were few in number but highly influential. In pre-1914 Europe, before the days of visas, work permits and even passports, it was perfectly possible to become, in effect, a stateless person and behave as a peripatetic world citizen. In the planning world the outstanding Odysseus was the young German expert, Werner Hegemann (1882–1936). Born in Mannheim, Hegemann studied in so many universities that it is difficult to keep track of them all. It would appear that by 1908 he had pursued studies in architecture, the history of art, and eventually economics, at Berlin, Munich, Paris, Strasbourg, Harvard and the University of Pennsylvania. He obtained his doctorate in Munich in 1908, but by this time he was spending much of his time outside Germany in the pursuit of the big-city housing studies which had first captured his imagination in 1905. His growing experience in the housing and planning fields, combined with his enormous energies, led to his being invited to play an important part in the organization of a series of planning exhibitions – Boston and New York in 1909, and then Berlin and Düsseldorf in 1910 and 1911 (Calabi, 1976, 56). In the massive two-volume study of world urban planning which he produced as a postscript to these last two exhibitions, he was at pains to point out that he had tried in recent years to spend time in each of the cities studied in the book, with the following results: Berlin, four years; Paris, two years; New York, Philadelphia, Boston, Chicago, Washington, two years in all; London and Letchworth, four months; Vienna, six weeks; Budapest, two weeks; and Stockholm, two weeks. The rest of his time, he added, had been spent in Munich or on shorter visits (Hegemann, 1913, 152). By the time this statement appeared in Germany, Hegemann was back in the United States, initially at the invitation of the People's Institute of New York (Hegemann, 1915, 1–2), but increasingly as an independently established lecturer, writer and planning consultant. In fact, by the time the United States entered the war, the bilingual and totally cosmopolitan Hegemann had become both the best known of Germany's younger generation of planning commentators, and one of the most admired of North America's scientific planners. He was to continue this pattern of life after the war, running a planning practice in the USA in partnership with Elbert Peets, and writing a literary landmark in each country: *The American Vitruvius* (1922), a study of the best in American urban design, and *Das steinerne Berlin* (1930), a devastating historical critique of the building and planning of Berlin. It took Hitler's rise to power to persuade him to settle permanently in the United States, but he saw little of this new age of nationalism, so alien to his ideals, for he died prematurely in 1936.

Patrick Abercrombie (1879–1957) also had much of the world citizen about him. An architect by training, he began to lecture at the School of Architecture, Liverpool University, in 1907. In 1909 he was appointed Research Fellow and Lecturer in the new Department of Civic Design, but in December 1910 he resigned the lectureship to devote his full time to study and to editing the new *Town Planning Review*. Under Abercrombie's guidance the *Review* grasped its opportunity as only the second journal in the world (and the first one in English) to be devoted exclusively to planning. For its early numbers he wrote a series of

planning studies of European cities which rivalled Hegemann's work in learning
and perception. He secured much material on American planning. He also became
a frequent attender of international conferences; he was at the Vienna housing
congress in 1910, and at Ghent in 1913. When war broke out he was a member
of the provisional council drafting a constitution for the International Union of
Cities, and he must have been the author of the *Review* editorial in 1914 lamenting the missed opportunity for world government which the Union had held out
(Hawtree, 1974, 189–91).

In the more restrictive post-war world, Abercrombie knuckled down to a
planning practice at home which ultimately allowed him to succeed Raymond
Unwin as the doyen of British planning. Though he never lost his international
awareness, he never realized his full potential as an international planner.

Thomas Adams (1871–1940) pursued a different course. His horizons con-
tinually broadened, from dairy farming in Midlothian to London journalism,
and then on to become secretary of the Garden City Association and manager
of Letchworth. After his resignation in 1906 he designed and promoted a number
of garden suburbs on behalf of private landowners (Hawtree, 1974, 133–43). In
1909 he joined the Local Government Board as an Inspector to work on schemes
submitted under the new Act. By now, however, he had travelled widely in
Germany and elsewhere and he chafed under the restrictions of the Local Government Board. In 1911 he visited the United States for the first time, and was
immediately excited by the vitality of American planning (*TPR*, 1911, 139).
More visits and contacts followed, and in 1914 Adams decided, despite his acceptance of the presidency of the Town Planning Institute, to take up an offer from
the Canadian government to serve its newly-founded Commission on Conservation.
In the 1920s Adams was to become involved in the regional planning movement
in the United States. He frequently returned to Britain and published books there,
but North America remained his professional home from 1915 until the end of
his career (see Armstrong, 1968).

Potentially the greatest international figure of all was Patrick Geddes (1854–
1932), whose vision of planning as creator of an entirely new world inspired many
in Britain and America, even if it did not always entirely enlighten them, in the
last years before the war. Geddes had made his first working visit to France, as a
biologist, in 1878, finding time to see the Paris exhibition of that year (Boardman,
1944, 37–40). International projects occupied much of the rest of his life; he
organized annual international summer schools at Edinburgh between 1887 and
1899 and the following year he moved his school to Paris for the international
exhibition. One of the themes which he pursued there was the need for social
and civic renewal as a substitute for war, and his efforts to promote international
harmony became even more serious in the new century (Boardman, 1944, 156;
Mairet, 1957, 99–108). A great admirer of German town planning, he devoted
part of his best-known planning book, *Cities in Evolution* (1915), to a report
on a tour of Germany. However, though Geddes lived the life of an international

figure, he enjoyed virtually no influence outside the English-speaking world. Like Adams, he did his greatest practical planning work abroad, but the invitation came not from North America but from India, and most of his work there in the 1920s went virtually unnoticed elsewhere (see Tyrwhitt, 1947).

It was much easier to be an intermediary than a full international figure. One was not required to shine in an alien ambience, and even a knowledge of foreign languages was not always necessary. The audience back home could rarely detect errors of fact or interpretation. So many intermediaries have already appeared in these pages that there is no point in reviewing them again in detail here — T. C. Horsfall, Georges Benoît-Lévy, Hermann Muthesius and Frederic C. Howe are perhaps the most outstanding examples in each of the four countries. Many were men of some leisure, and a patrician background often helped to put them at their ease in foreign company. More interesting, however, than their own qualities was the public willingness to give them a hearing which was a particular feature of the early 1900s. During these years, and even in Germany, foreign example reached the peak of its persuasive power. So general was the phenomenon that it cannot be explained away in terms of sublimated fears of foreign might or economic rivalry. It seems to relate more directly to the surge in creative internationalism which produced the huge leap in the numbers of international organizations after 1900. This was, for instance, the biggest growth-period of Esperanto, the international language invented by a Russian enthusiast in 1887. In fact, the *Comité permanent des Congrès d'Espéranto* (note the language chosen for its international title!) was set up precisely in this period, at Paris in 1906, only two years after another Paris-based body whose name lost something in the interests of internationalism, the *Fédération internationale de Football Association*. Admittedly, knowledge of Esperanto did not always aid communication, as Edouard Herriot discovered in 1906 when his delegation from Lyons was welcomed at a civic reception in Manchester. Several of Herriot's colleagues spoke Esperanto and persuaded him to dispense with interpreters, confident that there would be a sufficient number of Esperantolists among their Lancastrian hosts. And indeed there were, the only problem being the difference of accent which made the two sides completely incomprehensible to each other (Herriot, 1948, 212)! In fact, French was a more effective international language in these years; it was, for instance, the main language used by speakers at Ghent in 1913 (*TPR*, 1913, 209).

More effective, no doubt, than Esperanto as an aid to understanding foreign planning was the generalization of photographs in books and reviews after 1900, thanks to the perfection of the half-tone process in the 1890s. Slide lectures also became more frequent and popular now that foreign experiences could easily be recorded on the hand-held cameras developed in the 1890s by Kodak and other firms. These aids helped the intermediaries to make foreign theory and practice more palatable, and counteracted the occasional stodginess of the speeches and lectures which these indefatigable figures were prepared to give on

28 *A German municipal delegation visits Bournville, 19 May 1906. The well-fed mien of the 'first-class sleeping-car set' which dominated the early planning tours is clearly portrayed here. (Bournville Collection, Birmingham Reference Library)*

almost any occasion.

Most home-based planners no doubt acquired their initial knowledge of foreign example from these intermediaries. Of course, the exact impact of foreign influence on them is difficult to judge. Many, however, provided an earnest of their willingness to look abroad by joining one of the group tours which proliferated after about 1900. The pleasures of these excursions, which in the case of officials or political representatives were usually financed out of the public purse, attracted many nondescript figures who, while not even enthusiasts for planning, often returned with a favourable impression of foreign achievement and a greater readiness to learn from abroad. S. D. Adshead was prepared to argue that the social function of an international congress was as important as its utilitarian value (*TPR*, 1913, 234), and there was no doubt that attendance was boosted by an attractive venue. In 1910, for instance, over 150 people from Britain attended the international housing congress in Vienna (*TPR*, 1910, 159).

The international figures, the intermediaries, and the internationally-aware domestic planners all contributed to what the Italian historian, Giorgio Piccinato, has identified as 'una società internazionale urbanistica' in the last years before the war (Piccinato, 1974, 53). As Patrick Abercrombie pointed out at the time, a large core of experts could be found in attendance at all the conferences relevant to urban affairs (*TPR*, 1911, 138). Indeed, it is not entirely surprising to find that the only advertising carried by the *Annales* of the *Musée social* was for French and European railway services.

However, we must not forget those who were impervious to this atmosphere of international enthusiasm, the xenophobes. As they were rarely in evidence, their number and influence are very hard to measure. The clearest example of a xenophobe to have arisen from this study is John Burns, on whose ambivalent attitude to town planning we have already had occasion to comment. As perhaps the only man of working-class origin to exercise a major influence on urban planning anywhere in the world before 1914, Burns had no natural entrée into international society. Although he travelled abroad on trade union and political business, he was never at ease and always inclined to find fault. T. C. Horsfall and some of the other members of the National Housing Reform Council must have had a rude shock in 1906 when they found that the German example (which Burns seemed to confuse with France and perhaps even Italy) had no persuasive power for him:

> Mr. Cadbury had told them [Burns said] that it would take several generations to deal effectively with this problem, and he contrasted the efforts of Continental countries adversely to ourselves. He himself had been to the Continent to look at this and kindred problems, and he did not quite agree with the optimistic views as to the action taken by Continental countries. The Continental cities were often in appearance tidier, but not cleaner, than similar cities in this country. They were more orderly, but not more comfortable; and on the Continent, where centralised government existed, there

was a disposition, incompatible with English views of liberty and freedom, to put in the back street many evidences of poverty and untidiness that he was glad to say we still allowed to obtrude themselves in this country. We did not believe that every other man who was not a sanitary inspector or a policeman should be a fireman, and as this was still a free country the desire for liberty remained, and from the point of view of the independence of the people considerable benefit was conferred which he would not like to lose. (Aldridge, 1915, 177–8)

Even in 1910, when Burns, now the hero of the hour, opened the RIBA Town Planning Conference in London to the applause of the cream of the 'international society of urbanists', he clung to his British roots:

> I conceive the city of the future as Ruskin, Morris, Wren and Professor Geddes wished a city to be — that is, an enlarged hamlet of attractive, healthy homes... It is not an accident that the beautiful manor-house, the restful vicarage, the stately homes of England, and the beautiful public schools and colleges have turned out the Ruskins, the Kingsleys, the Morrises, the Nelsons, the Newtons, and the Darwins. (RIBA, 1911, 64)

Perhaps we might leave Burns in 1914, addressing the inaugural dinner of the Town Planning Institute, a body which had made a point of offering honorary membership to a number of distinguished foreign planners. By now, Burns was more kindly disposed to foreign example, but he clearly had his doubts about the number of free Continental trips which his department had indirectly approved. For him, British was still best:

> I think I have been too indulgent to local authorities in regard to conferences, but I think their officers might go to Bruges, Ghent, and Edinburgh — and Edinburgh is, I think, perhaps the noblest-planned city in the world — and places like Dusseldorf and also parts of London. I would advise you not to imitate and apply to English life, its towns and cities, what might be good in Washington or Berlin, what might be suitable for political, military, or social reasons in St. Petersburg or Moscow. (*TPR*, 1914, 8)

THE INTERNATIONAL DIFFUSION OF PLANNING: A THEORETICAL APPROACH

As leader of the faceless army of sceptics, Burns encourages us to look more carefully at the international planning movement. Was it really more than a permanent, circulating beano for people with independent means or expense accounts? Was the course of planning in each country really affected by what happened abroad or in the curious supra-national society of leading planners?

In applying our natural critical sense, however, we must be careful not to throw the baby out with the bath water. Planning, like other products of human ingenuity, was perfectly capable of participating in a process of international diffusion. It did so in three principal respects. First, planning, in so far as it was a process of design and therefore an artistic activity, was subject to the effects of *artistic influence*. Secondly, the specific control techniques and politico-legal instruments of planning, though initially developed in response to national or even local circumstances, were liable to adoption elsewhere through the processes of *innovation diffusion*. Finally, in a world divided into competing nation-states, conditions abroad could help *persuade*, or could be used to persuade, individuals to make decisions which they might not have made in response to national conditions alone.

The theory to support these three processes comes respectively from the history of art, economic history and social psychology. There is almost unanimous agreement among art historians and theoreticians that all artists are to a greater or lesser degree subject to the influence of other artists. Indeed, much art historiography consists of efforts to distinguish an artist's 'original' contribution from elements drawn from the work of others. The graphic and plastic arts may be viewed as an accretion of artificial images, and in the world of the artist such images are difficult to restrain within national boundaries. In fact, it takes an efficient tyranny to produce a purely national art form like 'Socialist Realism'. Such conditions were present nowhere in the world before 1914, and art was perhaps the most purely international of human activities at that time. Despite the gradual emergence of functionalism, architects continued to regard themselves primarily as artists until the very end of our period, and foreign images were incorporated readily into their buildings and designs for urban areas. In fact, the later nineteenth century saw an extraordinary growth of eclecticism which, in the principal form of the Art Nouveau craze, spilled over into the twentieth century.

The international diffusion of design imagery was so rich and varied that it is impossible to do it justice here. Two extreme examples may amuse as well as enlighten. In 1904 Raymond Unwin, in common with many other people in Britain, first became seriously aware of German planning through the efforts of T. C. Horsfall (Day, 1973, 104–5). So he visited Germany, read Camillo Sitte (probably in the French translation), and enjoyed himself. He especially liked the small German fortified towns such as Rothenburg, and he took many photographs of their crumbling walls, narrow streets, steep roofs and turrets. Though he had finished the master plan of Letchworth before the lessons of all this had really sunk home, he made up for it at Hampstead. He built a wall with Germanic turrets to separate the heath from part of the suburb. He built a shopping centre with gables and roofs of Teutonic steepness as a gateway to the suburb on the Finchley Road. At Letchworth he even proposed, but did not build, a railway-station roadbridge modelled on a medieval German drawbridge and barbican (see Unwin, 1911, 172, 174). All very trivial, perhaps, and yet the influence of these images went further. The German fortified town suggested to Unwin how the English village, which remained his residential ideal, could be reconciled with the city — simply divide the city into small communities physically separated by stretches of open space and even walls. The visual charm of this idea helped to root it deeply in the British planning consciousness, from which it was to re-emerge in the 1940s in Abercrombie's plan to divide London into a collection of physically distinct communities (Forshaw and Abercrombie, 1943, 21–9)

29 *Temple Fortune House, at the corner of Finchley Road and Hampstead Way, Hampstead Garden Suburb, before the First World War. Unwin liked to select a Germanic image to emphasize gateways and barriers, but it is clear that his wanderings with a sketchbook in Rothenburg and other mediaeval German towns had made a strong emotional impact on him. (Hampstead Garden Suburb Archives)*

The second example is also British, but the influence this time is American. The Port Sunlight of the 1890s was a pure evocation of the English village ideal, with winding streets, a neo-Gothic church, and carefully asymmetrical arrangements of cottages and public buildings, all in a collection of eclectic but basically Tudor styles. This arrangement, admittedly, was partially dictated by the presence

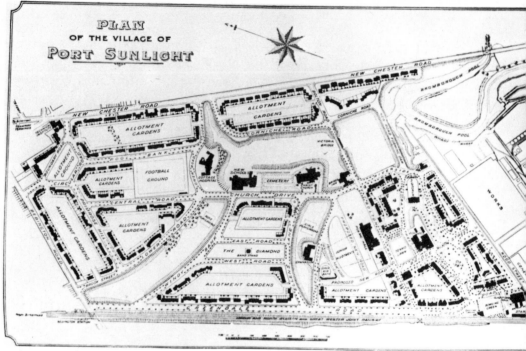

30   *Port Sunlight: pre-1909 development plan. (RIBA, 1911, 765)*

of a number of shallow creeks from the Mersey which, though drainable, were not worth the expense of filling in to allow building. W. H. Lever appears to have been perfectly happy with his creation until the City Beautiful movement began to impinge upon British architects in the early 1900s. He became involved in the 'Beautiful Bolton' movement, the most Americanized of the local civic improvement campaigns of the period, and patronized the preparation of boulevard and civic centre schemes for that dour textile town. This work brought him into close contact with Charles Herbert Reilly, head of the School of Architecture at Liverpool University since 1904. Liverpool's close commercial links with the United States had, since the 1890s if not earlier, made its businesses and architects more open to American architectural styles than those of any other British city (see Hughes, 1964). Under Reilly, its School of Architecture became a forcing ground for American ideas, and a strong opponent of the Arcadian tradition in British design. Instead, it looked for its inspiration, partly through the American prism, to the Ecole des Beaux-Arts. Lever came to be spellbound by all this neo-classical grandeur. Without the visual prospect which Reilly held out to him, he might never have endowed the Department of Civic Design at

31   (Opposite) *Port Sunlight replanned, 1909. The monumental character of this boulevard scheme reflects the interest of many British architects in the American City Beautiful movement. (RIBA, 1911, 764).*

~ A View of ~
PORT SUNLIGHT
: CHESHIRE :
INCORPORATING THE PREMIATED
DESIGN FOR THE CENTRAL BOULE-
VARD, PUBLIC LIBRARY AND
MUSEUM BY MR. E. PRESTWICH
AS SEEN FROM THE RAILWAY

Liverpool in 1909. The *Town Planning Review* might then never have appeared, and academic influences on the course of British planning might have been diffused elsewhere. Again, this is not mere triviality, the icing on the cake. One of the first acts of the new Professor of Civic Design, S. D. Adshead, was to organize a student competition for a plan to transform Port Sunlight. The result was a new system of rectilinear boulevards or parkways on the filled creeks, garnished with Versailles-like fountains and statues, and terminated by neo-classical monuments. The older buildings such as the church were incorporated as well; the *Town Planning Review* admired 'the ingenuity with which these *unrelated buildings* have been linked up to form a *complete scheme*' (author's italics) (*TPR*, 1910, 80). The new Port Sunlight was a charming oddity. More importantly, however, it expressed in extreme form the dominant mode of British civic design, a sometimes uneasy marriage of Beaux-Arts and bucolic, which Liverpool's leadership, consecrated by Unwin's general approval, kept in full vigour until after the Second World War.

The theory of innovation diffusion is also pure orthodoxy. It is assumed by economic historians that more efficient methods of achieving certain productive ends (inventions) become available over time (see Schmookler, 1966). Some are a by-product of experience, in that the man on the job comes to perceive an easier way of doing it. Others are the product of deliberate effort, which may well involve taking time and resources away from the job in hand, in order to perfect a better way of doing it; in other words, they require *investment*. It is theoretically possible for the same invention to be made independently in more than one place, but the adoption of inventions (innovation) is nearly always the product of a process of diffusion from the initial point of discovery. The invention is normally a saleable or stealable commodity, and it is much cheaper to purchase or steal it than to devote resources to re-inventing it. Only a complete lack of communication is likely to prevent innovation diffusion.

In the planning sphere there are two main types of innovation, the technical and the institutional. The American park system, Howard's garden city, and Hénard's roundabouts are examples of technical innovations, capable of being adopted in almost any town or country if the necessary resources are available. The garden city, however, also contains elements of the institutional innovation, and there is no clear dividing line between technical innovations and clearly institutional ones such as differential building regulations and use zoning. Extension planning, for instance, occupies an intermediate position. The international diffusion of institutional innovations encounters obstacles in the shape of differences between the political and legal structures of the various states. Even if these differences do not halt the spread of the innovation, they may lead to its substantial modification, and in these circumstances it may fairly be asked whether the process at work is not one of re-invention rather than innovation diffusion.

This doubt has arisen most forcibly of all in respect of zoning (see Logan,

1976; Mancuso, 1978). It can plausibly be argued that German zoning techniques, based on differential building regulations, were adopted in New York in 1916. In Germany the administration of differential building regulations had revealed the need for a modicum of use zoning, and the same conclusions were drawn in New York. However, use zoning had been recognized by the American courts, at least in respect of California, since the 1880s, and when zoning swept North America in the 1920s the dominant note was that of use zoning, and not differential building regulations. How German, then, is American zoning?

The same questions can be asked about the garden city, which on export from Britain became the dormitory suburb, and about extension planning, which was foreshadowed by a whole string of model suburbs in Britain before Horsfall brought the tablets of *Städtebau* from Germany. Would these innovations not have evolved to meet specific needs even without the foreign example? The challenge is fair but this is not the point at which to meet it, for the adoption of institutional innovations required political decisions. And in the moulding of political opinion foreign example again had a part to play.

We have seen throughout this book that anyone who owned a sufficiently large area of land could engage in town-building to his heart's content. What distinguished town planning from this ageless activity was the imposition of the plan on private owners. The necessary directive power had to be granted by public authority and, under the various liberal-democratic constitutions of the later nineteenth century, this meant that elected representatives, and ultimately the electorate, had to be convinced of the value of planning. It was also helpful if property-owners could be convinced, so that the courts could be kept out of the matter. The rise of town planning, whether locally generated or imported, depended ultimately on advocacy.

It is at this point that we can turn with some profit to the work of social psychologists on attitude change. Although their thinking is still in a state of flux, most social psychologists would agree that attitude changes in individuals are the product of one or more of three main categories of influence: rational-objective, social and emotional. In the first category, an individual's attitudes change either because he accepts a persuasive argument put to him with the deliberate intention of converting him to a new viewpoint, or because he assimilates new information which is not consonant with his existing beliefs, and is thus led to alter these beliefs and the attitudes based on them. In the second category, he alters his attitudes to conform to those of his social peers or betters, either to integrate himself more fully into a group (solidarity), to internalize an inferior social position (deference), or to support his aspirations to higher status. Prominent processes in this category are imitation, which applies principally to interactions between members of a group, and prestige suggestion, whereby an attitude associated with or advocated by a respected source is adopted without arousing the individual's normal critical faculties. In the third and final category, emotional experiences undermine existing attitudes and require the

Abb. 36. Gartenstadt-Zentrum. Ansicht der bearbeiteten Teilfläche.
Marktplatz mit Hallengängen. Amtsgebäude, Post usw.

ISOMETRIC VIEW OF CENTRAL SETTLEMENT

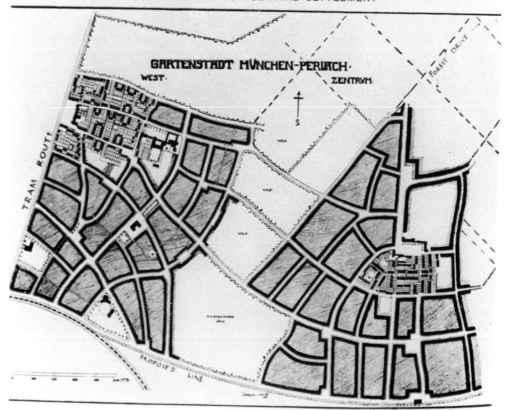

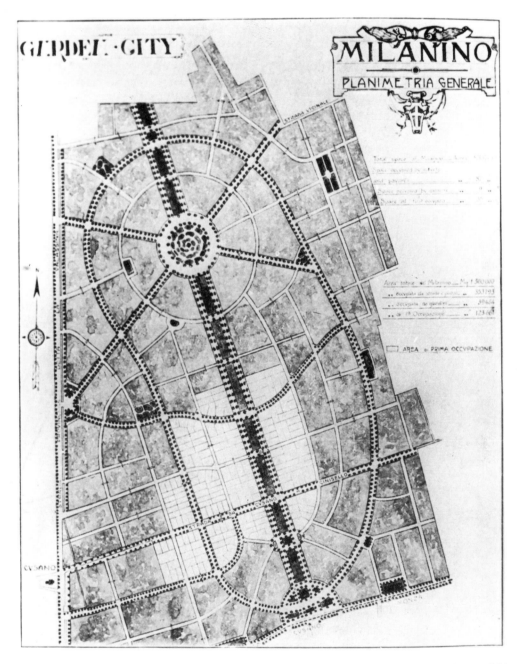

32 *'Some corner of a foreign field':* (Opposite) *a German 'garden city' (Perlach, Munich),
designed by Berlepsch-Valendàs, and* (above) *and italian version (Milanino, Milan). Both
were, in fact, garden suburbs. (TPR, 1910, plate 74; RIBA, 1911, 748)*

individual to establish new ones. The easiest example of this process to identify is trauma, which is defined as a compulsive reorganization of the mental field following an intense emotional experience, and often takes the form of a 'conversion' to a new set of beliefs. There is also evidence to suggest that fear can produce changes in attitudes (Beisecker and Parson, 1972, passim).

Although social psychologists disagree about the relative importance of these three categories of influence, most would accept that attitude change is usually the result of deliberate persuasion (Beisecker and Parson, 1972, 5). As the history of town planning is studded with deliberate persuasive efforts, both written and oral, we can therefore conclude that there is some connection between these efforts and the changes in attitudes which we can definitely detect. Furthermore, it follows therefrom that the methods of persuasion used in these efforts have some effect. Of course, if a variety of methods are used, there is no guarantee that any one of them is effective. However, if we find persuaders making extensive use of a particular method, and achieving attitude changes, we have strong grounds for assuming that that method is contributing to the effect. If it were not, the persuaders would presumably cease to use it.

It therefore follows that appeals to foreign example in planning are likely to have influenced the attitudes of those at whom they were aimed. Indeed, foreign example would appear to be a very potent force of persuasion. Foreign example is likely to present the individual with clearer alternatives to his existing beliefs than arguments based on domestic evidence. The foreign example may have an emotional appeal, either through semi-conscious associations with the exotic, or as an arouser of fear. Foreign example is likely to reach the average recipient through an individual of high status, a much-travelled man of the world, a clever linguist, or a distinguished foreign visitor. Prestige suggestion, therefore, is a strong possibility. Foreign example is also more likely to appeal to people of high education, whose ego-involvement in their beliefs is low; it was, therefore, likely to exercise a strong influence on the élite groups to whom an interest in planning was largely restricted before 1914. The very narrowness of the élite would also have made it very susceptible to social influence once attitudes affected by foreign example had become established within it. Finally, the foreign town-planning tour or conference would have been a very effective way of subjecting participants to the full range of influences, and of cementing their new attitudes, once established, through group activity.

THE FOUR COUNTRIES: CONNECTIONS AND INFLUENCES

Although it has been helpful to distinguish artistic influence, innovation diffusion, and persuasion by the use of foreign example, those who lived through our period were rarely aware of such clear divisions. Planning as an international phenomenon was too pervasive, too confusing. Even now, as we look back on the historical evidence, national, international, regional, local and personal factors intermingle constantly. We can, however, attempt in a very impressionistic way to establish how open each of our four countries was to foreign example. Let us begin with the most insular of them, France.

In this brief compass we can scarcely expect to uncover the secret foundations of French self-sufficiency and inner contentment. Theodore Zeldin, perhaps, has done most to explain their nineteenth-century forms (see Zeldin, 1973, 1977). No more cultivated upper and middle classes were to be found anywhere in the world. As for their international awareness, why, Paris had become, by the later nineteenth century, the very capital of world civilization, a secular Rome. Yet, perhaps because the world looked to France, the French scarcely felt the need to return the compliment. With their national society confirmed as early as the seventeenth century as the richest and most populous in Europe, a position which it retained until the early nineteenth century, they were spared self-doubt. Even in the course of the nineteenth century, when Britain, Germany and the United States outstripped France, the underlying stability of French society (despite various political shocks) reassured them. British industrial power excited some interest between 1815 and mid-century (see Bédarida, 1978, 13–17), but France herself seemed to be modernizing fast enough, while avoiding some of the horrors of the Manchesters and the Birminghams. America was too far away to worry about; the French could summon up little enough interest in their uncouth cousins in Canada, let alone a neighbouring breed of Anglo-Saxons. Few Frenchmen emigrated to North America during the century; more and more Americans turned up in Paris, some of them at the Ecole des Beaux-Arts, but few mastered the French language sufficiently to impress their hosts. In planning, perhaps, the French did not have a great deal to learn from Britain and the United States, but Germany was a different matter.

The French attitude to Germany has been a key influence on the course of world history. The rise of Germany in the nineteenth century was a brutal shock. Even after 1815 Western Germany, remoulded by Napoleon to the satisfaction of the Germans themselves, seemed a natural sphere of French influence. Soon, however, the opportunity was lost as German nationalism drew the most Francophile of states into the Prussian ambit. Napoleon III's belated attempt to resist led to the military disaster of 1870–1 and the loss of part of the homeland. France and the German Empire might have built up the strongest of cultural bonds through a French Alsace; in German hands, it soured their relationship and prepared the way for the First World War. In most fields French intellectuals cut themselves off from Germany after 1871; Henri Pirenne, the great Belgian historian, noted for instance how few French historians came to the International Congress of Historians at Berlin in 1908 (Lyon, 1974, 115–17). Many Germans, it must be said, looked down on the French, so the fault was not on one side alone, but it is clear that the exchange of planning ideas, which depended so much on personal contacts and prolific publication, could not flourish in this atmosphere. The only important German planning text to appear in French before 1914 was Camillo Sitte's *Der Städtebau nach seinen künstlerischen Grundsätzen*, which was published in Paris as *L'art de bâtir les villes* in 1902. And even then the translator, Camille Martin, so altered it to suit the current pro-medieval stance of his branch of the Public Art movement that Sitte's Renaissance sympathies were completely obscured (see Collins, 1965). (These distortions also caused great confusion in Britain and the United States where, in the absence of an English translation, planners and architects pounced on the French version, Sitte's German being astoundingly convoluted even by the standards of his time.) Stübben's *Der Städtebau* was apparently known in Paris, but only for its illustrations (Wolf, 1968, 18); it was symptomatic that Stübben's 1893 Chicago paper on planning should have appeared in French only because Charles Buls thought it worth publishing in Brussels (Stübben, 1895, 6–7). And in 1909, Charles Beauquier referred the Chamber to two articles by Stübben in the Brussels journal, *L'Art Public* (*DoPC*, 1909, so, 80).

Of course, we have already seen that these obstacles did not prevent knowledge of German planning from penetrating into France via the *Musée social* in the early 1900s. But it never made the impact that it did in Britain. There was no intermediary to compare with Horsfall, partly because few Frenchmen felt at home in Germany, and partly because to cite the German example in support of planning could easily be counter-productive. Edouard Fuster, the expert on German social policy, took more interest in British planning than the German variety (see *MSA*, 1908, 130). Edouard Herriot was more familiar with Germany than was J. S. Nettlefold, thanks to a pilgrimage to Bayreuth with Alsatian–Parisian friends in 1896 (Soulié, 1962, 21), but while Birmingham could influence Britain, the voice of Paris drowned that of Lyons. Finally, when Herriot went to Germany in 1913 to secure support for his big urban exhibition at Lyons, having had the idea for it while viewing the Dresden hygiene exhibition of 1911, he encountered frosty, uncooperative politeness in city after city, the result of deteriorating relations between the two countries (Soulié, 1962, 41). The virtual absence of German exhibits at the Lyons exhibition thus foreshadowed the war which cut it short (Herriot, 1948, 265). By 1914, it is true, the German example was being cited more frequently both inside and outside the Chamber of Deputies, with municipal landownership especially prominent. The main enthusiasm, however, came from people of Alsatian connections; elsewhere the admiration was rarely more than grudging. In 1913, for instance, the *Section d'hygiène urbaine et rurale* of the *Musée social* sent Robert Schloesing to Germany to study *Städtebau*, an initiative which culminated in Stübben's successful Paris visit in the following year. Yet when Schloesing reported on his visit, in March 1914, in the form of a public lecture at the *Musée social*, he secured the following response from the chairman, Georges Risler (reported here in indirect speech):

He [Risler] emphasized the importance of German technical prowess in town-extension planning. We had to learn to study the German effort and to take advantage of it. But he had no wish to forget the very glorious achievement of Haussmann and Alphand, and that of our great seventeenth- and eighteenth-century architects. He was delighted, he went on, to see that French architects were once again taking an interest in these questions. He reminded his listeners with what brilliance their names had shone, in recent years, in the prize-lists of the great international competitions. Several of them were in fact in the audience and he addressed them directly. After drawing applause by mentioning the name of one who was not there, Monsieur Hénard, he predicted that French art — which was so delicate, so adaptable to practical demands, and so flexibly articulated — was about to make a new and productive leap forward not only in the urban sphere, but in every other direction as well. To that end, it had only to follow that natural and national inspiration which rejected change for the sake of change alone. All that was required was utter obedience to the perfectly sure guidance of French taste. (*MSA*, 1914, 92)

The French indifference to German example helps to explain why the idea of extension planning failed to win much respect in France until it was taken up in Britain. Although British society as a whole exercised a diminishing attraction on the French as the nineteenth century moved towards its close, British prowess in housing reform could not be ignored by the small group of French enthusiasts. Louis-Napoleon's big housing grant of 1852, and the Mulhouse experiment of the following year which it helped to finance, were directly inspired by the British model-dwelling experiments of the 1840s. The detailed designs for workers' dwellings, as displayed at the 1851 exhibition in London, were considered and partially adopted in France. Louis-Napoleon even ordered a translation of Henry Roberts's influential treatise, which was published in France in 1850 as *Des habitations des classes ouvrières* (Guerrand, 1967, 103, 122). In Paris most of the model dwellings built under the Second Empire were blocks of flats, but when, in 1867, Napoleon III promoted an experiment with single-family houses, he employed an English company to build forty of them in the Avenue Daumesnil (Guerrand, 1967, 116).

Housing reformers' admiration for Britain was sustained through the 1870s and 1880s, and municipal dwellings, particularly those of Liverpool, aroused great interest when they were displayed at the Paris exhibitions. However, it was not until the turn of the century that the garden suburb and garden city concepts began to add an important new dimension to the British example. The period saw a modest revival of the 'Anglomania' which had affected France in the Restoration period. Partly a reflection of the growing strategic understanding between the two countries which culminated in the Entente Cordiale and the brilliant reign of a francophile Edward VII, it led to enhanced cultural interchange. H. G. Wells, for instance, was widely read in France, and Peter Wolf has argued that the French translations of *Anticipations* (1904), *When the Sleeper Wakes* (1905), and *The War in the Air* (1910) aroused French interest in the urban future. Wells was singled out as a convincing prophet by Robert de Souza, and by the Extension of Paris Committee (De Souza, 1913, 232–3; *Considérations*, 85). In 1902, furthermore, William Morris's *News from Nowhere* appeared in French (Wolf, 1968, 17).

These suburban and arcadian visions were increasingly backed by reality; Benoît-Lévy related in 1904 that it was not until he learned from Patrick Geddes and Charles Gide that model towns actually existed in Britain that he began to take the idea seriously — he had known that they were to be found in the United States and Australia, but such examples seemed too distant to be of much relevance to France (Benoît-Lévy, 1904, 2–10). On the other hand, it is clear that Benoît-Lévy's failure to capture the French urban reform movement was partly due to a deep-seated French resistance to the British suburban ideal. *La Construction Moderne*, for instance, which in the absence of more specialized journals exercised a big influence on urban environmental thinking, constantly derided Benoît-Lévy and the garden city idea. Faithful to the Parisian upper-class ideal of ultra-urbanity, it was impervious to Howardian or Wellsian perspectives. Indeed, in January 1904 it took Senator Paul Strauss, the housing reformer, to task for his enthusiastic remarks on the spreading city foreseen in *Anticipations*:

> Will our descendants really build themselves graceful cottages among the nondescript factories and chemical plants which are the classic monuments in [suburban] areas of this type? Will they make their homes on the debris of gasworks, when these have been supplanted by power stations? Or among those sanitary facilities which we hesitate to call by their true name, and which have become the native flora of these districts? (*CM*, 9[17], 1904, 193)

This sardonic, defensive and basically ignorant attitude greatly attenuated the impact of the British example in France. True, the British achievement in area clearance and parks and playgrounds, which were of special interest to French reformers, was quite often cited. But in the absence of really respected and influential intermediaries, the fact that most French reformers never went to England produced errors and distortions. Here is one example, a news item from *La Construction Moderne* (the italics are mine):

> *It is well known* that an English law *requires* municipalities to demolish and rebuild districts in which the death rate exceeds a certain figure. It was this law which Monsieur Chamberlain used to rebuild *the whole of the centre of Birmingham* when he was mayor of that city. (*CM*, 9[34], 1904, 408)

Perhaps a rosy view was what was needed to prod the indifferent into action. More likely, however, its effect on the average French sceptic was simply to betray the reformers' slackness and inability to convince. Ambroise Rendu's eulogy of the British 'Town Playing Bill', already cited, can scarcely have been persuasive. Georges Risler's conviction that by 1830 all English towns had been required to draw up extension plans was purely confusing (*MSA*, 1912, 425). The garden city was sold short by Benoît-Lévy's extraordinarily insensitive choice of the translation 'cité-jardin' — 'cité' might have seemed an inspiringly poetic synonym for 'ville' but in general usage it had come to mean an estate of workers' dwellings, and some of the grimmest blocks of flats to be found in France bore the name of 'cité'.

It was not until 1910 that direct knowledge of British practice began to be enhanced. With extension planning now formally adopted there, Britain could be regarded as an adequate surrogate for Germany. Georges Risler, for instance, wrote:

> We should like to offer a practical example to French philanthropists, one which it is easy to go and study among our [British] neighbours and which can be taken as a model. (Risler, 1910, 3)

The RIBA conference of 1910 attracted a small but distinguished French delegation and clearly reinforced Louis Dausset's and Robert de Souza's enthusiasm for planning. Indeed, in 1912 the City of Paris went so far as to send a delegation to join the British tour organized by the National Housing and Town Planning Council (*CM*, 27, 4 Aug. 1912, 531). The Nancy planning campaign also developed strong links with Britain. Nevertheless, a clear connection remains between the weakness of the French planning movement and its imperfect relations with a potentially amenable neighbour. The informed French public never really grasped the idea of urban planning, even in its limited British version.

It would be unfair, however, to blame defective French knowledge of Britain entirely on French indifference. If more British urban reformers had shown an interest in France, the French might have been drawn into a more fruitful debate in spite of themselves. But the French were caught in a vicious circle; their country had little to offer the foreign observer of urban affairs except its long aesthetic tradition and the fading grandeur of the Second Empire's improvements. The British school of pro-Beaux-Arts civic designers respected these examples; Inigo Triggs, for instance, whose very Christian name betrayed his aesthetic leanings, acknowledged a greater debt to Paris than to Berlin or Vienna:

> ...Paris was the pioneer, and her municipal authorities, acting under the guidance of Baron Haussmann, were the first to conceive the ideas of symmetry and spaciousness, of order and convenience, that have made Paris the finest city in the world. (Triggs, 1909, 33)

Even Patrick Abercrombie, a man of sounder judgment than Triggs, was moved to write, subject to a string of qualifications, that:

> Haussmann's modernisation of Paris in its comprehensive grasp of traffic, hygiene, light, and air, is the most brilliant piece of Town Planning in the world...(*TPR*, 1913, 103)

What was lacking, however, was the personal contact which bound British planners so closely to Germany. Even Raymond Unwin was happy to acknowledge the French aesthetic tradition, but the only contemporary French planning work that he singled out for special praise was Eugène Hénard's traffic-engineering theories (Unwin, 1911, 237–41). Hénard was also greatly admired by Triggs and other British planners, thanks to the attention won by his traffic analyses after about 1906 (Wolf, 1968, 45, 47). Hénard had even lent his diagrams personally to Triggs (Triggs, 1909, 122). Hénard alone, however, could not bring the British and French movements together.

The importance of two-way flows in the cultivation of foreign example is clearly demonstrated by the relationship between Britain and Germany. German influence was so prominent in our interpretation of the rise of planning in Britain that it would be pointless to go over the ground again here. We have not, however, directly considered what Britain could offer in return. If we do so, we find that, rather than being in Germany's debt, Britain was taking part in a fairly equal exchange of ideas. Germany offered Britain the institutional innovations which could permit the generalization of planning, but she had no technical innovations that could be of much interest to Britain, except in transport planning. Britain could offer two important institutions: a modern form of the leasehold tenure that had lapsed in Germany since early modern times, and area slum clearance. In other respects she was institutionally weak, but she was strong in techniques of low-density residential construction and design. While the British flocked to Germany after the turn of the century to view the wide streets and orderly districts produced by *Städtebau*, so did the Germans descend on England to view Port Sunlight, Bournville, Letchworth and Hampstead. Many British planners must have learned as much about German methods from German visitors in Britain as they did while on tour in Germany.

The first element of British design to be admired in Germany was landscape architecture; when the fortifications of Bremen were removed after 1802 they were replaced by gardens in the English style (Kabel, 1949, 44–5). German modernization after 1815 attracted a flood of British technicians and entrepreneurs. English firms provided Berlin's gas and later its water supply (Masur, 1971, 42). Even after Berlin municipalized the waterworks in 1873 during its big sanitary revival, the English manager, Henry Gill, stayed on as a municipal official – he was still there in the early 1890s (Pollard, 1893, 19–21). Many other German towns followed Berlin's example, and piped water led on to waterborne sewerage, an innovation which we have already seen imported virtually complete from Britain (see pp. 15–16). Here again, a British or partially British presence survived the installation period; William Heerlein Lindley (son of William Lindley, the railway engineer, who built a water and sewerage system for Hamburg after the fire of 1842) became *Stadtbaurat* at Frankfurt after helping his father build the sewerage system there. He held the post until 1896, thus becoming a collaborator of Adickes in his later years (Hartog, 1962, 23–4).

If Germany equalled or surpassed Britain in hygiene techniques after the 1870s, her reformers continued to look to Britain for inspiration in housing. This tradition dated back to 1847, the year in which Victor Aimé Huber and C. W. Hoffmann had founded their *Berliner gemeinnützige Baugesellschaft* in conscious imitation of the London model-housing associations already building at that time (Hegemann, 1963, 203). Their initiative was a virtual failure, but their successor as leader of the German housing movement, Julius Faucher, spent some time in England and, like them, championed the ideal of single-family housing (Hegemann, 1963, 240). Until the 1890s, it is true, the efforts of these upper- and middle-class housing reformers produced little practical result, but they were supplemented by the more enlightened of the workers' colonies built by employers in the Ruhr and other industrial provinces. Most of these settlements, flimsily built on cheap land, used small houses, and the employers, many of whom were in close business contact with Britain, used the English example to make a virtue of their low-density methods (Wurzer, 1974a, 19). The best-known of all was Alfred Krupp, who began to build houses for his steelworkers at Essen in the 1860s. A long stay in England in the winter of 1871 persuaded him that great advantages would attend the incorporation into his colonies of some of the virtues of English *Wohnkultur* (culture of the home) (Klapheck, 1930, 12–17). From then until the war his firm was constantly involved in the construction and enhancement of a series of settlements, increasingly based on the single-family house, which incorporated the latest refinements of English residential design as soon as they became available. Until the 1890s the results were dour and dreary, but as soon as the Port Sunlight/Bournville mode of design proved the practicality of a village-like environment, Krupp changed his methods. Sustained in his convictions by the nature and craft revival in Germany in the 1890s, he had begun by the early 1900s to build in a cottage-and-garden style consciously designed to evoke a pre-industrial golden age (Klapheck, 1930, 66–8).

By this time, German domestic architecture in general had been inspired by the spectacular leap forward in house design achieved in Britain in the 1890s thanks to the efforts of Shaw, Voysey and other architects (Berlepsch-Valendàs, 1911, 166–7). Their achievement was known in Germany before Hermann Muthesius was attached to the German embassy in London in 1896 specifically to study it. By the time he published his great work, *Das englische Haus*, in 1904, the British example was even better appreciated in Germany. However, Muthesius gave the British effort a final seal of approval. He anatomized British *Wohnkultur*, which he portrayed as permeating all levels of society, and acting as a potent means of education (Hartmann, 1977, 19). This was what German liberal and conservative reformers wanted to hear, and they welcomed further news from Britain about the integration of 'the English house' into the carefully planned community which the garden city and garden suburb techniques seemed to offer. For Berlepsch-Valendàs, the British approach to housing and residential planning, epitomized in the garden city idea, sought nothing less than 'the reconstruction of the conditions of human existence, especially in the sphere of housing, that most powerful of all factors in social life' (Berlepsch-Valendàs, 1911, 166–7).

Not everyone welcomed the surge of British influence. Theodor Fritsch, author of a proposal for a system of new towns, *Die Stadt der Zukunft*, published in 1896, was piqued when his ideas, ignored in Germany for several years, were suddenly hailed as the new gospel when restated in Howardian form by the *Deutsche Gartenstadtgesellschaft* (*Städtebau*, 1905, 25). Stübben was prepared to admit that the principle of decentralization of industry and population through *Gartenstädte* had been directly imported from Britain. However, he warned that it would need some modification in Germany, for he thought it scarcely possible under Continental conditions to build a whole town of small houses and gardens (Stübben, 1907, 306). Underlying these technical qualifications was a generally ambivalent attitude towards Britain among the informed public. Peter Hampe has tried to explain it in psychological terms as a father fixation, with Britain as the ageing parent outstripped by a vigorous son, still grudgingly respected yet to be overthrown at the first opportunity (Hampe, 1976, 76–8). Certainly, the growing political estrangement of the two countries complicated the already deeply-flowing counter-currents in German planning thought. Nevertheless, British influence in Germany was still on an upward path when war broke out. Raymond Unwin's *Town Planning in Practice* secured publication, under the more Germanic title of *Grundlagen des Städtebaus* (Foundations of town planning), the year after it appeared in Britain. The second edition appeared in both countries in the same year (Albers, 1975a, 16). Its exposition of the combination of formal and informal planning which Unwin had first achieved at Letchworth was greatly appreciated in Germany, where the mechanistic plans of Hobrecht's generation had provoked too extreme a reaction, in the form of Henrician meanderings. Berlepsch-Valendàs by now was coming to Britain every year to study the latest progress in planning on garden city lines (*TPR*, 1910, 246). The British visits of the *Deutsche Gartenstadtgesellschaft* were as popular as the Continental tours of the National Housing and Town Planning Council; in 1912 some 150 Germans descended on Hampstead Garden Suburb (*TPR*, 1913, 26).

In the complacent political climate which prevailed, at least in Prussia, in the new century, there was no hope of seeing one envied British institution, area clearance, generally introduced into Germany. Leasehold tenure, constantly advocated by the anglophile Rudolf Eberstadt, was too much at variance with the practices of the German property market to displace freehold, but it made some progress on municipal land at Ulm and elsewhere. On the technical side, however, the British contribution had come to be widely recognized by the time war broke out. Werner Hegemann's anglophilia probably led him to take too rosy a view of the technical innovations culled from Britain, but he singled out the detailed analysis of traffic pioneered by the Royal Commission on London Traffic, the clear distinction between traffic and residential streets, the terrace of small houses, as adopted by Bruno Taut at Falkenberg, and a whole range of refinements in low-density residential design (Hegemann, 1913, 157–8). Stübben, however, echoed Hegemann's respect for British residential design, and paid the British planning movement perhaps its biggest German compliment of these years:

> Our oft-cited German thoroughness (*Gründlichkeit*) is now being amplified in England by such vigorous enterprise (*Tatkraft*) that we have every cause to strive for further development, if we are not to be outstripped by our Anglo-Saxon cousins. (Stübben, 1911, 8)

This remark, almost the mirror-image of so many British eulogies of German planning, epitomizes the profound inter-relationship of urban environmental thinking in the two countries on the eve of war.

For most of our period the United States had little to offer Europe. It was noted, especially in Britain, for the vigour and rapid growth of its towns after the Civil War, but their rough appearance and corrupt government denied them any exemplary value. From as early as the 1850s the United States was the most important source of innovations in urban transport in the world. However, American urban transport generally remained less regulated by public authority than that of Europe, so few planning lessons could be drawn from the American experience. Public parks were, however, a different matter. American city parks began to outstrip those of Europe in both scale and the quality of their design from the 1850s. After about 1870, when European park creation flagged, the United States moved clearly ahead, with the idea of the park system transferring the whole issue onto a higher level. It was in North America that open space first emerged as a potential structural element for the entire city, while Europe continued to view the park as a reservoir or oasis in the middle of a mass of buildings. Even the next stage in European thinking, the idea of a belt of parkland or open country surrounding the town, which first emerged as a practical possibility in the 1890s (see Faludi, 1968–9), reflected the limitations of the European mind, unable to grasp the full implications of the spreading city which was already a reality in North America.

It was not until the 1890s that American parks and park systems first began to attract serious attention in Europe. Lord Meath, chairman of the Parks Committee of the newly-formed London County Council, went to the United States in 1890 to report on the park systems and their interlinking boulevards and parkways (*Garden City*, 1906, 59–60). However, most of the LCC area was fully built-up and the idea of a London park strategy was quickly forgotten. The French, as we have noted, began to hear of the American achievement via the reports of Forestier and Benoît-Lévy in the early 1900s. One of the earliest articles in *Der Städtebau*, in 1905, was a long, eulogistic review of the American park achievement by a German official (*Städtebau*, 1905, 113–23). By this time, the City Beautiful movement as a whole was beginning to attract European attention, if only for its paper qualities. We have already observed the impact of American monumental design on certain British architects, but the interest of German planners was an even bigger tribute. Werner Hegemann, of course, was a constant source of information, but the reputation of American planning did not depend upon his advocacy alone. The lavishly produced and profusely illustrated American planning report, designed to inspire a sceptical public, created a strong impression in Germany where *Städtebau* had become so much a dull routine. Better-informed observers were aware how much of these publications was simply window dressing, but exhibition organizers loved to give prominence to the intricate plans and stunning views which America could provide. Burnham's Chicago plan of 1909 made the strongest impression of all.

It was not simply, however, the superficial side of American planning which made an impact in Europe. The idea of city-wide development plans for established urban areas, of which the Washington and San Francisco schemes were early examples, was a particularly valuable inspiration to those who were struggling to drag Berlin out of the nineteenth century. The density and efficiency of public transport in American cities also suggested how Berlin's residential densities might be broken down. The influential pamphlet, *Gross-Berlin*, published in 1906 by the city's two architectural associations, drew attention to American planning developments (*Städtebau*, 1909, 127). Thereafter, the Berlin planning campaign, partly under Hegemann's guidance, incorporated several American features. The whole idea of holding an exhibition to stir up public concern was American-inspired, and it was no coincidence that Hegemann, who had already helped to put on planning exhibitions in New York and Boston, was invited to organize it. The accompanying planning competition was, of course, typical of German practice, but the debate which surrounded it had a distinctly transatlantic tone, and some of the entries incorporated American features. Perhaps the most striking innovation proposed in any entry was Rudolf Eberstadt's scheme for a system of green wedges, or interlocking open spaces running from the edge of the city into its very heart, which clearly drew on the American example (*TPR*, 1910, 168). With Hegemann's massive report on the Berlin competition giving lavish, indeed effusive, praise to almost everything American, the reputation of American planning in Germany was at its highest yet when war broke out:

> An objective consideration must persuade us to admit that Germany in general, and Greater Berlin in particular, have fallen far behind the Anglo-Saxon countries in the fields of transport and open space...It does not seem to be so much a basic national deficiency, as an inability to do without our French-Absolutist crutches, which has forced Germany to give up its leadership to the civic-minded (*selbstverwaltungsfähigen*) Anglo-Saxons. (Hegemann, 1913, 394)

For the French, the main lesson to be drawn from American planning was the civic improvement campaign. In the absence of effective legislation, French urban reformers faced much the same problems as the Americans in trying to stir up public opinion. Although American urban aesthetics, as a gargantuan interpretation of vaguely Beaux-Arts principles, did not impress the French, the idea of an aesthetically-based appeal to the upper classes was very appropriate to French, and especially Parisian, circumstances. Georges Benoît-Lévy gave a full report on these methods to the *Section d'hygiène urbaine et rurale* in 1908 (*MSA*, 1908, 330), and the *Musée's* Parisian open-space and planning campaign was partially modelled on this information. Also consciously based on the American example were the *Société française des espaces libres et des terrains de jeu*, founded in 1911 (*MSMD*, 1912, 349), the *Société des Amis de Paris* and their journal *Les Amis de Paris*, launched in 1911 (*TPR*, 1911, 235), and the unofficial Nancy extension plan (Hottenger, 1913, 35). Though the British also drew on this example, improvement campaigns like the 'Beautiful Bolton' movement were untypical of a reform activity which continued to concentrate on housing, an area in which America had almost nothing to offer. Chicago-type plans were far too ambitious to be considered, given the paucity of British planning powers even after 1909, and open spaces were not seriously considered outside the context of small residential areas. The poverty of the London planning debate, in comparison with that of Berlin, hindered full recognition of the breadth of American planning, and only in Liverpool, where City Engineer John A. Brodie was working on a city-wide system of planted boulevards linked to parks, were recognizably American techniques brought into use. Nor is this influence surprising, given that Brodie had joined the Liverpool University Department of Civic Design in 1909 (Cherry, 1974, 54). In fact, wherever we encounter American influence in Britain between about 1905 and 1914, it is almost always linked to the efforts of a school of neo-classicist architects and landscape architects to secure a bigger role in British urban design. This motive very largely accounts for the big American presence secured for the RIBA Town Planning Conference in 1910, and the lavish praise showered on American efforts at a number of points in its proceedings (e.g. RIBA, 1911, iii).

In relations between Britain and the United States, cultural affinity was outweighed by distance. It was much easier for the British planner to visit Germany than the United States, and only a few leading figures were able to view American efforts at first hand before 1914. Distance also affected the American view of Europe by making news of urban reform heavily dependent on the efforts of intermediaries such as Frederic C. Howe and Charles Mulford Robinson. Until the turn of the century some of the most influential intermediaries were British visitors, including James Bryce, the trenchant critic of urban corruption, and W. T. Stead, the slum reformer. From the 1840s the philanthropic housing movement in New York was closely linked to that of London (see De Forest and Veiller, 1903, I, 69–118) and the settlement houses were partly staffed by British emigrants or people with long stays in Britain behind them. From the 1890s, however, American urban reform began to pursue a more independent path, with American investigators travelling in greater numbers to Europe. Britain remained an important point of reference, but for physical planning visitors were increasingly tempted to study Germany, while young architects were drawn to Paris rather than London. Thus largely secure from the direct intrusion of European ideas, at a time when economic prosperity was eroding American deference to Europe in all but the aesthetic sphere, the leading American reformers could dictate the extent of American exposure to European ideas.

An early example of this method was provided by De Forest and Veiller's 1903 report on the New York tenement problem. The authors explained that they had, in line with previous housing inquiries, devoted much attention to European conditions and regulations. They had come to the conclusion, however, that the New York tenement house problem was the worst in the world, and they therefore proposed that conclusions and remedies should be sought primarily in the history of the tenement house in New York (De Forest and Veiller, 1903, I, 4). This partial detachment from Europe may do something to explain the difficulties of American planning, especially with respect to housing; in 1911, for instance, when Raymond Unwin, Thomas Adams and T. H. Mawson were invited over for the Third National Conference on City Planning, they found that in the absence of the customary strong contribution from Benjamin C. Marsh, they were the only ones to emphasize the social side of planning (*TPR*, 1911, 213). It also explains how a very precise control mechanism, the *Staffelbauordnung*, could be adopted in New York in 1916 without its justifying housing reform ideology. When German example was used in support of reforms to which American traditions were inimical, such as municipal landownership and land taxation, it had very little impact.

Only in aesthetics did the Americans remain susceptible to European currents which they could not control. This sense of inferiority was succinctly expressed by Burnham when, during the 1901 European tour which he had forced on his colleagues in the Washington Plan Commission, he wrote to his wife: 'We have much to learn and much to live out before we can equal old England or *any* place in Europe' (Hines, 1974, 147). This cringing deference could, however, lead directly to grotesque bravado, as on the occasion when Burnham's committee planning the Chicago exhibition buildings broke up in mad self-congratulation after Augustus St Gaudens, the sculptor, had suggested that it was 'the greatest meeting of artists since the fifteenth century' (Reps, 1965, 501). This bravado had its strongest expression in some of the civic centre schemes of the early 1900s, nearly all of which included a massive dome inspired by St Peter's or the Invalides. The Chicago exhibition had in fact led to the establishment of an American Academy in Rome, allowing American products of the Ecole des Beaux Arts, excluded from the Prix de Rome, nevertheless to dog the footsteps of the leading French urban designers. Burnham found as much inspiration in Rome as he did in Paris, and his extraordinary 600-foot high dome in his Chicago civic centre project formed a direct link between Brunelleschi and Albert Speer.

But in Progressive America, as in Nazi Germany, dreams of an ultimate world architecture surpassed the resources available to build it. Planning, even in the New World, had to be content with more modest achievements.

Seven

Urban Planning
The Pre-1914 Contribution

In 1914 most informed observers would have agreed that, even in Germany, urban planning still had a long way to go. Yet from a vantage-point in the last quarter of the twentieth century, the dimensions of the pre-First World War planning achievement cannot fail to impress. The practice of planning was defective or partial, except perhaps in Germany, but the idea of planning was firmly rooted almost everywhere. Certainly, the volume of planning activity has expanded since 1918. Urban planning has become more scientific, it has acquired an important social-welfare dimension, and it has been complemented by regional and national planning. However, the foundations for all of this had been laid before 1914; there have been no radically new departures since.

From this perspective, the last twenty-five years before the First World War take on a new importance. So far in this study they have appeared as no more than a phase of rapid but somewhat belated progress towards the rational ordering of city growth. However, if the idea of planning moved from birth to near maturity in this short period, then we have before us the most important episode in the whole history of public intervention in the urban environment.

That one of the twentieth century's most distinctive administrative activities should be a product of the nineteenth century need not surprise us. As industrial society spread across Europe and North America in the second half of the nineteenth century, its structural weaknesses came to be more clearly appreciated. At the same time, the idea gained ground that public intervention in social and economic processes could help counteract these defects. However, national and provincial governments remained reluctant to undertake a comprehensive reconstruction of society. Instead, they conceded much of the initiative in social reform to the authorities in the towns. It was after all in the towns, and particularly in the biggest cities, that the defects of industrialism were most obvious. It was even possible, and tempting, to believe that the problems were intrinsically *urban*, and therefore capable of resolution by the reform of urban processes alone. This assessment grew increasingly difficult to sustain as economic development proceeded and the urbanized proportion of the population rose, but it remained influential until world war and its aftermath brutally revealed its weaknesses. It was from this context that municipal socialism emerged, and it was from municipal socialism that the idea of planning was born.

In the early nineteenth century, as we have seen, public authority played a very limited role in the evolution of the urban environment. The urban administrations normally owned and maintained the street network and the drainage system. In many of the larger centres the authorities also enforced rudimentary building regulations in the interests of fire safety. Some also tried to control the emission of smoke and other nuisances. Finally, some authorities provided public places or buildings such as markets and exchanges. As the century went on, however, urban government tended to grow more ambitious. As the towns grew, and the facilities they required for economic and social efficiency increased in number and intricacy, private enterprise appeared more and more deficient. The more profitable privately-provided services tended towards monopoly, while the less profitable failed increasingly to attract the necessary capital as alternative investment opportunities expanded both at home and abroad. Underlying this latter problem was the inability of the poorest towndwellers to pay for services, such as piped water, which came to be considered essential for the good of the urban community as a whole. At first, many urban authorities tried to regulate the private suppliers of services, but in doing so they tended to reduce their attractiveness to private capital. Ultimately, they had no choice but to take over the services themselves.

The more capital intensive the service, the more carefully the authorities had to consider the relationship between its provision and the evolution of the town, if only to avoid wasting public money. This factor alone would have led the authorities towards planning. However, the authorities were also being drawn into a more ambitious regulation of the use of *private* land within the towns. The main stimulus here was the growing discrepancy between the housing environment generated in growing industrial and commercial towns with large populations of poorly-paid manual workers, and the quality of environment which came to be seen as necessary for the maintenance of physical and moral health. Just as the authorities chose to acquire certain services in order to ensure that all could benefit from them, so they sought to fix minimum standards for the privately-provided habitat. In fact, the logical conclusion of this intervention was direct public provision of workers' housing, but that point was only just being reached by the time of the First World War. Meanwhile, the authorities were drawn into an increasingly complex dialogue with private landowners and builders.

The whole tendency of the nineteenth century was thus to enmesh the authorities in the town-building process. On the one hand, they provided more and more of the infrastructure. On the other, they increasingly constrained the private owners and controllers of land in the development of their property. These parallel tendencies were bound in due course to generate the idea of public urban planning, in which both aspects of public activity would be combined, if only in the cause of efficiency, in an overall strategy of urban development.

Of course, if this gradual recognition of changing practical realities had been the only process at work, planning would have emerged locally at a multitude of points in time as each town passed some critical threshold. Indeed, for much of the nineteenth century we seem to be observing the early stages of just such a process. However, the ultimate widespread recognition and adoption of planning were conditioned by two other factors. There was planning's status as an innovation; and the participation of the urban authorities in broader political and cultural systems. These factors allowed planning to spread rapidly through the urbanized world by a process of national or provincial adoption.

First of all, however, planning had to be invented. This was no easy matter, for it required a specific combination of intellectual perception and practical activity which was achieved nowhere in the early stages of the industrial urbanization process. It was possible to carry on a very ambitious programme of public intervention in the urban environment without generating the idea of planning. Meanwhile, a far-sighted individual or group could come close to planning on a theoretical plane, without having the power to achieve the practical results which were needed to validate the idea.

In retrospect we can see that, during much of the nineteenth century, administrative practice was groping its way towards planning, especially in the larger cities. However, in the absence of a balanced distribution of specific interventions between the positive (public provision of facilities) and the negative (regulation of private land use) modes, or the necessary perception on the part of the administrators, the idea of planning could not emerge. Second Empire Paris, perhaps, came closest to planning without actually getting there. The authorities spent a hundred million pounds on public works in less than twenty years and introduced stricter and more refined building regulations. However, Haussmann's brand of intervention was too dependent on massive investment of public funds to achieve that essential quality of planning, the power to perpetuate itself. On the contrary, by stimulating a property boom over which the authorities had no control, the improvement programme was bound, sooner or later, to bring about its own demise. Furthermore, the authorities were so concerned to improve the centre that they allowed private interests to dominate the development of the periphery. There were too many gaps in the powers available for the strategy followed to amount to planning, and indeed one searches Haussmann's memoirs in vain for any appreciation of the idea of comprehensive urban planning, even though he wrote them as late as the early 1890s. Throughout, he portrays himself as a far-sighted engineer, and no more. If ambitious public works could not generate the idea of planning in Paris, they could scarcely do so elsewhere. Nor were building regulations, even in Liverpool and other advanced British towns, enough to create the concept of planning, especially as legal convention normally required them to be applied indiscriminately to the entire local authority area, without regard to internal functional distinctions. As for the grid plans of American cities, they were too much an embodiment of the selfish interests of the landowners to provide a clear path to planning.

While Paris approached planning in practice without generating the idea, a number of individuals created a theory of planning, without the practice. Outstanding was the Spanish engineer, Ildefonso de Cerdà, who produced a far-sighted extension plan for Barcelona in 1858, and justified it in a huge treatise, *Teoría general de la urbanización* (see Miller, 1978). Much of the book comprised an impressive theoretical model of comprehensive urban planning. However, Cerdà's ideas remained virtually unknown outside Spain, mainly because the Barcelona authorities declined to put his more radical proposals into effect. Cerdà wanted the greater part of each new block to be retained as open space, and the remainder developed with low buildings. The resulting city of gardens, served by rapid railed transport, would surely have spread Cerdà's thinking far and wide. Unfortunately, the authorities had no experience with such restrictive building regulations and, under pressure from the landowners in the extension zone, they allowed building to cover virtually the whole of each block, up to a generous maximum height. They also failed to provide the communal facilities planned by Cerdà as a focal point for each district. This partial application of Cerdà's plan produced results comparable to those of Hobrecht's Berlin extension, and cancelled out the persuasive power of his thinking. Meanwhile, in Germany, Baumeister's far-sighted study of town-extension planning, published in 1876, met a similar fate. It contained the germ of the idea of comprehensive planning, but the urban authorities were not yet ready to apply it in practice.

The circumstances in which planning was eventually invented can help us to see more clearly what had previously been lacking. It was not invented by an individual or a city, though both of these made their contribution. Instead, it was the creation of a national economic and administrative system, Germany, which exhibited a largely fortuitous combination of rapid urbanization, a general tolerance of government intervention in economy and society, and the survival of unusually powerful pre-industrial instruments of environmental control. Of the latter, the most productive was the absolutist institution of the extension plan. In being used, at first quite crudely, to control the growth of the expanding cities of mid-nineteenth-century Germany, the extension plan helped generate an intellectual and administrative dynamic which produced both the idea and the practice of planning. We have already traced this development in detail. Suffice it to say that planning was finally invented in this way between about 1890 and the early 1900s, as revival from the Great Depression generated a new phase of rapid urban growth. Frankfurt's introduction of building zones was the key administrative innovation, and Stübben's great manual provided the most convincing conceptualization of planning.

Admittedly, Germany's federal system complicated the legal emergence of planning. Moreover, the municipalities enjoyed a freedom of initiative which in some respects produced important variations in planning practice even within the

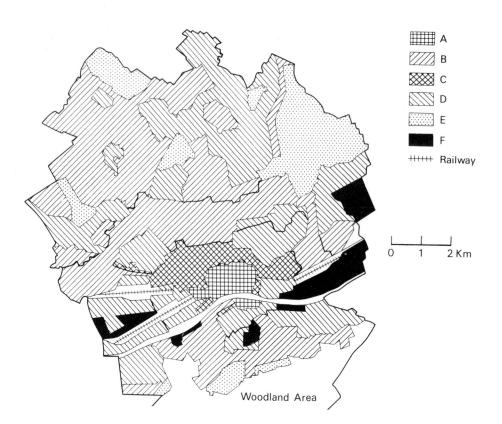

33   *Mature zoning: the Frankfurt building and use zone system* (Staffelbauordnung)*, c. 1910. It was the attribution of particular building types, and therefore particular uses, to districts within the city which allowed comprehensive urban planning to emerge in Germany from the early 1890s. This map, re-drawn from the original German source, therefore symbolizes the main conclusion of this study, that modern planning had been invented before the First World War. The inner city (A) is zoned industrial and residential. It has the most intensive site usage in the city (up to three-quarters of each site may be built up) and the greatest maximum height (20 metres up to cornice level). Around this business district, on the north bank of the Main, there is a high-density residential zone (C). Other residential zones (B) stretch out into the suburbs at progressively lower densities. On the outskirts lie a number of districts (E) designated for large detached houses* (Landhäuser)*. Large-scale manufacturing is concentrated in exclusively industrial areas (F) near the river and railways, but large areas of the inner suburbs are zoned for mixed industrial and residential use (D), at densities lower than those permitted in the centre. This preponderance of mixed areas in the inner districts of the city reflects its long-established physical structure; further out, where development is in progress or still awaited, the segregation of functions is more rigorous. This strategy implies growing commuting as the city expands. The maximum permitted number of storeys ranges from five in the centre to two in the* Landhausvierteln. *(Diagram based on map in Heights of Buildings Commission, 1913, facing p. 48)*

individual states. However, owing partly to Prussia's economic and demographic dominance of the German Empire, and partly to the Empire's great cultural unity, German planning was essentially a national movement. As a result, once it had been invented, the generality of towns quickly adopted it.

Certainly, by the early 1900s, planning was clearly associated in the eyes of foreign observers more with Germany as a whole than with individual German cities or states. As such, it clearly qualified for direct importation into the more centralized of the other highly-urbanized states by the initiative of their central governments or legislatures. In the atmosphere of international competitiveness which had been building up since the 1870s, planning could appear as one means of securing national efficiency, leading to the granting of planning powers to all urban areas. Planning could thus spread by a process of national leaps, with local urban conditions and historic practices almost entirely irrelevant to its progress.

However, even in Britain, where a national decision was taken in 1909 to adopt planning, the picture is not quite so simple. Parliament acknowledged the importance of local initiative by declining to *impose* planning on any town. As a result, a number of advanced cities set the pace in planning after 1909, just as their lobbying had done so much to secure the required legislation in the first place. Moreover, planning would doubtless have emerged in Britain from incremental processes even without the benefit of the German example. It might have been delayed a few years, but Ebenezer Howard's planning theories, developed without reference to Germany, would doubtless have combined with traditional British suburban design to produce the idea of comprehensive planning. In France, furthermore, we see a highly-centralized state which refused to adopt planning as a national policy until it grudgingly did so, in exceptional circumstances and in a disastrously slipshod manner, in 1919. In France, the essential base, in terms of a combination of intractable urban problems and existing administrative practices, was too weak to sustain the imported idea of planning, which faded or was distorted by some of its well-meaning French advocates.

Nor do the United States fit easily into a model of diffusion by national leaps. In fact, German example did not play a very important part here. Not only did the Federal government fail to show much interest in planning, but neither did most of the individual states. Much depended on city initiative, and at this level some of the biggest achievements were the work of unofficial bodies rather than of the municipalities or local boards. In terms of social policy the United States — the most prosperous nation of the four — did not feel that they had much to learn from Europe, and no serious military or economic threat was perceived. In consequence, no clear national pattern emerges in the development of planning in the United States, except in the debates of the small group of urban reformers. However, it also has to be said that in failing to import the German or British model of planning, the United States allowed their cities to muddle through with a very distorted and partial approach to environmental policy. After a burst of interest in the early 1900s, much of the social reform potential of planning was ignored, allowing planning to institutionalize itself as the handmaiden of private property interests and as a means of perpetuating social discrimination. Indeed, American planning has never recovered from this initial orientation.

However, American planning was not alone in serving primarily the interests of the richer sections of the population. In fact, in all four countries we have been observing the efforts of technocratic or social elites to set up a painless method of social reform which would remove the grievances of the poor while educating them into the values of their social superiors. From this point of view it is important to recognize that the years 1890–1914 were a time of growing social tensions, in which the idea of rationalizing the structure of cities acquired an unprecedented appeal. If lower rents, better housing and richer community facilities could remove the need for a major redistribution of income or wealth, then urban planning had a great deal to offer the middle and upper classes in addition to the simple creation of a pleasant urban environment. We cannot fail to note that the workers took very little interest in planning; instead, its biggest supporters were, in Germany, an elite of officials and academics; in Britain, a dying class of bourgeois social reformers connected with a threatened Liberal Party; in France, a minority of upper-class do-gooders with strong links with the Church and other conservative institutions; and, in the United States, urban big business.

Planning's basic appeal to these people lay in the prospect which it seemed to hold out of social peace achieved through no more than a rationalization of the land market, a reform which need not even harm the landowners, let alone the owners of commerce and industry and high-earning professionals. After 1914, it would become clear that most of this prospect was a mirage, and social reformers would increasingly turn their attention from land to capital. Indeed, the insertion of urban planning in a much broader programme of reform helps to explain its lack of development since 1918. Some of the key issues in the pre-1914 planning debate, such as the recoupment of betterment, remain largely unresolved today. On the contrary, urban landowners have been able to hold on to much of the economic power which was first unmasked by German reformers in the later nineteenth century. Meanwhile, planning's primary goal has become that of efficiency, and in that capacity it has become politically neutral, serving communist and capitalist state systems alike. Indeed, here lies the source of much of the frustration felt by planners in a world which has reduced them to the level of technicians.

Planning, then, throve on exaggerated hopes before the First World War. Nevertheless, its emergence in just twenty-five years from a morass of partial and often contradictory urban policies to the point where it caught the imagination of the whole of the urbanized world must rank as one of the most dramatic episodes in the whole history of public administration. We hope that this study has captured some at least of the excitement of this most creative, though ultimately disappointing, era in the evolution of urban planning.

Bibliography

This list includes only materials cited in the text. It does not pretend to be a full bibliographic guide to the question.

Abbreviations used in the text are as follows:

Aperçu	Commission d'Extension de Paris, *Aperçu historique* (1913)
BPP	*British Parliamentary Papers*
BSAMP	*Bulletin de la Société des Amis des Monuments parisiens*
Bulletin	*Bulletin des lois de l'Empire français; Bulletin des lois du Royaume de France; Bulletin des lois de la République française*
Centralblatt	*Centralblatt der Bauverwaltung*
CM	*La Construction Moderne*
CMPV	Conseil Municipal [de Paris], *Procès-verbaux*
CMRD	Conseil Municipal [de Paris], *Rapports et documents*
Considérations	Commission d'Extension de Paris, *Considérations techniques préliminaires* (1913)
DoPC	*Documents parlementaires, Chambre*
DPC	*Débats parlementaires, Chambre*
Hansard	*Parliamentary Debates* (House of Commons)
MSA	*Musée social, Annales*
MSMD	*Musée social, Mémoires et documents*
se	session extraordinaire
Sénat	*Débats parlementaires, Sénat*
so	session ordinaire
TPR	*Town Planning Review*

Abbott, Edith 1936: *The Tenements of Chicago 1908–1935*. Chicago: University of Chicago Press.

Abercrombie, Leslie Patrick 1945: *Greater London Plan 1944*. London: HMSO.

Adams, Frederick J. and Hodge, Gerald 1965: City planning instruction in the United States: the pioneering days, 1900–1930. *Journal of the American Institute of Planners*, 31(1), 43–51.

Adams, Thomas 1927: *Planning the New York Region: An Outline of the Organization, Scope and Progress of the Regional Plan*. New York: Committee on Regional Plan of New York and its Environs.

Addams, Jane 1911: *Twenty Years at Hull House, with Autobiographical Notes.* New York: Macmillan.

Adrian, Charles R. and Griffith, Ernest S. 1976: *A History of American City Government: The Formation of Traditions, 1775—1870.* New York: Praeger.

Albers, Gerd 1975a: *Entwicklungslinien im Städtebau: Ideen, Thesen, Aussagen 1875—1945: Texte und Interpretationen.* Düsseldorf: Bertelsmann.

Albers, Gerd 1975b: Der Städtebau des 19. Jahrhunderts im Urteil des 20. Jahrhunderts, in Schadendorf, Wulf (ed.): *Beiträge zur Rezeption der Kunst des 19. und 20. Jahrhunderts.* Munich: Prestel Verlag, 63—71.

Aldridge, Henry R. 1915: *The Case for Town Planning: A Practical Manual for the Use of Councillors, Officers and Others Engaged in the Preparation of Town Planning Schemes.* London: National Housing and Town Planning Council.

Allan, C. M. 1965: The genesis of British urban redevelopment with special reference to Glasgow. *Economic History Review*, 2nd series, 18, 598—613.

Anderson, R. D. 1977: *France 1870—1914: Politics and Society.* London: Routledge and Kegan Paul.

Armstrong, Alan H. 1968: Thomas Adams and the Commission of Conservation, in Gertler, L. O. (ed.): *Planning the Canadian Environment.* Montreal: Harvest House, 17—35.

Armytage, Walter H. G. 1961: *Heavens Below: Utopian Experiments in England 1560—1960.* London: Routledge and Kegan Paul.

Ashworth, William 1954: *The Genesis of Modern British Town Planning: A Study in Economic and Social History of the Nineteenth and Twentieth Centuries.* London: Routledge and Kegan Paul.

Ashworth, William 1975: *A Short History of the International Economy Since 1850.* London: Longman, 3rd ed.

Aspinall, P. J. 1978: *The Evolution of Urban Tenure Systems in Nineteenth Century Cities* (CURS Research Memorandum, no. 63). Birmingham: Centre for Urban and Regional Studies, Birmingham University.

(Association Française pour l'Avancement des Sciences) 1926: *Lyon 1906—1926.* Lyons: A. Rey.

Bangert, Wolfgang 1936: *Baupolitik und Stadtgestaltung in Frankfurt a.M.: ein Beitrag zur Entwicklungsgeschichte des deutschen Städtebaues in den letzten 100 Jahren.* Würzburg: Verlag Konrad Triltsch.

Baratier, Edouard (ed.) 1973: *Histoire de Marseille.* Toulouse: Privat.

Barnett, Canon and Mrs S. A. 1909: *Towards Social Reform.* London: T. Fisher Unwin.

Barraclough, G. 1957: *The Origins of Modern Germany.* Oxford: Basil Blackwell.

Bastié, Jean 1964: *La croissance de la banlieue parisienne.* Paris: Presses Universitaires de France.

Baumeister, Reinhard 1876: *Stadt-Erweiterungen in technischer, baupolizeilicher und wirthschaftlicher Beziehung.* Berlin: Ernst und Korn.

Baumeister, Reinhard 1887: *Moderne Stadterweiterungen.* Hamburg: Verlag Richter.

Bédarida, François 1978: Introduction to Tristan, Flora, *Promenades dans Londres*, edited by F. Bédarida. Paris: François Maspero, 11—43.

Beisecker, Thomas D. and Parson, Donn W. (eds.) 1972: *The Process of Social Influence: Readings in Persuasion.* Englewood Cliffs: Prentice-Hall.

Bell, Colin and Rose 1969: *City Fathers: The Early History of Town Planning in Britain.* London: Barrie and Rockliff.

Bellet, Daniel and Darvillé, Will 1914: *Ce que doit être la cité moderne: son plan, ses aménagements, ses organes, son hygiène, ses monuments et sa vie.* Paris: H. Nolo.

Benoît-Lévy, Georges 1904: *La cité-jardin.* Paris: Jouve.

Benoît-Lévy, Georges 1905: *Cités-jardins d'Amérique.* Paris: Jouve.

Bergel, Jean-Louis 1973: *Les servitudes de lotissement à usage d'habitation.* Paris: Pichon et Durand-Auzias.

Berger-Thimme, Dorothea 1976: *Wohnungsfrage und Sozialstaat: Untersuchungen zu den Anfängen staatlicher Wohnungspolitik in Deutschland (1873–1918).* Frankfurt: Peter Lang/Berne: Herbert Lang.

Berlepsch-Valendàs, Hans Eduard von 1911: *Die Gartenstadtbewegung in England, ihre Entwickelung und ihr jetziger Stand.* Munich/Berlin: R. Oldenbourg.

Besson, Michèle 1971: *Les lotissements.* Paris: Berger-Levrault.

Best, G. F. A. 1973: Another part of the island, in Dyos, H. J. and Wolff, M. (eds.): *The Victorian City*, vol. I. London: Routledge and Kegan Paul, 389–412.

Bliss, William D. P. (ed.) 1908: *The New Encyclopedia of Social Reform.* New York/London: Funk and Wagnall.

Boardman, Philip 1944: *Patrick Geddes: Maker of the Future.* Chapel Hill: University of North Carolina Press.

Born, Karl Erich 1976: Structural changes in German social and economic development at the end of the nineteenth century, in Sheehan, James J. (ed.): *Imperial Germany.* New York/London: New Viewpoints, 16–38.

Bournville Village Trust 1955: *The Bournville Village Trust, 1900–1955.* Bournville: Bournville Village Trust.

Bridenbaugh, Carl 1955: *Cities in the Wilderness: The First Century of Urban Life in America 1625–1742.* New York: Alfred A. Knopf, 2nd ed.

Briggs, Asa 1952: *History of Birmingham, vol. 2: Borough and City 1865–1938.* London: Oxford University Press.

Brown, Kenneth D. 1977: *John Burns.* London: Royal Historical Society.

Brunner, Arnold W., Olmsted, Frederick Law and Arnold, Bion J. 1911: *A City Plan for Rochester: A Report for the Rochester Civic Improvement Committee, Rochester, N.Y.* Rochester: Rochester Civic Improvement Committee.

Buder, Stanley (1967) The model town of Pullman: town planning and social control in the Gilded Age. *Journal of the American Institute of Planners*, 33(1), 2–9.

Burg, David F. 1976: *Chicago's White City of 1893.* Lexington: University Press of Kentucky.

Burke, Peter 1975: Some reflections on the pre-industrial city. *Urban History Yearbook*, 13–21.

Burnham, Daniel H. 1905: *Report on a Plan for San Francisco.* San Francisco: City of San Francisco.

Burnham, Daniel H. and Bennett, Edward H. 1909: *Plan of Chicago.* Chicago: The Commercial Club.

Calabi, Donatella 1976: Werner Hegemann, o dell'ambiguità borghese dell'urbanistica. *Casabella*, 428, 54–60.

Cannadine, David 1977: Aristocratic indebtedness in the nineteenth century: the case re-opened. *Economic History Review*, 2nd series, 30(4), 624–50.

Carrière, Françoise and Pinchemel, Philippe 1963: *Le fait urbain en France.* Paris: Armand Colin.

Chalklin, C. W. 1974: *The Provincial Towns of Georgian England: A Study of the Building Process, 1740—1820.* London: Edward Arnold.

Chandler, Tertius and Fox, Gerald 1974: *3000 Years of Urban Growth.* New York/London: Academic Press.

Chapman, S. D. (ed.) 1971: *The History of Working Class Housing.* Newton Abbot: David and Charles.

Cheney, Charles Henry 1917: *Procedure for Zoning or Districting of Cities.* San Francisco: California Conference on City Planning.

Cherry, Gordon E. 1974: *The Evolution of British Town Planning.* Leighton Buzzard: Leonard Hill.

Cherry, Gordon E. 1975: *Factors in the Origins of Town Planning in Britain: The Example of Birmingham, 1905—1914* (CURS Working Paper, no. 36). Birmingham: Centre for Urban and Regional Studies, Birmingham University.

Chevalier, Louis 1958: *Le choléra, la première épidémie du XIXe siècle: étude collective.* La Roche-sur-Yon: Imprimerie centrale de l'Ouest.

Chickering, Roger 1975: *Imperial Germany and a World Without War: The Peace Movement and German Society, 1892—1914.* Princeton, NJ: Princeton University Press.

City Plan Commission, Newark, New Jersey 1913: *City Planning for Newark.* Newark, NJ: L. J. Hardham Printing Co.

Collini, Stefan 1976: Hobhouse, Bosanquet and the State: philosophical idealism and political argument in England 1880—1918. *Past and Present,* 72, 86—111.

Collins, George R. and Christiane C. 1965: *Camillo Sitte and the Birth of Modern City Planning.* New York: Random House.

Commission d'Extension de Paris 1913: *Aperçu historique.* Paris: Préfecture du Département de la Seine.

Commission d'Extension de Paris 1913: *Considérations techniques préliminaires (la circulation — les espaces libres).* Paris: Préfecture du Département de la Seine.

Commission on Building Districts and Restrictions 1916: *Final Report, June 2, 1916.* New York: City of New York, Board of Estimate and Apportionment, Committee on the City Plan.

Committee on the City Plan 1914: *Development and Present Status of City Planning in New York City: Being the Report of the Committee on the City Plan, December 31, 1914, Together with Papers Presented at a Meeting of the Advisory Commission on City Plan, December 17, 1914.* New York: City of New York, Board of Estimate and Apportionment, Committee on the City Plan.

Committee on Town Planning of the American Institute of Architects [George B. Ford, ed.] 1917: *City Planning Progress in the United States, 1917.* Washington: Journal of the American Institute of Architects.

Les congrès internationaux de 1681 à 1899: liste complète 1960. Brussels: Union of International Associations.

Les congrès internationaux de 1900 à 1919: liste complète 1964. Brussels: Union of International Associations.

Creese, Walter L. 1966: *The Search for Environment: The Garden City, Before and After.* New Haven/London: Yale University Press.

Crossick, Geoffrey 1977: The emergence of the lower middle class in Britain: a discussion, in Crossick, G. (ed.): *The Lower Middle Class in Britain.* London: Croom Helm, 11—60.

Darley, Gillian 1975: *Villages of Vision*. London: Architectural Press.

Day, Michael G. 1973: Sir Raymond Unwin (1863—1940) and R. Barry Parker (1867—1947) a study and evaluation of their contribution to the development of site-planning theory and practice (2 vols). MA thesis, Manchester University.

Day, Michael G. and Garstang, Kate 1975: Socialist theories and Sir Raymond Unwin. *Town and Country Planning*, 43, 346—9.

De Forest, Robert W. and Veiller, Lawrence (eds.) 1903: *The Tenement House Problem* (2 vols). New York: Macmillan.

De Souza, Robert 1913: *Nice, capitale d'hiver*. Paris/Nancy: Berger-Levrault.

Delafons, John 1962: *Land-Use Controls in the United States*. Cambridge, Mass.: Joint Center for Urban Studies, MIT and Harvard University.

Des Cilleuls, Alfred 1877: *Traité de la législation de la voirie urbaine*. Paris: [no publisher given].

Dewhirst, Robert K. 1960—1: Saltaire. *Town Planning Review*, 31, 135—44.

Dickinson, Robert E. 1961: *The West European City: A Geographical Interpretation*. London: Routledge and Kegan Paul, 2nd ed.

Douglas, Roy 1976: *Land, People and Politics: A History of the Land Question in the United Kingdom, 1878—1952*. London: Allison and Busby.

Dupeux, Georges 1974: *La société française 1789—1870*. Paris: Armand Colin, 7th ed.

Dyos, H. J. 1961: *Victorian Suburb: A Study of the Growth of Camberwell*. Leicester: Leicester University Press.

Dyos, H. J. 1968: The slums of Victorian London. *Victorian Studies*, 11 supp., 5—40.

Dyos, H. J. and Aldcroft, D. H. 1969: *British Transport: An Economic Survey from the Seventeenth Century to the Twentieth*. Leicester: Leicester University Press.

Eberstadt, Rudolf 1893: *System und Princip in der Berliner Stadtverwaltung: ein Beitrag zur Communalreform*. Berlin: Verlag Hugo Steinitz.

Eberstadt, Rudolf 1909: *Handbuch des Wohnungswesens und der Wohnungsfrage*. Jena: Gustav Fischer.

Egli, Ernst 1967: *Geschichte des Städtebaues, Band III: die neue Zeit*. Zurich/Stuttgart: Eugen Rentsch Verlag.

Engeli, Christian and Haus, Wolfgang 1975: *Quellen zum modernen Gemeindeverfassungsrecht in Deutschland*. Berlin: Kohlhammer.

Exposition de la 'Cité Moderne' organisée par la Chambre de Commerce de Nancy et la Société Industrielle de l'Est, Nancy, 4—17 mai 1913, *Bulletin de la Chambre de Commerce de Nancy*, 11(53), juillet-août 1913 (special number).

Faludi, Andreas 1968—9: Vienna's green belt. *Transactions of the Bartlett Society*, 7, 101—25.

Fein, Albert 1972: *Frederick Law Olmsted and the American Environmental Tradition*. New York: George Braziller.

Ferguson, T. 1963—4: Public health in Britain in the climate of the nineteenth century. *Population Studies*, 17(3), 213—24.

Fishman, Robert 1977: *Urban Utopias in the Twentieth Century: Ebenezer Howard, Frank Lloyd Wright, and Le Corbusier*. New York: Basic Books.

Ford, James 1936: *Slums and Housing, With Special Reference to New York City: History, Conditions, Policy*. Cambridge, Mass.: Harvard University Press.

Forestier, J. C. N. 1906: *Grandes villes et systèmes de parcs*. Paris: Hachette.

Forshaw, J. H. and Abercrombie, Leslie Patrick 1943: *County of London Plan*. London: Macmillan.

Fraser, Derek 1979: *Power and Authority in the Victorian City*. Oxford: Basil Blackwell.

Gaillard, Jeanne 1977: *Paris, la ville 1852–1870*. Paris: Editions Honoré Champion.

Garner, John S. 1971: Leclaire, Illinois: a model company town (1890–1934). *Journal of the Society of Architectural Historians*, 30(3), 219–27.

Gaskell, S. Martin 1976: Sheffield City Council and the development of suburban areas prior to World War I, in Pollard, S. and Holmes, C. (eds.): *Essays in the Economic and Social History of South Yorkshire*. Barnsley: South Yorkshire County Council, 174–86.

Geddes, Patrick 1915: *Cities in Evolution: An Introduction to the Town Planning Movement and to the Study of Civics*. London: Williams and Norgate.

Gibbon, Sir Gwilym and Bell, Reginald W. 1939: *History of the London County Council, 1889–1939*. London: Macmillan.

Girard, Louis 1952: *La politique des travaux publics du Second Empire*. Paris: Armand Colin.

Goldfield, David R. 1977: Pursuing the American dream: cities in the Old South, in Brownell, B. A. and Goldfield, D. R. (eds.): *The City in Southern History: The Growth of Urban Civilization in the South*. Port Washington: Kennikat Press, 52–91.

Griffith, Ernest S. 1974: *A History of American City Government: The Progressive Years and their Aftermath, 1900–1920*. New York/Washington: Praeger.

Guerrand, Roger-H. 1967: *Les origines du logement social en France*. Paris: Les Editions Ouvrières.

Guillou, Jean 1905: *L'émigration des campagnes vers les villes*. Paris: Arthur Rousseau.

Gurlitt, Cornelius 1904: Der deutsche Städtebau, in Wuttke, R. (ed.): *Die deutschen Städte*, vol. I. Leipzig: Friedrich Brandstetter, 23–45.

Guttenberg, Albert Z. 1977: City encounter and 'desert' encounter: two sources of American regional planning thought. Paper presented at the 17th Annual Conference of the Western Historical Association, Portland, Oregon, 14 October 1977.

Hampe, Peter 1976: Sozioökonomische und psychische Hintergründe der bildungsbürgerlichen Imperialbegeisterung, in Vondung, K. (ed.): *Das wilhelminische Bildungsbürgertum: zur Sozialgeschichte seiner Ideen*. Göttingen: Vandenhoeck und Ruprecht, 67–79.

Hardy, Dennis 1979: *Alternative Communities in Nineteenth Century England*. London: Longman.

Hartmann, Kristiana 1977: *Deutsche Gartenstadtbewegung: Kulturpolitik und Gesellschaftsreform*. Munich: Heinz Moos Verlag.

Hartog, Rudolf 1962: *Stadterweiterungen im 19. Jahrhundert*. Stuttgart: Kohlhammer Verlag.

Haussmann, Georges 1890–3: *Mémoires* (3 vols). Paris: Victor-Havard.

Haw, George 1900: *No Room to Live: The Plaint of Overcrowded London*. London: Wells, Gardner, Darton and Co., 2nd ed.

Hawtree, Martin G. 1974: The origins of the modern town planner: a study in professional ideology. PhD thesis, Liverpool University.

Hays, Forbes B. 1965: *Community Leadership: The Regional Plan Association of New York*. New York/London: Columbia University Press.

Hegemann, Werner 1911: *Der Städtebau nach den Ergebnissen der allgemeinen Städtebau-Ausstellung in Berlin nebst einem Anhang: die Internationale Städtebau-Ausstellung in Düsseldorf. Band 1*. Berlin: Verlag Ernst Wasmuth.

Hegemann, Werner 1913: *Der Städtebau nach den Ergebnissen der Allgemeinen Städtebau-Ausstellung in Berlin nebst einem Anhang: die Internationale Städtebau-Ausstellung in Düsseldorf. Band 2: Verkehrswesen, Freiflächen*. Berlin: Verlag Ernst Wasmuth.

216 Bibliography

Hegemann, Werner 1915: *Report on a City Plan for the Municipalities of Oakland and Berkeley.* Oakland/Berkeley: Municipal Governments of Oakland and Berkeley [etc.].

Hegemann, Werner 1963: *Das steinerne Berlin: Geschichte der grössten Mietskasernenstadt der Welt.* Berlin: Ullstein (slightly abridged re-edition of the work first published by Jakob Hegner, Lugano, in 1930).

[Heights of Buildings Commission] 1913: *Report of the Heights of Buildings Commission to the Committee on the Height, Size and Arrangement of Buildings of the Board of Estimate and Apportionment of the City of New York, December 23, 1913.* New York: City of New York, Board of Estimate and Apportionment, Committee on the Height, Size and Arrangement of Buildings.

Heiligenthal, Roman 1929: *Städtebaurecht und Städtebau. Band 1: Die Grundlagen des Städtebaus und die Probleme des Städtebaurechtes, Städtebaurecht und Städtebau im deutschen und ausserdeutschen Sprachgebiet.* Berlin: Deutsche Bauzeitung.

Heinrich, Ernst 1962: Der 'Hobrechtplan'. *Jahrbuch für Brandenburger Landesgeschichte,* 13, 41−57.

Hemleben, Sylvester John 1943: *Plans for World Peace Through Six Centuries.* Chicago: University of Chicago Press.

Hénard, Eugène 1903−6: *Les transformations de Paris* (8 fascicules). Paris: Librairies-Imprimeries Réunies.

Hennebo, Dieter 1974: Der Stadtpark, in Grote, L. (ed.), *Die deutsche Stadt im 19. Jahrhundert: Stadtplanung und Baugestaltung im industriellen Zeitalter.* Munich: Prestel Verlag, 77−90.

Hennock, E. P. 1973: *Fit and Proper Persons: Ideal and Reality in Nineteenth-Century Urban Government.* London: Edward Arnold.

Herriot, Edouard 1948: *Jadis: avant la première guerre mondiale.* Paris: Flammarion.

Herzfeld, Hans 1962: Berlin als Kaiserstadt und Reichshauptstadt 1871−1945, in his *Ausgewählte Aufsätze.* Berlin: Walter de Gruyter, 281−313.

Hines, Thomas S. 1974: *Burnham of Chicago: Architect and Planner.* New York: Oxford University Press.

Hobhouse, Hermione 1975: *A History of Regent Street.* London: Macdonald and Jane's.

Hofmann, Wolfgang 1964: *Die Bielefelder Stadtverordneten: ein Beitrag zu bürgerlicher Selbstverwaltung und sozialem Wandel 1850 bis 1914.* Lübeck/Hamburg: Matthiesen Verlag.

Hofmann, Wolfgang 1974: *Zwischen Rathaus und Reichskanzlei: die Oberbürgermeister in der Kommunal- und Staatspolitik des Deutschen Reiches von 1890 bis 1933.* Stuttgart: Verlag W. Kohlhammer.

Hofmann, Wolfgang 1978: Preussische Stadtverordnetenversammlungen als Repräsentativ-Organe, in Reulecke, J. (ed.): *Die deutsche Stadt im Industriezeitalter.* Wuppertal: Peter Hammer Verlag, 31−56.

Hohorst, Gerd, Kocka, Jürgen and Ritter, Gerhard 1975: *Sozialgeschichtliches Arbeitsbuch: Materialien zur Statistik des Kaiserreichs 1870−1914.* Munich: Verlag C. H. Beck.

Holderness, B. A. 1976: *Pre-industrial England: Economy and Society, 1500−1750.* London: Dent.

Horsfall, T. C. 1895: *The Government of Manchester.* Manchester: Cornish.

Horsfall, T. C. 1900: Housing of the labouring classes. Unpublished lecture, Manchester Central Library, 370. 942 Ho 1.

Horsfall, T. C. 1904: *The Improvement of the Dwellings and Surroundings of the People: The Example of Germany.* Manchester: Manchester University Press.

Hottenger, Georges 1913: *Nancy et la question d'extension des villes* (extracts from *Bulletin de la Société Industrielle de l'Est*, nos. 105, 106). Nancy: Imprimeries Réunies de Nancy.

Howard, Ebenezer 1965: *Garden Cities of Tomorrow*. London: Faber and Faber, amended edition of the work first published in 1902.

Howe, Frederic C. 1905: *The City, the Hope of Democracy*. London: T. Fisher Unwin.

Hughes, J. Quentin 1964: *Seaport: Architecture and Townscape in Liverpool*. London: Lund Humphries.

Improved Means of Locomotion as a First Step towards the Cure of the Housing Difficulties of London, Being an Abstract of the Proceedings of Two Conferences Convened by the Warden of Robert Browning Hall, Walworth, with a Paper on the Subject by Charles Booth 1901. London: Macmillan.

Johnson, James H. 1967: *Urban Geography: An Introductory Analysis*. Oxford: Pergamon Press.

Jones, Gareth S. 1971: *Outcast London: A Study in the Relationship between Classes in Victorian Society*. Oxford: Clarendon Press.

Jourdan, M. G. 1890: *Recueil de règlements concernant le service des alignements et des logements insalubres dans la Ville de Paris*. Paris: Préfecture du Département de la Seine.

Jourdan, M. G. 1900: *Recueil de règlements concernant le service des alignements et de la police des constructions dans la Ville de Paris*. Paris: Préfecture du Département de la Seine.

Kabel, Erich 1949: *Baufreiheit und Raumordnung: die Verflechtung von Baurecht und Bauentwicklung im deutschen Städtebau*. Ravensburg: Otto Maier Verlag.

Kantor, Harvey A. 1973: The City Beautiful in New York. *New-York Historical Society Quarterly*, 57(2), 149–71.

Kantor, Harvey A. 1974: Benjamin C. Marsh and the fight over population congestion. *Journal of the American Institute of Planners*, 40(6), 422–9.

Kellett, J. R. 1978: Municipal socialism, enterprise and trading in the Victorian city. *Urban History Yearbook*, 36–45.

Kennedy, P. M. 1975: Idealists and realists: British views of Germany, 1864–1939. *Transactions of the Royal Historical Society*, 5th series, 25, 137–56.

Klapheck, Richard 1930: *Siedlungswerk Krupp*. Berlin: Ernst Wasmuth.

Köllmann, Wolfgang 1969: The process of urbanization in Germany at the height of the industrialization period. *Journal of Contemporary History*, 4, 59–76.

Krabbe, Wolfgang R. 1974: *Gesellschaftsveränderung durch Lebensreform: Strukturmerkmale einer sozialreformerischen Bewegung in Deutschland der Industrialisierungsperiode*. Göttingen: Vandenhoeck und Ruprecht.

Lampard, Eric E. 1973: The urbanizing world, in Dyos, H. J. and Wolff, M. (eds.): *The Victorian City*. London: Routledge and Kegan Paul, vol. I, 3–57.

Land Enquiry Committee 1914: *The Land: The Report of the Land Enquiry Committee, vol. II: Urban*. London: Hodder and Stoughton.

Latreille, André (ed.) 1975: *Histoire de Lyon et du Lyonnais*. Toulouse: Privat.

Lavedan, Pierre 1952: *Histoire de l'urbanisme: époque contemporaine*. Paris: Henri Laurens.

Lavedan, Henri 1959: *Histoire de l'urbanisme: Renaissance et temps modernes*. Paris: Henri Laurens.

Lavedan, Pierre 1975: *Histoire de l'urbanisme à Paris*. Paris: Hachette.

Law, C. M. 1967: The growth of urban population in England and Wales, 1801–1911. *Institute of British Geographers, Transactions*, 41, 125–43.

Lee, J. J. 1978: Aspects of urbanization and economic development in Germany, 1815–1914, in Abrams, P. and Wrigley, E. A. (eds.): *Towns in Societies: Essays in Economic History and Historical Sociology.* Cambridge: Cambridge University Press, 279–94.

Lees, Andrew 1975: Debates about the big city in Germany, 1890–1914. *Societas*, 5(1), 31–47.

Lees, Andrew 1979: Critics of urban society in Germany, 1854–1914. *Journal of the History of Ideas*, 40(1), 61–83.

Leonard, Charlene Marie 1961: *Lyon Transformed: Public Works of the Second Empire 1853–1864.* Berkeley/Los Angeles: University of California Press.

Lépidis, Clément and Jacomin, Emmanuel 1975: *Belleville.* Paris: Henri Veyrier.

Lloyd, T. H. and Simpson, M. (eds.) 1977: *Middle Class Housing in Britain.* Newton Abbot: David and Charles.

Logan, Thomas H. 1976: The Americanization of German zoning. *Journal of the American Institute of Planners*, 42(4), 377–85.

Luard, Evan 1977: *International Agencies: The Emerging Framework of Interdependence.* London: Macmillan.

Lubove, Roy 1962: *The Progressives and the Slums: Tenement House Reform in New York City 1890–1917.* Pittsburgh: University of Pittsburgh Press.

Lubove, Roy 1967: *The Urban Community: Housing and Planning in the Progressive Era.* Englewood Cliffs: Prentice-Hall.

Lyon, Bruce 1974: *Henri Pirenne: A Biographical and Intellectual Study.* Ghent: E. Story-Scientia.

McEvedy, Colin and Jones, Richard 1978: *Atlas of World Population History.* London: Allen Lane.

McKay, John P. 1976: *Tramways and Trolleys: The Rise of Urban Mass Transport in Europe.* Princeton: Princeton University Press.

McKelvey, Blake 1963: *The Urbanization of America (1860–1915).* New Brunswick: Rutgers University Press.

Mairet, Philip 1957: *Pioneer of Sociology: The Life and Letters of Patrick Geddes.* London: Lund Humphries.

Mancuso, Franco 1978: *Le vicende dello zoning.* Milan: il Saggiatore.

Mander, John 1974: *Our German Cousins: Anglo-German Relations in the 19th and 20th Centuries.* London: John Murray.

Marchand, C. Roland 1972: *The American Peace Movement and Social Reform.* Princeton: Princeton University Press.

Marschalk, Peter 1978: Zur Rolle der Stadt für den Industrialisierungsprozess in Deutschland in der 2. Hälfte des 19. Jahrhunderts, in Reulecke, J. (ed.): *Die deutsche Stadt im Industriezeitalter.* Wuppertal: Peter Hammer Verlag, 57–66.

Marsh, Benjamin Clarke 1909: *An Introduction to City Planning: Democracy's Challenge to the American City.* New York: author.

Masterman, C. F. G. (ed.) 1901: *The Heart of the Empire: Discussions of Problems of Modern City Life in England, with an Essay on Imperialism.* London: T. Fisher Unwin.

Masur, Gerhard 1971: *Imperial Berlin.* London: Routledge and Kegan Paul.

Matzerath, Horst 1978: Städtewachstum und Eingemeindungen im 19. Jahrhundert, in Reulecke, J. (ed.): *Die deutsche Stadt im Industriezeitalter.* Wuppertal: Peter Hammer Verlag, 67–89.

Matzerath, Horst and Thienel, Ingrid 1977: Stadtentwicklung, Stadtplanung, Stadtentwicklungsplanung: Probleme im 19. und im 20. Jahrhundert am Beispiel der Stadt Berlin. *Die Verwaltung*, 10(2), 173–96.

Medalen, Charles 1978: State monopoly capitalism in Germany: the Hibernia affair. *Past and Present*, 78, 82—112.

Mellor, Roy E. H. 1978: *The Two Germanies: A Modern Geography*. London: Harper and Row.

Miller, Bernard 1978: Ildefonso Cerdà: an introduction. *Architectural Association Quarterly*, 9(1), 12—22.

Mitchell, B. R. 1975: *European Historical Statistics, 1750—1970*. London: Macmillan.

Mollat, Michel (ed.) 1971: *Histoire de l'Ile-de-France et de Paris*. Toulouse: Privat.

Money, L. G. Chiozza 1905: *Riches and Poverty*. London: Methuen.

Niethammer, Lutz 1976: Wie wohnten Arbeiter im Kaiserreich? *Archiv für Sozialgeschichte*, 16, 61—134.

Nolen, John (ed.) 1916: *City Planning: A Series of Papers Presenting the Essential Elements of a City Plan*. New York/London: D. Appleton and Co.

Olsen, Donald J. 1964: *Town Planning in London: The Eighteenth and Nineteenth Centuries*. New Haven/London: Yale University Press.

The 1,978 International Organizations Founded Since the Congress of Vienna: Chronological List 1957. Brussels: Union of International Associations.

Pahl, R. E. 1970: *Patterns of Urban Life*. London: Longman.

Peisch, Mark L. 1964: *The Chicago School of Architecture: Early Followers of Sullivan and Wright*. London: Phaidon Press.

Peterson, Jon A. 1976: The City Beautiful movement: forgotten origins and lost meanings. *Journal of Urban History*, 2(4), 415—34.

Piccinato, Giorgio 1974: *La costruzione dell'urbanistica: Germania 1871—1914*. Rome: Officina Edizioni.

Pinkney, David 1958: *Napoleon III and the Rebuilding of Paris*. Princeton, NJ: Princeton University Press.

Plan of Proposed Street Changes in the Burned District and Other Sections of San Francisco (Joint Report of Committee on Extending, Widening and Grading Streets and Committee on Burnham Plans — Submitted to Board of Supervisors, May 1906) 1906. (San Francisco City Library, * f 352.7 Sa 52).

Pollard, James 1893: *A Study in Municipal Government: The Corporation of Berlin*. Edinburgh/London: William Blackwood and Sons.

Proceedings of the Third National Conference on City Planning. Philadelphia, Pennsylvania, May 15—17, 1911 1911. Boston.

Radicke, Dieter 1974: Die Berliner Bebauungsplan von 1862 und die Entwicklung des Weddings: zum Verhältnis von Obrigkeitsplanung zu privatem Grundeigentum, in Poeschken, G., Radicke, D. and Heinisch, T. J. (eds.): *Festschrift für Ernst Heinrich*. Berlin: Universitäts-Bibliothek der TU Berlin, 56—74.

Rauchbach, Wolfgang 1969: Der Gedanke einer inneren Kolonisation: Betrachtungen zum 100. Todestag von Victor Aimé Huber. *Stadtbauwelt*, 38/9, 212—15.

Rebentisch, Dieter 1978: Industrialisierung, Bevölkerungswachstum und Eingemeindungen: das Beispiel Frankfurt am Main 1870—1914, in Reulecke, J. (ed.): *Die deutsche Stadt im Industriezeitalter*. Wuppertal: Peter Hammer Verlag, 90—113.

Reps, John W. 1965: *The Making of Urban America: A History of City Planning in the United States*. Princeton: Princeton University Press.

Reps, John W. 1967: *Monumental Washington: The Planning and Development of the Capital Center*. Princeton: Princeton University Press.

Reynolds, Josephine P. 1948: The model village of Port Sunlight. *Architects' Journal*, 107, 492–6.

Reynolds, Josephine P. 1952–3: Thomas Coglan Horsfall and the town planning movement in England. *Town Planning Review*, 23(1), 52–60.

RIBA, *see* Royal Institute of British Architects.

Riis, Jacob A. 1902: *The Battle with the Slum.* New York: Macmillan.

Risler, Georges 1910: *Les nouvelles cités-jardins en Angleterre: le soleil et l'habitation populaire.* Paris: Société d'Economie Sociale.

Ritter, Gerhard A. and Kocka, Jürgen (eds.) 1974: *Deutsche Sozialgeschichte: Dokumente und Skizzen. Band II: 1870–1914.* Munich: Verlag C. H. Beck.

Rivière, Louis 1904: *La terre et l'atelier: jardins ouvriers.* Paris: Librairie Victor Lecoffre.

Robinson, Charles Mulford 1901: *The Improvement of Towns and Cities, or the Practical Basis of Civic Aesthetics.* New York/London: G. P. Putnam's Sons.

Robinson, Charles Mulford 1903: *Modern Civic Art, or the City Made Beautiful.* New York/London: G. P. Putnam's Sons.

Robinson, Charles Mulford 1916: *City Planning with Special Reference to the Planning of Streets and Lots.* New York/London: G. P. Putnam's Sons.

Robson, William A. 1948: *The Government and Misgovernment of London.* London: Allen and Unwin, 2nd ed.

Rodger, Richard 1979: The law and urban change: some nineteenth-century Scottish evidence. *Urban History Yearbook*, 77–91.

Rouleau, Bernard 1967: *Le tracé des rues de Paris: formation, typologie, fonctions.* Paris: Editions du Centre National de la Recherche Scientifique.

[Royal Institute of British Architects] 1911: *Town Planning Conference, London, 10–15 October 1910: Transactions.* London: RIBA.

Saunders, Ann 1969: *Regent's Park: A Study of the Development of the Area from 1086 to the Present Day.* Newton Abbot: David and Charles.

Saville, John 1957: *Rural Depopulation in England and Wales, 1851–1951.* London: Routledge and Kegan Paul.

Sax, Emil 1869: *Der Neubau Wien's im Zusammenhange mit der Donau-Regulirung: ein Vorschlag zur gründlichen Behebung der Wohnungsnoth.* Vienna: A. Pichler.

Schmookler, Jacob 1966: *Invention and Economic Growth.* Cambridge, Mass.: Harvard University Press.

Schou, August 1963: *Histoire de l'internationalisme, III: du Congrès de Vienne jusqu'à la première guerre mondiale.* Oslo: H. Aschehoug.

Schultz, Stanley K. and McShane, Clay 1978: To engineer the metropolis: sewers, sanitation and city planning in late-nineteenth-century America. *Journal of American History*, 65(2), 389–411.

Scott, Mel 1969: *American City Planning Since 1890.* Berkeley/Los Angeles: University of California Press.

Shaw, Albert 1895: *Municipal Government in Continental Europe.* London: T. Fisher Unwin.

Sheehan, James H. 1971: Liberalism and the city in nineteenth-century Germany. *Past and Present*, 51, 116–37.

Siegfried, André 1946: *Mes souvenirs de la IIIe République: mon père et son temps: Jules Siegfried, 1836–1922.* Paris: Editions du Grand Siècle.

Simmons, Jack 1974: *Leicester Past and Present* (2 vols). London: Eyre Methuen.

Simon, John 1890: *English Sanitary Institutions, Reviewed in Their Course of Development and in Some of Their Political and Social Relations.* London: Cassell.

Singer, H. W. 1941: An index of urban land rents and house rents in England and Wales, 1845–1913. *Econometrica*, 9, 221–30.

Sjoberg, Gideon 1960: *The Pre-industrial City: Past and Present.* New York: Free Press.

Smellie, K. B. 1957: *A History of Local Government.* London: Allen and Unwin, 3rd ed.

Smith, P. J. 1980: Planning as environmental improvement: slum clearance in Victorian Edinburgh, in Sutcliffe, A. (ed.): *The Rise of Modern Urban Planning, 1800–1914.* London: Mansell, 99–134.

Sorlin, Pierre 1969: *La société française I. 1840–1914.* Paris: Arthaud.

Soulié, Michel 1962: *La vie politique d'Edouard Herriot.* Paris: Armand Colin.

Stübben, J. 1895: *La construction des villes: règles pratiques et esthétiques à suivre pour l'élaboration des plans de villes* (Rapport présenté au Congrès international des Ingénieurs de Chicago, 1893 – traduit par Charles Buls). Brussels: Lyon-Claesen.

Stübben, J. 1907: *Der Städtebau.* Stuttgart: Alfred Kroner Verlag, 2nd ed.

Stübben J. 1911: Vom Städtebau in England, in Brix, J. and Genzmer, F. (eds.): *Städtebauliche Vorträge*, 4(8), 5–52.

Stübben, J. 1920: Die Entwicklung des deutschen Städtebaus und ihr Einfluss auf das Ausland. *Stadtbaukunst alter und neuer Zeit*, 8, 113–16; 9, 129–33; 10, 151–4.

Summerson, John N. 1945: *Georgian London.* London: Pleiades.

Sutcliffe, Anthony 1970: *The Autumn of Central Paris: The Defeat of Town Planning, 1850–1970.* London: Edward Arnold.

Sutcliffe, Anthony 1974a: A century of flats in Birmingham 1875–1973, in Sutcliffe, A. (ed.): *Multi-Storey Living: The British Working-Class Experience.* London: Croom Helm, 181–206.

Sutcliffe, Anthony 1974b: Introduction, in Sutcliffe, A. (ed.): *Multi-Storey Living: The British Working-Class Experience.* London: Croom Helm, 1–18.

Sutcliffe, Anthony 1976: A nation of reluctant townsfolk. *The Geographical Magazine*, 48(5), 290–6.

Sutcliffe, Anthony 1980: Zur Entfaltung von Stadtplanung vor 1914: Verbindungslinien zwischen Deutschland und Grossbritannien, in Fehl, G. and Rodríguez-Lores, J. (eds.): *Städtebau um die Jahrhundertwende: Materialien zur Entstehung der Disziplin Städtebau.* Cologne: Deutscher Gemeindeverlag/Verlag W. Kohlhammer, 138–70.

Taylor, Graham Romeyn 1915: *Satellite Cities: A Study of Industrial Suburbs.* New York/London: D. Appleton and Co.

Thienel, Ingrid 1973: *Städtewachstum im Industrialisierungsprozess des 19. Jahrhunderts: das Berliner Beispiel.* Berlin/New York: Walter de Gruyter.

Tims, Margaret 1961: *Jane Addams of Hull House 1860–1935.* London: Allen and Unwin.

Town Planning in Theory and Practice 1908 (Report of a Conference arranged by the Garden City Association...London...25 October 1907). London: Garden City Association.

Triggs, H. Inigo 1909: *Town Planning: Past, Present and Possible.* London: Methuen.

Tyrwhitt, Jacqueline (ed.) 1947: *Patrick Geddes in India.* London: Lund Humphries.

Unwin, Raymond 1911: *Town Planning in Practice: An Introduction to the Art of Designing Cities and Suburbs.* London: T. Fisher Unwin, 2nd ed.

Veber, Adrien 1899: *La suppression des octrois.* Paris: Giard et Brière.

Ville de Nancy 1977: *Nancy: architecture 1900* (exhibition catalogue). Nancy: Ville de Nancy.

Vondung, Klaus (ed.) 1976: *Das wilhelminische Bildungsbürgertum: zur Sozialgeschichte seiner Ideen.* Göttingen: Vandenhoeck und Ruprecht.

Ward, Edward J. (ed.) 1913: *The Social Center.* New York/London: D. Appleton and Co.

Warner, Sam Bass Jr. 1962: *Streetcar Suburbs: The Process of Growth in Boston, 1870–1900.* Cambridge, Mass.: Harvard University Press and MIT Press.

Warner, Sam Bass Jr. 1968: *The Private City: Philadelphia in Three Periods of Its Growth.* Philadelphia: University of Pennsylvania Press.

Webb, Sidney and Beatrice 1913: *English Local Government: The Story of the King's Highway.* London: Longman, Green and Co.

Webb, Sidney and Beatrice 1922: *English Local Government: Statutory Authorities for Special Purposes.* London: Longman, Green and Co.

Weber, Adna Ferrin 1899: *The Growth of Cities in the Nineteenth Century: A Study in Statistics.* New York: Macmillan.

Werner, Frank 1978: *Stadtplanung Berlin: Theorie und Realität. Teil I, 1900–1960.* Berlin: Verlag Kiepert, 2nd ed.

White, B. D. 1961: *A History of the Corporation of Liverpool, 1835–1914.* Liverpool: Liverpool University Press.

Wiebenson, Dora 1970: *Tony Garnier: the Cité Industrielle.* London: Studio Vista.

Williams, Michael 1974: *The Making of the South Australian Landscape.* London/New York: Academic Press.

Wilson, William H. 1964: *The City Beautiful Movement in Kansas City.* Columbia: University of Missouri Press.

Wohl, Anthony S. 1977: *The Eternal Slum: Housing and Social Policy in Victorian London.* London: Edward Arnold.

Wolf, Peter M. 1968: *Eugène Hénard and the Beginning of Urbanism in Paris 1900–1914.* The Hague: International Federation for Housing and Planning.

Woods, Robert A. (ed.) 1898: *The City Wilderness: A Settlement Study, by Residents and Associates of the South End House.* Boston/New York: Houghton, Mifflin and Co.

Wurzer, Rudolf 1974a: Die Gestaltung der deutschen Stadt im 19. Jahrhundert, in Grote, L. (ed.): *Die deutsche Stadt im 19. Jahrhundert: Stadtplanung und Baugestaltung im industriellen Zeitalter.* Munich: Prestel Verlag, 9–32.

Wurzer, Rudolf 1974b: Eugen Fassbender. *Stadtbauwelt*, 44, 299.

Youngson, A. J. 1966: *The Making of Classical Edinburgh, 1750–1840.* Edinburgh: Edinburgh University Press.

Zeldin, Theodore 1973: *France 1848–1945. Vol. I: Ambition, Love and Politics.* Oxford: Clarendon Press.

Zeldin, Theodore 1977: *France 1848–1945. Vol. II: Intellect, Taste and Anxiety.* Oxford: Clarendon Press.

Index